Transport for Travel and Tourism

TRANSPORT FOR TRAVEL AND TOURISM

B.S. Badan
Harish Bhatt

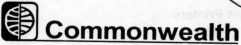
Commonwealth

Transport for Travel and Tourism

© Reserved

First Published : 2007

ISBN   81-311-0067-7

Published by :

Ajay Verma
For COMMONWEALTH PUBLISHERS
4831/24, Prahlad Street,
Ansari Road, Darya Ganj,
New Delhi - 110002
Ph. : 23272541, 23257835
Fax : 91- 011- 23257835
e-mail : campusbooks@hotmail.com

Printed at :
Roshan Offset Printers
Delhi

PREFACE

Tourism can be defined as the act of travel for the purpose of recreation, and the provision of services for this act. It is a service industry, comprising a number of tangible and intangible components. The tangible elements include transportation systems—air, rail, road, water and now, space; hospitality services, accommodation, foods and beverages, tours, souvenirs; and related services such as banking, insurance and safety and security. The intangible elements include: rest and relaxation, culture, escape, adventure, new and different experiences.

Travel and tourism is a major industry in the world and is at the top of the league of invisible earners of foreign currency. Many sovereignties, along with their respective countries and states, depend heavily upon travel expenditures by foreigners as a source of taxation and income for the enterprises that sell services to these travellers. Consequently the development of tourism is often a strategy employed either by a non-governmental organization or a governmental agency to promote a particular region for the purpose of increasing commerce through exporting goods and services to non-locals.

During recent years the tourism industry has witnessed unprecedented growth. Increasing consumer demand for educational and participatory travel experiences has resulted in a variety of specialty niche markets such as ecotourism, cultural-heritage tourism, and agritourism. New paradigms link strategic tourism planning with sustainable development.

The leisure and tourism industry is one of the leading global economic activities, a multi-billion-dollar industry with

700 million international travellers per year around the world. Tourism is a motor for employment and income creation and, especially in poor countries, a vehicle for development. But today it is not sufficient to simply create employment without regard for the quality of jobs and the social and environmental effects of tourism in vulnerable areas. A growing number of organizations, including the tourism industry leadership, are increasingly conscious of the risks and are adopting a more responsible attitude.

The present publication provides an authoritative look at how to manage travel and tourism industry in a better way. It introduces the complexities of the tourism system so that they will be better positioned to eventually assume the managerial challenges and responsibilities in a diverse and challenging industry. The latest advancements in tourism theory and thinking, retaining the thoroughness of content, diversity of applications, regional and international issues, economic significance, tourism operators and the role of technology in the tourism industry etc. are also described elaborately. Numerous regional and global case studies and examples are included to provide an appropriately broad geographic context. This work will be highly informative and useful to students, researchers, policy makers, managers and working groups of travel and tourism industry.

B.S. Badan
Harish Bhatt

Contents

Contents

1

Transport for Travel and Tourism

Introduction

Transport and tourism are synonymous. That is transport is indispensable to the operation of the travel and tourism industry and, therefore, a knowledge of how it works is essential. This chapter begins by summarising the principal features of a transport system that are common to all the major forms or modes. The particular characteristics of each of the modes and current issues relating to tourism are then described. Finally, the contribution of transport to environmental impacts is discussed.

The Importance of Transport

Transport is important to the travel and tourism industry for four reasons:

(i) Tourism implies movement

Virtually all tourism is based on experiencing different locations, for which transport facilities are essential. Not so widely recognised, however, is the scale and extent of the transport businesses that underpin that travel. For international tourism, airlines are the principle mode of travel (although globally, ground travel—by car or train—remain the most commonly used forms of transport) and, for example,

British Airways—the largest airline in the UK—in 2000 had a turnover of £8,940m, employing 65,640 people. Even so, BA is small by comparison with the giants of the US industry.

At the same time, transport investment and infrastructure are vital to the commercial development of tourism in an area. Indeed, the historical role of the railways in the development of the British seaside resorts in the 19th Century was mirrored by the contribution of air travel to the emergence of many international tourist destinations, such as The Gambia, the Maldives and the Caribbean islands, during the 20th Centuary. For example, traditionally the few visitors to the smaller Greek islands arrived by ferry from Athens (Piraeus) and the more adventurous still do, but the time taken (and inherent complexity) would be unacceptable to the mass market. It was only when an enterprising tour operator persuaded the authorities to allow military airfields to be used for charter flights that large-scale commercial development could begin.

This illustrates the important concept that, after cost, the main constraint on people's ability to travel is not distance but time; certainly, the growth of long-haul holidays shows that distance is not necessarily a deterrent as long as the journey can be made easily and rapidly. Conversely, some destinations, such as the St. Moriz area of Switzerland and Positano/Amalfi on the Neapoliltan Riviera, have remained exclusive partly because they are difficult to reach quickly and are, thus, only available to those with time to spare or fast personal means of transport.

(ii) Transport is a product of the travel industry

Despite the growing importance of Internet sales, travel agents generate a large proportion of their income from selling transport services, as distinct from holiday packages —in particular tickets for air and rail travel, together with car hire, coach and ferry services. World-wide, typically 75 percent of all air tickets are sold by travel agents. Commission is paid on these sales, and it is necessary for the travel agent to have knowledge of services and facilities available.

(iii) There is overlap between components of the travel industry

Some travel agents and tour operators are offshoots of transport companies, and vice-versa; the same organisation which puts the package together or sells it may be involved in providing the transport. Ferry companies, airlines, railways and coach operators offer extensive tour programmes of various kinds, while most charter airlines are connected financially with tour operators (the outstanding UK example being Britannia Airways, a subsidiary of Thomson Travel Group). The Virgin Group controls hotels, long-and short-haul aviation and two UK rail franchises, in addition to other activities outside transport.

(iv) The quality of transport is important in the travel business

A tour operator contracting hotel accommodation seeks assurances about the standard of rooms, meals and other facilities. Less attention tends to be given to the choice of transport, but poor transport arrangements can spoil a holiday just as easily. However, people are increasingly conscious of quality and expect service of a high standard. Where that quality is lacking and an operator refuses compensation, successful legal action is possible—as occurred after a coach driver smoked throughout a holiday.

Elements of Transport Systems

Although various modes of transport perform different functions and have individual strengths and weaknesses, they all feature five essential elements in common:

- a *Way* or route on which travel occurs;
- *Vehicles* that perform that movement;
- *Terminals* between which they travel;
- *Control and communication systems* through which safety is ensured and those involved are kept informed; and
- *Skilled management and staff* who bring the element together.

All these make up a transport system, and it is important to recognise the contribution of each.

The way

In the case of sea and air travel, the way is natural and 'free'. In principle, therefore, it can be used without restriction or cost, although safety demands that most air movements are subject to an air traffic control system, while ports and inland waterways usually involve artificial works which are charged for. Roads require construction and maintenance to reach a standard suitable for modern traffic; this is normally done by a public authority and the cost recovered by taxation on fuel and the use of vehicles. Occassionally, as with French autoroutes, a private company builds and maintains the route and then charges users a direct toll to use it.

Rail systems similarly require construction and, by their nature, can only be used by very specialised vehicles. Historically, most railways were built by the companies which owned and operated vehicles on them, but nowadays it is increasingly common for the track to be in different hands from the operator. Since the way is exclusive, the congestion found on roads can be avoided but the specialised nature of rail construction incurs high costs which can only be justified by high levels of traffic.

The vehicle

This is the carrying unit on which people travel—the train, ship, coach or aircraft. Sometimes separate 'motive power' is used to haul carrying units, the obvious example being railway engines, but usually the power to achieve movement is produced within the carrying unit itself. Over the years, the trend has been for the average size of vehicle to increase in order to accommodate increased demand and obtain economies (for example, the introduction of the 'jumbo' jet in the 1970s). However, this can result in the inability to service some destinations (as with cruise ships) or demand heavy investment to accommodate them, such as in longer airport runways.

The terminal

The terminal could be defined as the place where people begin and end their journeys but, in practice, this is rarely true; few people live next to transport terminals and even fewer would like their holiday hotel to be next to the airport (although airport hotels do of course exist for other purposes). In fact, the terminal performs two functions. Firstly, it facilitates transfer or interchange between modes. For example, passengers boarding an international flight at a major airport might arrive by one of a variety of means, including:

- railway,
- their own or a friend's car,
- taxi,
- another aircraft (interlining),
- hire car,
- scheduled bus or coach,
- touring or transfer coach.

Thus, a major function of an airport is to allow the smooth interchange from and to these other modes of transport.

The second function of a terminal is to consolidate traffic. Passengers normally 'interline' or change aircraft, because no convenient direct service exists. Therefore, the airport acts as a hub, a process which exists in most forms of transport and is becoming increasingly common. In this case, aircraft from regional centres feed into a major interchange, maximising the range of through-journey opportunities for passengers and creating higher passenger numbers for carriers.

Control and communication systems

For safety reasons, aircraft are subject to air traffic control systems which monitor not only take-off and landing but their movement while airborne. Similarly, railways are subject to control systems, traditionally referred to as 'signalling' but usually far more technically advanced than this suggests. It is these systems which make air and rail relatively safe in terms of accidents per passenger-kilometre.

In contrast, we enjoy a right to take a car or other vehicle onto the road system, however busy and congested it is. The purpose of control here is to improve safety and restrict movements once we are there, through traffic lights, roundabouts, speed limits, and so on. Similarly, once out of port ships can generally sail where their owners wish, although rules of navigation dictate how they should move when close to each other, and masters use navigational aids to avoid shallows and other dangers.

At airport or rail terminals, there are usually information screens which not only list arrivals and departures, but also give "real time" information stating when the next or delayed services are expected to arrive. This is possible because those operating the control systems are permanently in contract—through radio and electronically—with the aircraft or trains they monitor and thus know exactly where they are. This is not usually the case with road vehicles, unless they are linked to a tracking system which reports their movements back to a control centre and so on to waiting passengers.

Management and staff

It is easy to underestimate not just the numbers of personnel involved in a major transport business but also the complexity of management. For example, a company such as GNER, the franchise which operates trains between London, North-East England and Scotland, employs 3,000 to operate its 112 departures per day and carries 14m passengers each year, requires all the usual management functions, such as HR, finance, IT and marketing, in addition to those carrying out specialist operating duties.

The following sections now consider different modes or forms of transport.

Road Transport

The private car

In most developed countries, the private car is the most popular form of transport for leisure travel. Not only can it reach most destinations easily and luggage can be easily handled, but also car owners can make extra 'marginal' journeys at a low cost which becomes lower still as more people are carried. This popularity and convenience of the car is demonstrated by a survey of visitors to Stratford-on-Avon which found that 66 percent arrived by private car; 17 percent by touring coach; 6 percent by hire car; 5 percent by train, and 6 percent by other means. More generally, over 80 percent of visitors to the English country-side travel by car, a proportion which rises to ninety percent in some national parks.

The car's widespread availability has brought about two major developments within tourism:

(i) *The use of a family car for holidays abroad*

There has been a rapid growth in independent overseas travel by private car, although crossing water adds disproportionately to total holiday costs, thus discouraging both island residents from holidaying abroad and those on 'the other side' from coming in. For this reason, together with the attraction of warmer weather, residents of France, Germany and Holland are much more likely to use their car for a holiday on the European mainland than to travel to the United Kingdom.

(ii) *Car rental*

Because people value the use of a car for mobility at home, but a destination is beyond the possible range for taking one's own, the car hire business has developed rapidly in resort areas. Hire cars are also available at airports and rail terminals for business or leisure use. Some holidays include 'fly-drive' as an integral part of the package, while others offer optional car hire at discounted rates within the resort.

Given the rapid growth in car ownership and usage, attention is inevitably focused on the environmental impacts of the car, particularly in more fragile areas. Many national parks, for example, are developing policies to encourage the use of alternative forms of transport. At the same time, one approach to 'managing' independent car-borne leisure travel by tourism bodies is to designate recommended routes. These can be lengthy stretches of major roads passing through scenically attractive areas, such as the Romantischestrasse and Weinstrasse in Germany, where the object is to persuade travellers to stop and spend in historic towns along the route. On a more local basis, 'scenic drives' may be promoted along a common theme such as fruit trees in blossom. These are geared more to the 'Sunday afternoon' motorist looking for somewhere to go, and may have the ulterior motive of attracting drivers away from popular destinations and roads which become congested.

Taxis and private hire cars

The role of taxis is, in effect, halfway between private and public transport. Visitors may well use taxis on a casual basis to reach locations where they lack the confidence to use public tansport, whilst they may also find it the easiest way of reaching a city centre from an airport. Equally, a taxi may be an alternative to a hired car to reach an attraction which is not accessible by public transport. Sometimes it is accepted practice, for example when cruise ships call into a port, for visitors to hire a taxi with a driver for the time available; the driver knows the main attractions and takes his passengers for a personalised tour. Taxis are also used by tour operators and their resort representatives for transferring small numbers of visitors between airports and hotels.

Cycling

For the first half of the twentieth century, cycling was one of the commonest forms of transport, used for travel to work, school and leisure alike. While that has continued in some places (notably in some University cities and in Holland), the growth in car ownership has both led to cars replacing cycles for these journeys and made conditions more dangerous and unpleasant for the cyclists remaining.

Nevertheless, cycling has more recently re-emerged as a leisure activity, particularly in the form of 'mountain' bikes. Families often travel by car on holiday or for a day out with cycles fixed to the back or roof of their car to an area where quiet roads or tracks are available, whilst some bus and rail operators adapt vehicles to carry cycles and so offer a public transport alternative. Opportunities for leisure cycling have also increased. In the UK, for example, the charity Sustrans (Sustainable Transport) is using funds raised from local authorities and others to develop a national network of cycle routes.

The National Cycle Network is a visionary project to provide a 10,000-mile network of cycle routes.

Originally launched with a £43.5 million grant from the Millennium Commission, the Network involves the active participation of more than 400 local authorities, the Department of the Environment, Transport and the Regions, and other public and private bodies.

The Network is a linked series of traffic-free paths and traffic-calmed and minor roads connecting urban centres and the countryside, and reaching all parts of the UK. These will provide a safe, attractive, and high quality network for cyclists and a major new amenity for walkers and wheelchair users.

More than 5,000 miles of signed and mapped routes opened in June 2000. Ten thousand miles will be completed by 2005. The Network will connect with hundreds of further extensions.

Among the 10,000 km already open, a 'Sea to Sea' route from the Irish to the North Sea has been created and the target is to achieve 17,000 km of track. The routes are not all in open countryside; it is estimated that over 20 million people will live within 3 km of a point on the network, so it will be possible to use it for local leisure and travel to work or education. Inevitably, some of the network will be in the form of cycle lanes along roads carrying other traffic, but the maximum use is being made of disused routes, such as old rail tracks and canal towpaths.

Scheduled bus and coach

Scheduled services are those that run to a fixed timetable and are not subject to cancellation if demand is insufficient. These are the forms of transport normally used

least by tourists, but are important for particular locations
and purposes:

Fig. 1.1 : Sustrans cycle routes

Long-Distance Leisure Journeys

In the UK, this market is dominated by two organisations, National Express and Scottish Citylink. Both run
networks of inter-urban coach services and are, primarily,
planning and marketing bodies which charter in coaches to
meet their needs from large and small operators across the

country. However, the image of one large organisation is created by a requirement that coaches on long-term contract are of a specified design and painted in a standard colour scheme. Virtually all demand is leisure-oriented in some form and its scale is such that National Express schedules around 700 coaches on an average day, with more on a short-term basis to meet peak demands. Most European countries do not have long-distance coach networks of the same kind because their Governments have preferred to encourage use of their railways, but they are expanding slowly.

Local Services

These are used by tourists principally for short-distance travel within towns and cities; London Transport Marketing (1996) found that about 45 percent of overseas visitors used its buses during their say, while just under 40 percent used taxis. Buses are also used to an extent to reach rural attractions from the bigger accommodation centres. For example, in North Wales a 'Snowdon Sherpa' system of connecting minibuses was originally intended to help solve parking problems at the foot of Snowdon, but has been developed to provide longer distance access from towns such as Liandudno and Portmadoc. In some countries, particularly Switzerland, extensive and high quality rural services are promoted strongly to tourists and are used as an environ-mentally-friendly alternative to local car hire.

The bus has a fairly captive market among visitors to some islands, the systems in Tenerife, Malta and Majorca all being well used. That in Tenerife (TITSA) is modern and professional, while the Maltese system traditionally uses ancient buses which are almost a working museum and tourist attraction in themselves; however, modernisation is now taking place.

Also included in this category are local sightseeing tours, which are common in larger cities but have also been expanding in smaller historic centres. The London survey mentioned above found these to be used by over 20 percent of overseas visitors. In the UK they commonly use old

double-deck buses with the roof removed, which have a low
purchase price and are a novelty for most visitors.

'Touring' Coaches

These refer to non-scheduled services offered for leisure
purposes. At one extreme is the day trip, designed either for
the resident population or to take visitors to attractions in
the wider area; the latter, of course, are often organised in
conjunction with tour operators and sold by resort
representatives. Within the resident market, demand has
moved away from the traditional seaside resort towards
theme parks and locations associated with television series.
Major shopping centres and developments can attract large
numbers. The Metro Centre near Newcastle can accommodate 370 coaches and receives close to this number in the
weeks before Christmas, while the hypermarkets of Calais
are popular further south. Other growth sectors have been
open-air museums such as Beamish and Ironbridge, where
the school trip market is important. The total value of the
market for UK residents taking coach tours (i.e. at least one
night away) is estimated at £643m per annum, with a further
£396, coming into the UK from overseas groups.

Beyond the day trip come weekend and mid-week
breaks and extended tours of between seven and fourteen
days. These include both more traditional tours and also
'shuttle' operations, where parties are ferried to their
accommodation with a minimum of stops, and then return
home one or two weeks later.

Structure of the industry

The road transport industry includes all sizes of
operator, with fleets varying from one coach to a thousand or
more. However, the bigger fleets, which outside the UK are
still often publicly owned, tend to concentrate on local bus
work, and in the coach sector small firms predominate, many
of whom sell direct by word of mouth, newspapers or through
a small number of local agents. The elderly form a large part
of the coach tour market, but growth can be achieved

provided new customers are attracted; it is an expanding and increasingly prosperous sector of the population.

As coach operators do not normally have the bargaining strength to negotiate attractive rates with hotels and ferry companies, specialist tour wholesalers offer to coach firms a package of accommodation, if necessary with overnight stops, and ferry bookings at reasonable prices expressed as a figure per head (subject to a minimum break-even number). Operators have then only to add coach operating costs and a profit margin to arrive at a selling price for the tour.

Rail Transport

The railways no longer hold the dominant position in leisure passenger transport they enjoyed in the nineteenth and early twentieth centuries. Although demand still exists for rail transport to traditional coastal resorts for day trips and holidays, commuters and business travellers are now more numerous on these routes than holidaymarkers.

However, rail is important in certain niche markets and, where investment in new vehicles and infrastructure takes place, it can increase ridership and market share. Most European systems have developed more commercial approaches which identify distinct styles of operation, and set appropriate targets for them. We shall consider each of these principal sectors in turn and then look at the involvement of the private sector in preserved and narrow-gauge railways.

Inter-City services

The main characteristic of Inter-City services is that they provide fast, high-quality regular services—often running every hour—between principal centres. Business travellers are an important market and for them first-class coaches are provided with restaurant cars and possibly other services such as computer plug-in points. Fares are relatively high, through a higher charge for First Class, discriminatory pricing on the busiest trains and possibly a premium for travel on Inter-City trains as opposed to others. Not surprisingly, perhaps, Inter-City services are normally the most profitable in a rail system.

Most West European countries have invested heavily in new high-speed rail systems, some running internationally. (e.g. the Thalys service from Paris to Brussels, Cologne and Amsterdam). Maximum speeds of up to 300 kph enable these trains to compete effectively not just with the car but with airlines, and they have taken much of the airlines' previous market share for centre-to-centre traffic. On Inter-City routes as a whole, however, few trains can be filled with business customers alone and other types of customer are encouraged through pricing mechanisms such as Senior and Young Person's Railcards and APEX tickets. Sales to visitors from overseas can also be important, for which most European railways maintain international offices. Unlimited travel tickets (in Britain the Britrail Pass) are also available, but are normally sold only through these offices to avoid their use by domestic customers. For example, many young Americans use the British system to attend the Edinburgh Festival each summer.

Regional services

These are passenger routes outside the main conurbations that are slower, make more stops and sometimes offer lower standards of comfort. Although it is hard to distinguish precisely, there are two broad categories, which we might call 'Express' and 'the rest'. Express routes are those which come closest to Inter-City in terms of fast services between regional centres, using trains of a high standard with limited catering services; examples are Newcastle-Leeds-Liverpool in the UK and Dusseldorf-Kassel in Germany. These Express routes also come closest to Inter-City in their financial performance, being expected to cover at least their direct operating costs.

The rest are a financial liability to any rail organisation and exist mainly for political and social reasons. They may fit the description 'branch lines' although, in the UK, most such lines were closed in the 1960s; an exception is in Cornwall, where a number of branch lines remain open because of a continuing role in bringing visitors to the area. More commonly, these routes are 50 km or more in length, connecting outlying towns and remote areas to the core system. It is accepted that these lines cannot be profitable and are therefore, subsidised by central or regional Governments.

However, opportunities exist to improve their financial performance because, as rural tourism and interest in outdoor activities has grown, so too has the potential for their use by visitors. Many such lines pass through National Parks and other scenically attractive areas where environmental pressures make it sensible to encourage access by rail rather than by road. The cost structure of railways means that it costs little or nothing to carry additional leisure traffic, and the income can be used almost entirely to reduce losses. Well-planned marketing pro-grammes to increase such patronage are therefore likely to be highly cost-effective.

Urban services

Urban railways are often operated by local as opposed to nationally-controlled organisations. In much of Europe, new systems are being built and existing ones adapted. For example, in Stuigart and other German cities the traditional street trams run by city authorities have been modernised and diverted underground in city centres, while the suburban trains of the state railway (DB) also run in tunnels under the centre. Visitors to cities, who often do not have private transport with them, will use local rail services if they are made attractive enough and promoted as an integrated system.

In London, 9 percent of all journeys on the Underground system are made by tourists and a survey found that 76 percent of visitors had used the Underground system the previous day. Additionally, nearly 30 percent of all overseas visitors to London used the national rail system at some time during their stay.

Ownership and control of railways

Historically, most large railways, like major airlines, have been owned by the state, not only because they are seen as having political or strategic importance, but also because they tend not to be commercially viable. Most railways are still Government-owned, although they may be set more specific commercial targets and be run in a more businesslike way than hitherto.

The international trend to privatisation has not yet affected most rail systems. However, the EU has encouraged member states to separate the provision of *infrastructure* (track, control and stations) from the *operation* of the trains themselves. Some countries are, therefore, setting up track-owning companies or authorities from which train operators 'rent' paths or slots. The UK Government's decision was firstly to separate the various elements of service provision and then privatise them in turn. An infrastructure company (Railtrack)—recently nationalised by the Government—own all public track (other than that locally run in the major cities), the control systems and some stations. 25 Train Operating Companies (TOCs) pay access charges for use of the system, own the remaining stations, and lease the trains they run from leasing companies. Their income is obtained from fares and Government subsidy.

However, the ownership of trains is of little interest to passengers, who seek reliability, reasonable fares and comprehensive and unbiased information. These factors are particularly important to tourists who are unfamiliar with a system, and integrated charging can be important in marketing rail-based travel. For example, tour operators sell packages based on accommodation together with rail travel, which is periced on a zonal system according to distance from the destination. It would seriously undermine the marketing of these packages if some TOCs excluded their services or charged on a different basis.

Tourist and private railways

Although the large, public rail organisations make an important contribution to the movement of tourists, there are also railways which exist purely as tourist attractions or holidays in their own right.

Firstly, it is possible to run privately-owned locomotives (usually steam) over parts of the public rail system; the number of preserved locomotives makes this commonest in the UK. Secondly, the national rail systems can be used for luxurious trains, of which the Venice-Simpton Orient Express (VSOE) is the best known example. Here, privately-owned coaches are hauled by electric locomotives provided by the various national railways.

Alternatively, a private organisation may run a self-contained railway. These normally involve steam locomotives and, usually, these are lines which have been closed to conventional traffic, although some were never intended for passenger travel at all. For example, most of the narrow-guage railways in North Wales, collectively promoted as the Great Little Trains of Wales, were built to carry slate from quarries to the sea. The popularity of such lines can be increased by attractive scenery and nearby major tourist attractions. The Keighley and Worth Valley Railway in West Yorkshire, for instance, has its headquarters at Haworth where visitors to the Bronte literary associations are numbered in hundreds of thousands.

The appeal of these preserved railways which are open throughout a season must be to a mass market where they compete with totally different attractions. However, although they must meet the same safety standards as a 'public' line, which involves considerable expense, they are helped by only having to run when they judge the market demands it and by the use of volunteers to carry out driving, manual and clerical work.

The Channel Tunnel and Eurostar

The Channel Tunnel between Folkestone in Kent (UK) and Coquelles near Calais (France) opened in May, 1994. It is a rail tunnel through which two distinct types of passenger service operate – the Shuttle and Eurostar.

The Shuttle service is designed to carry cars, coaches and goods vehicles with their drivers and passengers, and operates only between terminals at either end of the tunnel. It competes directly with cross-Channel ferries, particularly those between Dover and Calais, but its effect has also been felt on the longer crossings north and west of the Straits of Dover. In 2000, the Shuttle carried 2.8m cars and 79,000 coaches.

Conversely, Eurostar is a high-speed Inter-City service which operates principally from London to Brussels and Paris. Jointly owned by the National Express Group and British Airways in the UK, and by the Belgian and French state railways, its scheduled time of 3 hours from London to Paris and 2 hours 40 minutes to Brussels makes it particularly attractive to business travellers between city centres. By 2000, Air France had lost 60 percent of its Paris-London market to Eurostar, which carried a total of 7.1m passengers in that year. However, competition between Eurostar and the airlines has succeeded in expanding the total market.

Between Folkestone and London, Eurostar trains currently run over the slow and congested tracks also used by local commuter trains. A fast Rail Link to continental standards is under construction, the first section of which should be completed in 2003, with the more difficult London section to follow in 2007. This will further improve journey time and reliability, so increasing the threat to the airlines.

Shipping

Much of Britain's growth as an industrial nation and as the centre of an empire was connected with its shipping industry. In the Victoria era, large companies such as Cunard and P&O emerged, involved in the transport of goods to and from overseas centres and the movement of emigrants and business people. However, while cargo shipping still exists in a modern, mainly containerised, form, the greater speed of aircraft made it impossible from the 1950s onwards for ships to compete for passengers, and this business has largely disappeared. Shipping is now important to tourism in three forms:

(i) Local ferries

These operate principally inland on lakes but also over short distances along coastlines and in long inlets, such as the

Norwegian fjords. These features often occur in moun-tainous areas which are attractive for tourism, and the lakes are part of the scenery that is marketed. Such terrain often makes overland travel difficult and it can be much quicker to travel from one side of a lake to the other by water than round the edge (for example from the French southern side of Lake Geneva to Lausanne in Switzerland on the northern bank). Similarly, it is an easier journey by water from one resort to another along the Italian Riviera than on land by road. Thus, ferries may form part of a local transport network for residents, but use by tourists is likely to predo-minate.

Such ferries have been a feature of the English Lake District since late Victorian times. The Furness Railway, wishing to reach the heart of the Lakes at Bowness and Ambleside, built a branch from its main line to the southern tip of Windermere at Lakeside, where a terminal and an imposing hotel were built, and its passengers could then travel by steamer along the lake. Today, the Lakeside and Haverthwaite Railway runs steam trains along the northern part of the line, connecting with the ships of Windermere Lake Cruises. The fact that original craft are still in use is one of the attractions, and in this way visitors are offered a package of travel by vintage train and ship.

(ii) Sea-going ferries

These are distinguished by typically longer crossing times and, particularly with islands, their history is much more of necessity as opposed to leisure.

Traditionally, people wishing to travel from Britain to Europe or from Ireland to the UK mainland reached the port by train. Crossed by ferry and continued by rail on the other side. Nowadays, however, the majority of passengers travel with vehicles which are also carried on the ferry these being known as 'Roll-on/Roll-off or 'RoRo' ferries. Domestic routes, such as those to Ireland and the Scottish islands, continue to be important. Just under a million cars and many foot passengers travel by sea to or from Ireland every year, while the Scottish services, operated by Caledonian Macbrayne

(West Coast) and P&O (Orkney and Shetland), in addition to being 'lifelines', have also become involved in tourism travel. Between them they carry about 250,000 cars annually.

Holidays involving taking the family car, and sometimes a caravan, to or from the European mainland enjoyed steady growth for many years and packages were developed, including ferry crossings and either fixed bookings or a series of "go-as-you-please" hotel vouchers. In recent years, however, the ferry companies have experienced increasing difficulties. From Table 1.1 it is evident that, over a ten year period, traffic on the Straits of Dover and English Channel routes began to fall in 1995, while on the North Sea the decline began earlier in 1993 (although a recovery can be seen from 1998 onwards).

Table 1.1 : Accompanied cars travelling by ship between the UK and European mainland, 1990-1999.

	Accompanied cars by ship (thousands)									
	1990	1991	1992	1993	1994	1995	1996	1997	1998	1999
North Sea	650	730	734	697	632	609	547	518	532	586
Straits of Dover	2,346	2,624	2,715	3,173	3,627	3,309	3,383	3,739	3,193	2,856
English Channel	1,140	1,257	1,295	1,369	1,436	1,422	1,292	1,357	1,370	1,349
ALL ROUTES	4,137	4,611	4,744	5,238	5,695	5,340	5,222	5,614	5,095	4,790

Source: Transport Statistics Great Britain 2000, DETR.

The Principal cause of this was the opening of the Channel Tunnel, where the shuttle service between Folkestone and Calais takes 35 minutes compares with at least 75 minutes by ferry. By mid-1996, the Shuttle was estimated to have around 45 percent of traffic across the Straits of Dover, equivalent to the combined business of the two largest ferry companies, and the over-capacity led to fierce price competition, particularly at off-peak times. Thus, although the total market continued to increase, ferry turnover fell, a problem aggravated in 1999 by the ending of duty-free sales within the EU.

Cruises

Like ferries, cruising has a long history. Developed from the luxurious liners that sailed across the Atlantic and so far-flung colonies, cruise ships traditionally had an image of being expensive and oriented towards rich, elderly passengers.

The strength of cruising is that it combines the opportunity to 'sample' a variety of destinations with an elegant lifestyle, with the added benefit that the accommodation travels to the destination. The main disadvantage is that, due to the labour costs of providing high standards of service, cruising is expensive. For example, the average price of cruise holidays bought in the UK in 1995 was an estimated £1,049.

Sometimes, cruises may depart from and return to tourists' home country but, since most cruise destinations are a substantial distance from customers' homes, it is often impractical to sail from the country of origin. As a result, the 'fly-cruise' has become increasingly popular accounting for around 70 percent of the UK cruise market. Not only to customers can fly to join the ship at a suitable point, but also the cruise is able to consolidate passengers of different nationalities and so maximise carryings. For example, the world's largest cruise market is the USA and its principal cruising area the Caribbean; most cruises start at or near Miami, which both American and European customers can reach quickly by air.

In recent years, the traditional image of cruising as an expensive form of travel for more elderly customers has been addressed by cruise operators. The Caribbean, for example, has become an attractive destination for the young, partly due to the water-sports opportunities offered and partly by changing the style of shipboard activity towards the gym and swimming pool, and by moving towards healthier food. At the same time, the problem of high costs have also tackled by introducing short 'mini-cruises' at a low cost and hoping customers will then trade up and by reducing levels of service, including food (although in surveys, high standards of food and drink are highly rated). Moreover, tour operators have increasingly featured cruises in their brochure range, normally by selling the products of an existing operator. Airtours took this a stage further in 1995 by introducing cruises under their own name, targeted at the market in which the company already traded. As a result of these changes, UK sales of cruises increased from 30 1,900 in 1994 to 740,000 in 2000; as new destinations were brought on stream, the Caribbean lost some of its dominant position but still accounted for 41 percent of UK sales in 1999 (Coulson 2001).

For destinations, cruise ships do not always represent a suitable form of tourism. Cruise passengers tend to buy relatively little on shore, whilst the arrival of a cruise ship with 1,500 passengers can put enormous strains on local facilities. Thus, some Caribbean islands having developed an exclusive image for a small but wealthy market, fear that cruise business may lead to environmental damage and loss of this clientele. At least one island has withdrawn facilities for berthing cruise ships and, as shipping companies introduce new ships able to carry up to 6,000 passengers in their pursuit of economies of scale, this is likely to increase if indeed ports are able to accommodate vessels of this size.

Air Transport

Air travel is the means of transport most associated with the tourism industry, since it is a fundamental element of the mass package tour. This perception is confirmed by figures showing the number of UK residents leaving the UK by the three alternatives of air, sea and the Channel Tunnel (Table 1.2). The figures also demonstrate that, while business travel and visiting friends and relatives (VFR) are important, holidays are the predominant reason for travel by all the modes.

Table 1.2 : Overseas visits by UK residents, 1999 ('000s).

	Holiday	(of which inclusive tour)	Business	VFR	Other	Total
Air	25,282	14,998	6,400	4,974	854	37,510
Sea	6,483	2,923	875	1,069	1,640	10,427
Tunnel	2,898	1,135	886	554	1,605	5,994
Total	35,023	19,077	8,161	6,598	4,100	53,881

Source: Travel Trends 1999, HMSO.

However, the UK aviation market is small by comparison with that of the USA, as can be seen by comparing passenger numbers passing through major airports and carried by the largest airlines (Table 1.3 and 1.4).

Table 1.3 : Passengers at major airports, 1998.

	Airport	Total Passengers (million)	International Passengers (million)
USA	Atlanta Hartsfield	73	4
USA	Chicago O'Hare	72	9
UK	London Heathrow	60	53
USA	Dallas Fort Worth	60	4
USA	Los Angeles	59	15
Germany	Frankfurt /Main	42	34
USA	San Fransisco	39	7
France	Paris Charles de Gaulle	38	34
Netherlands	Amsterdam Schipol	34	34

Source: ICAO, reproduced in Transport Statistics 2000 (DETR).

It can be seen from Tables 1.3 and 1.4 that, although the USA dominates the world's aviation industry, only a small proportion of its passengers fly internationally. British Airways, though eleventh in terms of total passengers carried, has the highest figures for *international* passengers and passenger kilometers. Similarly Heathrow, with 54.8 million international and 7.1 million domestic passengers in 1999, has the world's highest number of international users.

The USA's dominance can be explained by its advanced economy and its large geographical area, which not only contains a large population but creates a greater market for domestic travel within the country.

The relatively high cost of air travel and the need to site airports at some distance from city centres mean that the greater speed of aircraft only becomes an asset above a certain distance, usually about 500km. Below this rail, and sometimes car, can achieve comparable centre-to-centre time, the exception being where water forms a barrier. This is why, until the Channel Tunnel was opened, air had a near-monopoly of business travel over the fairly short distances between London and Brussels or Paris.

Table 1.4 : Passengers carried and kilometers traveled on scheduled flights by major international airlines, 1997.

	Airline	Total Passengers (millions)	Int. Passengers (millions)	Total Pass. km (billions)	Int. Pass. km (billions)
USA	Delta	103.1	7.2	160.3	36.9
USA	United	84.2	12.3	195.3	76.2
USA	American	81.1	17.1	172.1	55.9
USA	US Air Piedmont	58.7	2.3	66.9	6.9
USA	Northwest	54.6	9.5	115.8	52.4
USA	Continental	38.8	4.9	70.9	17.4
Japan	All Nippon	36.8	3.0	51.2	18.3
Germany	Lufthansa	35.7	22.6	71.5	66.4
France	Air France	32.7	15.5	70.0	52.4
Japan	JAL	31.8	11.3	79.1	62.0
UK	British Airways	29.5	24.3	101.5	99.1

Source: ICAO, reproduced in Transport Statistics 2000 (DETR).

Of the 151 million passengers who passed through British airports in 1999, 133.5 million were making international journeys and only 17.5 million domestic. The latter market comprises principally:

- Journeys linking cities over the magic distance where air becomes advantageous (e.g., London-Giasgow).
- Services to offshore islands as in Scotland, Northern Ireland and the Channel Islands.
- Interlining, where passengers transfer to or from an international flight.

Scheduled and charter aviation

The air passenger market can be divided in principle between scheduled traffic, where seats are purchased individually, and charter, where blocks of seats or the entire capacity of an aircraft, perhaps for a season, is sold to an intermediary. Most charter operations are in the form of Inclusive Tour Charters (ITCs), and it is the growth of these which made the European package holiday available to a mass market. More recently, long-haul destinations have been included in charter operations.

Charter operators achieve a much lower seat cost than the conventional scheduled flight, for a number of reasons:

- They usually fit more seats into a given type of aircraft than would a scheduled airline; a Boeing 757 would typically seat 180 for British Airways but 228 in charter use. The extra space is an important selling point to scheduled passengers, so it is difficult for the same aircraft to be used for a mix of scheduled and charter flights.

- The charter operator achieves a greater number of flying hours per day from its aeroplanes. The Managing Director of Monarch Airlines, claiming 11.7 flying hours per day compared with 6.8 hours at British Airways, commented:

By a combination of differential pricing and clever marketing by the tour operators, charter airlines are able to sell capacity at times of day that are unthinkable for scheduled carriers and thus achieve very high levels of utilisation.

For example, Figure 1.2 shows a flight plan for a Boeing 757 of Britannia Airways as it was scheduled to operate on Fridays during summer 1997:

Depart	Palma	0120	Arrive	Birmingham	0340
"	Birmingham	0620	"	Naples	0905
"	Naples	1005	"	Birmingham	1250
"	Birmingham	1425	"	Corfu	1735
"	Corfu	1835	"	Birmingham	2155
"	Birmingham	2320	"	Palma	0140

Fig. 1.2 : A charter flight plan.

- Whereas the scheduled airline may assume a relatively low load factor (i.e., percentage of seats filled), the charter operator assumes that 95 percent or more of seats will be filled. Furthermore, if this seems unlikely to be achieved, the operator will 'consolidate' groups of customers from different flights in a single departure. This results in the last-minute changes to flight arrangements that are unpopular with customers but keep costs down to the price they are willing to pay. The scheduled airline's lower load results from the fact that it must fly at scheduled times, irrespective of demand. Conversely, the charter operator flies only when the break-even load factor (typically 95 percent) has been achieved.

- Charter airlines are usually much smaller then scheduled airlines, which are often national 'flag-carriers' and in many cases state-owned, and therefore have relatively lower administrative costs. In particular, because the charter airline sells its seats in blocks to a few customers, its marketing costs are much lower. For example, Monarch Airlines claimed an advertising budget of £10,000 in relation to a turnover of £111 million, and that its only other marketing costs were the salaries of a sales director, three salesmen and a typist-altogether no more than 0.2 percent of turnover. Conversely, British Airways' 2000 turnover of £8,940m was much greater, but its 'selling costs' were 13 percent of this figure, mainly as a result of agent commissions and its reservation system.
- They normally offer a lower standard of in-flight catering and, unlike many scheduled operators, charge for all drinks and other services, such as the use of headphones.
- They generally use smaller and regional airports, where handling and landing charges are lower than at the major international airports.

Despite the low prices achieved by charter operators, under certain circumstances scheduled operators also serve the ITC market. For example, blocks of seats on scheduled flights are commonly sold at discounted prices to tour operators willing to pay above the charter rate (for example, fly-cruise customers), whilst some tour operators offer destinations where demand cannot justify charter flights and, therefore, there is no option but to buy scheduled capacity. Some scheduled airlines also mount their own holiday programmes using existing flights, and switch aircraft which fly business routes during the week to serve holiday destinations at weekends.

Conversely, some charter airlines, knowing they will have spare capacity on particular flights, now sell 'seat-only' tickets, but their development has been limited. Despite the demand for cheap individual bookings to holiday destinations, charter operators sometimes feel it is not worth the cost of setting up the necessary distribution system, whilst countries wishing to protect their scheduled airlines discourage 'seat-only' sales through their regulatory system.

'No-frills' airlines

Perhaps the most significant recent development within Europe has been the growth of 'no-frills', or low-cost scheduled airlines such as Buzz, Easylet, Go and Ryanair. This has been made possible by the relaxation of regulatory controls within the EU, but what distinguishes these airlines is the adoption of the same cost-cutting practices as charter airlines. There are variations in their systems, but generally:

- They use Internet or telesales bookings, thereby avoiding commissions to agents.
- They aim for high utilisation of aircraft through a long operational day and short turnrounds (20 minutes in the case of Ryanair). This is facilitated by carrying no cargo and limited catering.
- If catering is provided at all, it is basic and charged for, leading to a smaller cabin crew requirement.
- Regional airports are used, where low handling charges are negotiated.
- Aircraft have a high seating density similar to charter airlines.
- Tickets are only sold for single sectors, eliminating complex financial reconciliation, handling of baggage and transfers at connecting airports.

Although the 'no-frills' airlines carry out extensive promotion of very low lead-in fares, they also charge at levels closer to their established rivals—but still good value—at peak times and when demand enables them to. Thus, while in April, 2001 it was possible to fly with Ryanair from Stansted to Frankfurt/Hahn for £7 each way (plus airport departure tax), a flight to Ancona on a summer weekend in July, 2001 was priced at £77 each way.

Currently, these airlines hold no more than a 6 percent share of the total scheduled market within Europe, and not all are trading profitably. However, the leading operators are introducing new routes and expanding capacity at rates exceeding 20 percent per annum and it is clear that a large market is awaiting the opportunity of low-cost European travel.

Regulation in Transport

Regulations is important because it has a major effect on the price, availability and quality of transport services for tourism.

Forms of regulation

Traditionally two types have been recognised:

(i) Safety or quality controls

External safety control, such as the high standards of maintenance and operating procedures required with aircraft, is generally accepted as socially beneficial and, therefore, this form of regulation generally attracts controversy only when it is shown to be absent. For example, the sinking of SS Titanic in 1912 led to regulation ensuring that every ship carries sufficient lifeboats for all its passangers. Quality controls include the professional qualifications of ships' masters, airline pilots and coach drivers, their working hours and the mechanical condition of the equipment they use.

(ii) Quantity controls

These may restrict entry to a route, the timetable offered or fares charged and are, therefore, far more controversial. Where deregulation has occurred in recent years, as in the US domestic air market and the British bus and coach industries, it is primarily the removal of quantity controls that has taken place.

In recent years, regulation has been imposed for further reasons—consumer protection and environmental reasons. Operators of air-based holidays are required to hold an Air Travel Organiser's Licence (ATOL), which is issued by the Civil Aviation Authority (CAA) in return for a financial bond. The purpose is to protect customers against the risk of either losing holidays they have paid for or of being stranded at the destination. All such organisers must display an ATOL number and logo in their publicity. Scheduled airlines carrying inclusive tour passengers and coach tour operators are now also subject to bonding.

The prime example of environmental controls is where limits are placed on night movements of aircraft at airports in the interest of local residents. Coach operators can also experience restrictions on the routes they use in areas congested by high levels of tourist traffic.

Who are the regulators?

The task of regulation is carried out partly by public bodies and partly by private or industry-based organisations, although often to meet a Government's wishes. In the UK, Government bodies include the CAA, which exercises both 'quantity' and 'quality' control over British air carriers, is responsible for the Air Traffic Control system and operates a number of airports. Traffic Commissioners issue Operators' Licences (now issued according to safety criteria only) to bus and coach operators, and monitor their behaviour. Local councils control the issue of licences to taxi operators and, through powers to subsidise, can secure the availability of tourist-oriented bus and rail services.

Governments also support international bodies, among which is the International Civil Aviation Organisation (ICAO), a United Nations body which is mainly concerned with the technical side of air operations. In particular, it is concerned with the improvement of technical standards and with helping developing countries to bring their facilities to international standards. Similarly, following marine disasters such as the loss of the 'Herald of Free Enterprise' at Zeebrugge in 1987, the International Marine Organisation (IMO) has been studying the design of RoRo ferries, and new requirements of bulkheads to divide up vehicle decks are being brought into effect.

ICAO works closely with the International Air Transport Association (IATA), a trade organisation representing most international airlines. IATA is concerned with technical matters (hence its liasion with ICAO), and also provides financial and legal services for its members. However, it is best known as the body which still decides many of the fares charged by international airlines, a task which is delegated to it by individual Governments.

Regulation in international air transport

While control of domestic air routes is determined by the individual state, the international industry requires regulation at various levels. Indeed, whether a route between two states should exist at all is, firstly, a political decision made by the Governments concerned rather than the airlines. This is known as a *bilateral agreement* and specifies the number of airlines that are to operate the service. It is normally either 'dual designation', in which case only two airlines may operate (usually one from each country), or 'multiple designation', which allows a number of airlines to fly the route.

The agreement sometimes specifies that the fixing of detailed times and fares should be delegated to IATA, subject to Government confirmation. It also specifies which of a number of possible 'freedoms' apply. These 'freedoms' grant the airlines of one country the following rights:

1st the freedom to fly over another country's territory without landing.

2nd the freedom to land for technical, non-traffic reasons, such as refuelling.

3rd the freedom to set down passengers, mail and freight taken on in the airline's the home country.

4th the freedom to pick up passengers, mail and freight destined for the home country of the airline.

5th the freedom to start flights in the home country (A), pick up passengers, mail and freight in country (B) and convey to country (C). An example of this 5th Freedom would be an American airline operating New York-London-Frankfurt which was permitted to carry London-Frankfurt traffic.

6th the freedom to start in country (A), and operate via the home country (B) to country (C). Here an example would be a route operated by the Chinese airline Cathay Pacific from Bangkok through its base at Hong Kong and on to Tokyo in Japan.

The granting of the first and second freedoms is normally automatic. The third and fourth are negotiable, although possession of these freedoms forms the basis of most international services. The 5th and 6th freedoms are less commonly agreed although the deregulation of air services within Europe should in principle mean that all European airlines now enjoy all of these freedoms.

An airline wishing to take advantage of a bilateral agreement must next satisfy the licensing requirements of each state involved. This is normally a formally but gives the 'host' country an opportunity to ensure that visiting airlines meet its own quality standards. Similarly, the aspiring airline must meet its own state's requirements, partly on a quality basis but also to be recognised as a party to the bilateral agreement relevant to its intended destination.

The above applies to scheduled routes, but it cannot be assumed that a free market exists in the charter business, about which each state makes its own policy decision. Quality controls still exist to the same standards and in the USA, for example, where quantity controls are absent following deregulation of the domestic industry in the 1970s, there appears little need for a charter industry. On the other hand, most European countries favour charter flights as encouraging the growth of tourism whilst, until recently,

Australia discouraged them, thereby delaying the growth of long-haul holidays.

Regulation within Europe

Despite the existence since 1993 of a Single European Market within the EU, the aviation industry is still strongly oriented to individual states. In 1992 the EU agreed its 'Third Aviation Package', which was a complex series of liberalisation measures. However, the most important points may be summarised as follows:

- In general, Governments can no longer control the fares charged by airlines.
- The bilateral agreements between EU member states are replaced by the freedom for airlines based in one state to fly between any of them. Not only can an airline fly any route from its home state to another EU state, but it can fly between two others; for example, the Irish-registered Ryanair flies between the UK and Germany. This is sometimes referred to as the 7th freedom.
- An EU-based airline can now also fly internally within another member state. For example, Lufthansa could operate on the Paris-Nice route. This is known as 'cabotage' or the 8th Freedom.

However, it must be remembered that at least one of most city-pairs served by airline routes lies outside both the USA and the EU, where most deregulation/liberalisation has occurred. In these cases, bilateral agreements normally still have dual designation and the route can be served only by the two partners' national airlines.

Strategic alliances

The nationally or place of ownership of an airline is important in determining where it is permitted to fly. In the past this was not a problem, because most international routes were 'dual designation' with access limited to the national (and usually state-owned) airlines of the destination countries. Now that other airlines are permitted to compete on these routes, and that they are increasingly owned by the private sector, the issue of nationality becomes, important. That is, if an airline, through changes in shareholdings, loses its national status it also loses the right to operate on routes based in its 'home' country.

Aviation, like most industries, is becoming global and economies of scale are identified from having world-wide coverage. However, the obvious approach of mergers between airlines may be closed to them because of their effect on national status. Airlines have, therefore, taken the alternative approach of forming strategic or marketing alliances designed to achieve the benefits of scale without losing national identity. There is no rigid formula but the following are common features:

- Cross-shareholdings at a level below 50 percent.
- Collaboration in maintenance of aircraft and stocking of spare parts.
- Mutual provision of handling services at "home" airports.
- Code-sharing, that is, the attachment of the flight code of one partner to the operation of another. For example, a KLM flight from Amsterdam to Berlin may also be listed with a flight number of its American partner North West Airlines. This is to encourage a concept of through or connecting flights and to give a stronger presence on computer reservation screens.
- Jointly-planned scheduling to optimise connections at hub airports and maximise utilisation of aircraft.
- Inter-availability of tickets, standardised pricing and common reservation systems.
- Shared Frequent Flyer programmes, encouraging brand loyalty among customers.

Cost Structures, Capacity and Utilisation
Fixed and variable costs

Like any business, transport experiences a mixture of fixed, variable and semi-variable costs. Similarly, what the economist calls 'joint costs' are experienced, the most important of which is that at some time a vehicle will probably have to return to the place where it began its journey. Therefore, the cost to a carrier of operating a journey must include coming back, and purely one-way traffic must pay exceptionally well if it is to be. This does not necessarily mean returning directly; airlines, for example, often perfect are known as 'W formations' where routes are linked together, either to give good or to serve destinations where the airline lacks back-up resources (Figure 1.3).

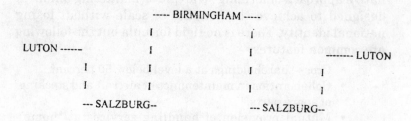

Fig. 1.3 : The W formation.

The incidence of fixed and variable costs determines what marginal costs will be, that is, the cost of providing an additional unit of capacity or the saving from removing a unit. Transport's units of production come in 'lumps' of fixed sizes; if a coach tour operator runs only 50-seat coaches, the minimum that can be added to or removed from an operation is this number.

Marginal costs can be very low or very high. The cost to the operator of an additional passenger on a train or plane which has empty seats is minimal; in the case of the train it is literally the carboard in the ticket, while an airline must pay airport handling charges for each passenger and provide meals, but other cost changes are negligible. However, the point is eventually reached where no capacity remains and the marginal cost of the next passenger is then extremely high.

The significance of marginal costs varies between the modes of transport. Variable costs have traditionally formed a much greater proportion of total costs in road transport than rail, because rail provides its own track which must be paid for regardless of the level of use. Road users, on the other hand, pay for their track through taxation, which (especially fuel tax) varies directly with use. Variable costs are also high for airlines because of the high fuel consumption of aircraft. These differences are important because they affect the benefit to the operator from increasing or reducing the level of service.

Utilisation and load factors

We have already noted that one of the ways in which charter and 'no-frills' airlines are able to keep costs down is by maximising utilisation of their aircraft. This is because the high fixed costs remain the same regardless of distance or sectors covered; the fixed cost per flight or per passenger falls as it is spread over a greater number. Similarly, we have seen that total cost varies little with the number of passangers being carried and that costs are at their lowest per head when the load factor is maximised. It is therefore in operators' interest:

- ' To maximise the distance operated in service.
- Given fixed vehicle capacities, to maximise *use* of that capacity profitably in terms of the number of passengers being carried. Thus, it is usually not in operators' interest to create more capacity if it will remain partly unused.

Contributory revenue

When assessing the financial performance of a route, it should not necessarily be considered in isolation. Frequently, one part of a transport system feeds another, passengers transferring from a local to a long-distance service at an interchange point. If the local service, such as a rail branch line, is deemed to be uneconomic and closed, passangers using it for access to Inter-City routes will not necessarily make their own way to the railhead and many are likely to use cars for the whole journey. Thus, if the capacity of the Inter-City service remains the same, the seat stays empty and the fare income (much more than that for the local service) is lost. For this reason, it is worth looking at the contributory element in a loss-making service, since it could well be worth retaining as a 'loss leader' for the commercial route. Many airlines' domestic routes are loss-making in themselves but are retained because they feed traffic, which might otherwise be lost to a competitor, to profitable international routes.

Industry Performance and Marketing

The glamour associated with air travel and the enormous investment in aircraft and airports may suggest that aviation is highly profitable but, in general, this is not so. Scheduled airlines rarely achieve significant profits, and no large rail system is commercially viable. The challenge for these businesses, therefore, is to improve their load factors to nearer the levels of charter airlines. However, whilst this could easily be done by filling seats at low fares, it does not necessarily maximise revenues; for example, business travellers on airlines making last-minute journeys and willing to pay & hire fare may find their chosen flight is full. The answer lies in yield management.

Reference has already been made to transport capacity being in 'lumps' of fixed sizes. The problem for operators in filling that capacity is that, with a few exceptions, demand for their product is 'derived'—it is not wanted as an end in itself but as a means to something else. People fly to Spain to acquire a suntan and, therefore, want a flight in August and not February. The carrier thus experiences peaks in demand which hinder attempts to secure full utilisation of capacity and which may mean that some equipment is not in use for part of the day or year.

Operators must first ensure that the costs of any under-used equipment are correctly allocated and fully recovered, probably in the form of peak premium charges. However, action can also be taken to minimise the effect of the peak. Some of this action may be operational, for example, by leasing extra vehicles for peak requirements, but the price mechanism can help towards this objective too, both by persuading some peak customers to switch and by generating new business outside the peak. Provided again that costing is accurate and fixed costs are allocated to the peak operations, lower but still profitable prices can be offered for this new business because only the marginal variable and semi-variable costs, plus ideally some contribution to fixed costs, need be recovered.

Elasticity of demand

Use of the price mechanism to influence patronage levels presumes that the public will in fact respond—what economists call 'price-elastic' demand. However, a number of hurdles must be overcome by the transport operator. Firstly, elasticity of demand can relate to factors other than price, in particular quality of service issues. Therefore there are limits to the extent to which price alone will affect patronage.

Secondly, it is important not to be too successful. Low prices which result in demand exceeding supply will bring a call for extra resources with a high marginal cost that would not be recovered. Finally, every operator has its existing customers who are paying the full price. It is vital not to allow these to 'trade down' to lower prices, a process known as revenue dillution, and so some kind of barrier or distinction must be created between the high- and low-price products in order to retain high-price traffic. This is the explanation of many of the restrictive conditions attached to reduced fares, which will now be examined.

Product differentiation and price discrimination

Transport operators have long practiced branding in the form of separate First and Second Class or Economy provision, Pullman cars and so on. These maximised revenue by ensuring that customers willing to pay a higher price did so, and the revenue is secured by a providing higher quality in some way—more comfortable and guaranteed seats, availability of meals, a quiet atmosphere for working, and so on. Much more widespread than in the past, however, is the carriage of passengers in the same facilities at widely differing prices, where barriers of an invisible kind are erected.

The best illustration of this are the rules conventionally attached to airlines' APEX fares, which are sometimes as low as 30 percent of Economy. These are subject to a limited number of seats on particular flights, often around midday when demand is low, a minimum advance booking period of 14 days, which is unsuitable for urgent business trips; a 'no refund or cancellation' condition; and, a rule that a Saturday night must fall between the outward and return journeys, which conflicts with the business traveller's normal desire to be home for the weekend but is acceptable to leisure travellers. These all minimise the 'dilution' of revenue from the valued business market but, as the number of reduced price offers has increased, can lead to a situation where passengers seated alongside pay fares varying by up to 300 percent. Airlines have therefore developed a 'business' or 'Club' class for those paying the full Economy fare, creating a separate cabin with better meals and other privileges. In turn, this has undermined the need for First Class and most airlines have now abolished it within Europe.

However, the operator's objective is to maximise not just seats filled but revenue, and both can be achieved by skillful use of market intelligence and sales data. Just as a tour operator observes sales carefully before deciding when and how far to discount, an airline can decide when, where and how many APEX seats to release. Thus, the ratio can vary not just between flights but day by day, the process aided by equipping aircraft with moveable screens and curtains to adjust the balance between Business and discounted passengers. Information from Computer Reservation Systems assists airlines in making these decisions, and load factors can be further improved by the use of Standby tickets, which are only validated close to the time of departure and when seats have not been filled by other means.

Seat reservations and overbooking

Air passengers assume that when a booking is confirmed a seat is assured, but this is not necessarily the case. Full-price scheduled tickets have a refund facility which airlines are anxious to retain for fear of upsetting high-fare regular business travellers. These, uncertain when they will be able to travel, sometimes buy several tickets in the knowledge that they can obtain a refund on those not used. The loss resulting from 'no-shows' can be considerable, so a practice has developed of systematic overbooking, whereby levels of 'no-shows' are established from records and a flight for which 5 percent of passengers typically fail to report might be overbooked by 3 percent. Sometimes the gamble fails and passengers with valid tickets find there is no room. On long-haul flights, it may be possible to upgrade some to First, while others are encouraged or obliged, with a variety of inducements, to transfer to other flights. The European Union has introduced a Regulation fixing levels of compensation for overbooked passengers and setting priorities in selection.

Environmental Impacts of Transport

All tourism activities have their damaging effects on the local and wider community, but transport has some of the most visible and severe of these. Few would consider airports and their surroundings physically attractive, air pollution levels are normally high, and the route to resorts is often littered with the ugly but necessary support business on which mass tourism depends. Even in the resort itself, we may notice large areas taken up by car parking both on and off the street, the smell of vehicle exhausts and nose-to-tail traffic at busy times. There are also the less obvious consequences, such as climate change.

Ample evidence exists of people's concern at these problems. For example, a survey of residents' attitudes to tourism in Stratford-on-Avon confirmed that traffic congestion, parking problems and general environmental damage were seen as disadvantages of the town's tourism business. 88 percent of residents believed that traffic congestion needed to be relieved, but there was not the same consensus on how to achieve it! As car ownership grows, both visitors and residents find it more difficult to imagine a lifestyle without it, while business in host areas consider car-borne trade vital to their prosperity. As a result, people's desire for action in general is contradicted by a wish that it should not affect them personally.

Nevertheless, attitudes may be changing slowly. A view has emerged in Europe that, rather than restrictions on car use deterring visitors, *too much* traffic can be a deterrent. Switzerland has a group of car-free villages which promote themselves jointly on that strength, and they have experienced growth in their share of the tourism market. An economic as well as an environmental case therefore exists for promoting sustainable forms of transport. Also, it is easy to forget that not everybody owns a car. Ownership rates vary widely between countries and regions but, even in prosperous areas, 10-15 percent of households may have no car, a figure which rises to over 50 percent in cities. Therefore, a resort or business which limits itself to car access ignores a substantial part of the market whilst, at some attractions, scarce land has to be devoted to car parking which, if visitors arrived by other means, could be put to more productive use.

A number of approaches to environmentally-friendlier transport are possible. Greater use of walking, horse-riding and cycling can be encouraged by the development of specialised routes. Local traffic management and restriction schemes can be implemented, but these tend to have no effect on the total number of cars coming into an area. The signing necessary to advise motorists of a restriction can itself be visually intrusive, but perhaps the biggest problem is the likely objections from businesses and residents.

An alternative approach is to encourage use of public transport, either for the 'trunk' journey to the holiday area or for local journeys within it. However, car-owners take their motorised lifestyle for granted and find the alternative inconvenient, probably expensive and unsuited to their image, and many projects have failed to achieve their objectives. As a minimum, in order to attract car users public transport must offer high quality in its operation and promotion, have reasonable and simple integrated pricing, appear 'seamless' and create an impression of user-friendliness. It helps if it can be sold as an attraction in itself, for example through the use of vintage equipment. Even this may not be enough and , therefore, to achieve any significant transfer from cars, it may be necessary to introduce traffic restrictions alongside. Here, here the pill can be sweetened with assurances that funding is committed to a high-quality alternative.

Two kinds of location lend themselves particularly to intervention of the kind described, namely, historic towns and protected rural areas, such as National Parks. In both cases, visitors are attracted by the traditional and 'heritage' aspects. Thus, conventional approaches to traffic planning, involving the widening of roads, demolition of buildings and construction of car parks, would remove the essential attraction of the visit and so threaten visitor numbers. As a result, many historic town centres are now pedestrianised, and the removal of traffic to achieve this is often by a Park and Ride scheme which allows car users to park on the outskirts and use a dedicated bus (occasionally a train) to the centre.

National Park areas have found it more difficult to achieve progress, but the Lake District, for example, is currently developing a 'Strategic Gateway' west of Kendal. This will seek to intercept car traffic approaching the congested centre of the National Park by providing a Park and Ride facility on its outskirts.

2

Issues in
Tourist Transport

Introduction

The demand for tourist transport was discussed in terms of the commercial opportunities, it affords operators who are able to understand and harness it. To meet the demand for tourist transport, businesses and operators can employ a range of concepts to analyse what they need to do to match supply to demand. First, some of the broader issues affecting the supply of tourist transport, particularly a conceptual framework in which both the traveller's and the transport provider's perspectives are considered to try and maximise the commercial and non-commercial opportunities within the tourism industry. We discuss that how operators and the transport sector employ particular management tools (e.g., logistics and information technology applications) and business strategies to provide the tourist as a user and consumer of the transport system with a range of opportu-nities to enhance their overall tourist experience. While the two chapters examine supply issues in different ways—looking at the complexity of analytical and operational issues separated into discrete sections—in reality one needs to view these two elements in a holistic manner as they are inter-twined in the real world.

It is also important to emphasise the broader tourism context in which tourist transport exists. The recent study by Harris and Masberg (1997) that examined vintage tram operations in 26 North American cities indicates how the supply of a mode of transport can be harnessed for tourism and yet is not able to generate tourism without appropriate infrastructure to support it. Harris and Masberg (1997) argue that while trams may constitute a cultural icon influencing tourists to visit a destination, a pool of attrac-tions is needed to get visitors to use trams to tour within the destination. In other words, the supply of transport itself is not sufficient to stimulate tourism development but can be a catalyst if it is integrated as part of a wider strategy to develop attractions, accommodation and an urban tourism experience. This example serves to illustrate the significance of developing various approaches and concepts which promote a broader understanding of transport supply issues. A similar argument can also be developed for transport modes such as car hire which support tourist activities, although in a number of cases. Where transport is the tourist experience (e.g., cruising and vintage railways), supply issues may assume an even greater significance as the entire experience is directly dependent upon the service the operator provides.

There is a relative paucity of research on supply issues in tourism and transport studies (Eadington and Redman 1991). Witt et. al., (1991) consider that the:

> Subset of transport studies that directly relates to tourism is relatively neglected...(and)...it is a major task of research to bring together the work done in transport studies with that more specialised work on tourism ...(as)... many of the relevant studies are privately commissioned and often not widely disseminated. (Witt et. al., 1991:155-6)

The absence of any synthesis of supply-related research which integrates tourism and transport into a more cohesive framework led Sinclair to argue that the 'literature on transportation and its implications for domestic and international tourism merits separate analysis'. The efficient management and operation of transport systems for tourists require that demand issues are analysed in relation to supply since the two issues coexist and they determine the future pattern of use and activities within the tourist transport system.

The supply of tourist transport has been dealt with in various popular tourism textbooks (e.g., Holloway 1989; Lavery 1989), which consider the characteristics, principles and organisation associated with each mode of tourist transport. In a book such as this, it is inappropriate to reiterate the empirical discussion of different modes of transport in these publications since it would inevitably result in a descriptive listing which is documented elsewhere. Furthermore, a variety of good accessible publications also document many of the issues associated with different modes of tourist transport, using up-to-date market intelligence compiled by transport analysts. (The former Economist Intelligence publications and the subsequent travel and tourism intelligence journals such as *Travel and Tourism Analyst, International Tourism Reports* and their occasional reports are essential reading.) The commences with a discussion of theory related to supply issues; this is followed by a framework which develops the context in which both the traveller's and the transport provider's perspectives are considered in relation to an underlying concern for service quality. The concept of transaction analysis is introduced as a method of understanding the central role of transport in the supply of tourist travel. Transaction analysis assists in assessing the transport supplier's involvement in the distribution chain and the ways in which they may influence and control the chain and service quality in the supply of transport services. To illustrate the extent of one transport operator's involvement in the distribution chain, a case study of Singapore Airlines is examined.

Theoretical Perspectives on Tourism and Transport Supply Issues

Despite the rapid growth in research studies in tourism in the 1980s and 1990s, those publications which make a contribution to the advancement of knowledge and our understanding of the subject are still comparatively few.

This is certainly the case in relation to supply issues and one explanation may be related to the fact that :

Tourism supply is a complex phenomenon because of both the nature of the product and the process of delivery. Principally, it cannot be stored, cannot be examined prior to purchase, it is necessary to travel to consume it, heavy reliance is placed on both natural and human-made resources and a number of components are required, which may be separately or jointly purchased and which are consumed in sequence. It is a composite product involving transport, accommodation, catering, natural resources, entertainment, and other facilities and services, such as shops and banks, travel agents and tour operators.

Thus many business supply components which are combined to form the tourism product, and because they operate in different markets, it makes it difficult to analyse supply issues. In fact, it proves even more complex when seeking to separate out one element of the tourism product (i.e.transport) to identify the range of supply issues affecting an individual element.

Probably the most influential and pertinent publication to date which assists in addressing supply issues in a theoretical framework is a recent synthesis of *The Economics of Tourism*. Sinclair and Stabler infer that one can explain how firms operate under different conditions and therefore it may be possible to identify factors which affect supply issues in relation to tourism in general, and transport in particular. While it is not possible to present a detailed analysis here, the main principles outlined by Sinclair and Stabler are discussed as they focus on four market situations:

- perfect competition,
- contestable markets,
- monopoly,
- oligopoly.

In this discussion, attention is directed to the transport sector.

Perfect Competition

In economic models of conditions of perfect competition, a number of assumptions exist:

- There are a substantial number of consumers and firms, implying that neither can affect the price of an undifferentiated product.
- There is free entry to and exit from the market, assuming that there are no barriers.

Sinclair and Stabler (1997) explain how a perfect market operates and how prices are derived, with the tendency towards a break-even price in a situation where consumers derive a benefit. However, in the real world, many economists believe that markets are not perfectly competitive.

Contestable Markets

In this situation, there are 'insignificant entry and exit costs, so that there are negligible entry and exit barriers. Sunk costs which a firm incurs in order to produce and which would not be recoupable if the firm left the industry, are not significant'. Due to technology, information and supply conditions are available to all producers and while producers cannot change prices instantaneously, consumers can react immediately. The key principle here is that new and established firms are able to challenge rival business through pricing strategies. Firms in contestable markets are seen to operate in a similar way to those in perfect markets, since they charge similar prices for a product; existing operators cannot charge more than average cost because more competitors would enter the market. Due to low sunk costs and low entry/exit barriers, rivals establish to compete.

Monopoly

This is probably best described as the opposite of perfect competition, where a major business or firm is able to exercise a high level of control over the price of the product and level of output. The implications are that firms operating in a monopolistic market charges prices above the average cost of production to generate high profit levels, os consumers pay a price higher than that which would exist in a competitive market. In many countries, domestic air and rail networks operate under monopoly conditions even though it can be against the interests of consumers.

In some cases, a monopoly condition may be more beneficial than competition, as in the case of deregulation in the transport industry. In such situations, an influx of new entrants following deregulation may lead to smaller firms being taken over by larger businesses. On monopoly routes this results in higher prices which are detrimental to consumers' interests. Sinclair and Stabler (1997) also examine other scenarios where monopoly conditions may be beneficial to the wider public good in tourist transport operations. Where governments have privatised state transport interests, one outcome has been a greater degree of concentration of operations among a small number of operators. However, where monopoly situations exist, regulation by the state is normally imposed to prevented higher prices and supernormal profits.

Oligopoly

An oligopoly exists where a limited number of producers dominate the transport sector. Williams highlights the situation in relation to tourism and transport since 'tourism has a highly dualistic industrial structure which is polarised between large numbers of small firms (typically in retailing, accommodation services) and a small number of large companies (for example, in air transport)'.

In an oligopoly, each firm controls its price and output levels and there are entry and exit barriers. An oligopoly market situation is characterised by supply conditions dependent in part upon the output and pricing decisions of competitors. In an ideal world, oligopolies prefer prices to be set at levels where the profits are maximised for all producers in that industry sector. If the firms colluded to set prices, it could lead to a monopoly and higher profits for producers if they restricted the supply. Sinclair and Stabler (1997) point to the impact of inter-airline pricing and route-sharing agreements to achieve joint profits in an oligopolistic situation. In an oligopolistic market, producers can alter output and prices while taking account of their competitors' likely reactions.

In their overview of the air travel market, Sinclair and Stabler (1997) argue that

> Although a domestic monopoly or oligopoly structure has been common, with a single state-supported airline or a small number or competing airlines, deregulation has made some markets competitive in the short run. In the international market some routes are competitive, being served by many carriers. Most of the others are served by at least two carriers, indicating an obligopolist market, although a few routes are served by a single carrier which may be tempted to exercise monopoly powers. (Sinclair and Stabler 1997 : 81)

In the terms of the remaining transport sectors, Sinclair and Stabler conclude that :

> The structures of the bus, coach and rail sectors are similar to that of air travel in that they too, experience the problems of high capital costs, fixed capacity, peaked demand, the need for feeder routes to sustain profitable ones. Some state support and regulation characterise these modes.

It is apparent that where a large number of small firms operate in the transport sector a competitive market exists. In contrast, where a limited number of firms operate, akin to an oligopoly or at the extreme, a monopoly, different conditions affect the supply of transport services for tourists. What emerges from the excellent analysis of supply conditions in tourism is that various criteria influence the competitive conditions which exist in different markets, and factors such as the degree of market concentration or price leadership affect the extent and nature of inter-firm competition. For example, French (1996) examines the advent of 'no frills' airlines in Europe and the effect on the market. In a similar vein, Peisley (1997) examines the case of the Channel Tunnel as a new market entrant and its impact on the cross-Channel ferry market. Here the competition led to a reduction in yields with a competitive price war. The result has been a greater degree of concentration in the ferry market with the merger of P&O and Stena Line. Thus, in any analysis of transport supply issues, a range of criteria need to be investigated in different market conditions. These are based on Sinclair and Stabler :

- The number and size of firms.
- The extent of market concentration.
- Entry and exit barriers.
- Economies/diseconomies of scale and economies of scope.
- Costs of capital, fixed capital and costs of operation.
- Price discrimination and product differentiation.
- Pricing policies (e.g., price leadership, price wars, and market-share strategies).

The final two points are examined concerned with the strategies business pursue in competitive markets. In the case of the first five points, which pertain to market structures, Sinclair and Stabler identify a range of data sources available to researchers. In the airline sector, some data sources on demand also contain evidence on supply such as ICAO, IATA and industry bodies. Other sources, such as company annual reports, also contain interesting data. Therefore, having outlined some of the principal theoretical considerations affecting the supply of transport for tourism, attention now turns to a conceptual framework

—the supply chain. This enables one to recognise the theoretical issues and to appreciate how the criteria associated with competitive markets may affect the organisation and delivery of supply.

The Supply Chain in Tourist Transport Services

Prior to the innovative synthesis by Sinclair and Stabler (1997), there was an absence of detailed research on the supply of tourism and transport services. This has acted as a major constraint on the development of literature in this area, and with the exception of research by transport economists, economists' interest in supply issues has been limited, if not peripheral to the main studies in the area. The situation has been compounded by the image of supply research in tourism and transport studies, which is sometimes perceived as descriptive, lacking intellectual rigour and sophisticated methods of study, since 'generally there is little research on the tourism (and transport) industry and its operation which is analytical in emphasis'. This is perpetuated by the treatment of supply issues in many general tourism texts which broadly discuss 'passenger transportation', since there are methodological problems in differentiating between the supply and use of transport services by the local population for travel to work, leisure and recreational travel purposes and more specific tourist use. In fact, Sinclair and Stabler argue that 'categories as transport...are very broad and benefit from disaggregation into sub-makets with different structures and modes of operation'. Thus it is not surprising to find that research has focused on established areas of tourism and transport supply, notably:

- Descriptions of the industry and its operation, management and marketing.
- The spatial development and interactions which characterise the industry at different geographical scales.
  Source: Sinclair and Stabler.

Studies of transport systems within tourism research have been characterised by a preoccupation with how their operations are organised to provide a service to travellers and how the international nature of transport facilitates tourism activities and development. This approach to research on tourist transport systems is rooted in economics, as emphasised, based on the concept of the 'firm', developed by Coase (1937) and discussed further by Buckley and Casson (1985). In the context of tourism and transport supply, Buckley (1987) notes that the analysis of a firm or company is characterised by certain relationships within the organisation and with its purchasers or consumers. The external process of selling a product or service involves a transaction between two parties following an agreement to purchase, often though not exclusively, using a monetary transaction. Commercial transactions are based on agreed conditions and enforced within a framework of contractual obligations between the parties. Therefore, transaction chains develop to link the tourist with the suppliers of services in tourism and the 'tourism product or service' is defined as the sum of these transactions. Such research highlights the significance of the 'chain of distribution' for transport and tourism services, which is the method of distribution of the service from production through to its eventual consumption by tourists. A more general discussion of the distribution chain in tourism can be found in Holloway (1995).

Transaction Analysis

Buckley (1987) describes some typical transaction chains for tourism which identify the integral role of transport services in linking origin and destination areas (Figure 2.1). The nature of the specific supply chain depends upon a wide range of factors which are internal and external to individual firms in the transport sector. For example, what is the primary force driving the supply system? Is it driven by pull factors, where a tourist destination may market a region and supply transport services on a state-owned airline to stimulate demand for tourism? Or is it driven by push factors, where the trourist generates the demand, and the transport and accommodation sectors respond to this as a commercial opportunity? The overall business environment, government predisposition to tourism and planning constraints may have a moderating influence on the supply system. In addition, transaction analysis illustrates the significance of 'agents' in the system, corporate policy in transport provision and contractual arrangements in the supply chain.

Much of the existing knowledge available on these issues has been generated through interviews with mangers in each sector of the transport industry about their commercial practices (e.g., contracting arrangements, profit margins and global strategies). It is rare to find researchers being given access to commercial information on supply (and demand) issues, due to the confidential and sensitive nature of the data, and the perceived threat it might pose to a company's competitive advantage if rival operators obtained such information. In some cases this amounts to paranoia among companies, as media coverage of the British Airways and Virgin Atlantic libel case in 1992-93 highlighted. The result is that the relationship between transport supply and tourist use remains poorly understood, with commercial research primarily concerned with the effect of pricing transport services, the behaviour of consumers and the outcome in terms of use and profitability for producers. It is within this context that Buckley's (1987) research proves useful in understanding the nature of relationship which may exist in the supply chain.

From Buckley's four chains (Figure 2.1), it is evident that a variety of distribution systems exist for the sale and consumption of transport services by tourists. One of the critical issues in the distribution system for the seller is access to superior information on available services, so that these can be sold to the consumer. There are various studies which document tourism and transport retailing, where the agent or broker is normally paid a commission on their sales. The travel agent comprises a convenient one-stop location for tourists to buy tourism services as an inclusive

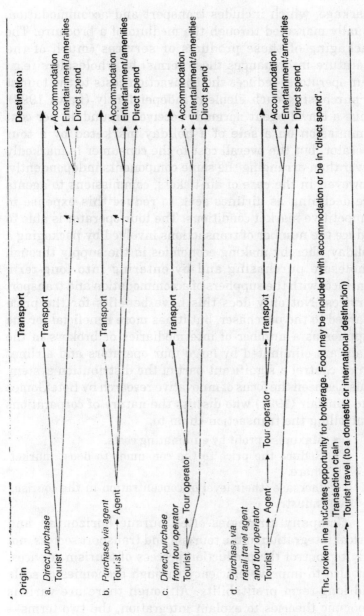

Fig. 2.1. Four types of tourism transaction chain.

package; which includes transport and accommodation, usually marketed through the medium of a brochure. The packaging of these products or services (much of the literature interchanges these terms) by wholesalers (e.g., tour operators) reduces the transaction costs to the tourist of purchasing each element independently (Laws 1995). Thus a travel agent normally receives around 10 per cent commission on a sale of a holiday marketed by a tour operator, but the overall cost to the consumer is markedly lower than arranging the same components independently. However, in the case of air tickets, commissions to agents are declining as airlines seek to reduce this expense in competitive market conditions. The tour operator is able to reduce the number of transactions involved by packaging a holiday; thereby making economies in the supply through wholesale purchasing and by entering into long-term contracts with the suppliers of accommodation and transport services. Not only does this have benefits for the price charged to the purchaser, but it has more beneficial for the supplier as a number of intermediaries or brokers in the chain are eliminated by large tour operators and airlines which control a significant part of the distribution system. This has been the focus of innovative research by Bote Gomez and Sinclair (1991) who discuss the nature of corporations controlling the transaction chain to:

- Maximise profit by eliminating costs.
- Reduce the price to the consumer to boost market share.
- Increase their level of concentration in the tourism industry.

Company strategies often pursue horizontal and verical integration in the tourism and transport sectors, not only to control the production process of tourism services, but also to improve efficiency through economies of scale and long-term profitability. Although there are various economic theories to explain integration, the two terms— vertical and horizontal integration—have received little detailed analysis.

Integration in the Tourism Sector: Implications for the Supply of Tourist Transport

According to Bote Gomez and Sinclair (1991):

- Integration is based on the concept of common ownership which may involve the coordination or control of the production process or may have no direct effect on it.

Table 2.1: Integration in the UK package holiday business in 1998.[1]

	Thomson	Cooks Sunworld[2]	Airtours	Inspirations	First Choice
		Operator/parent company			
Retail outlets	Lunn Poly	Thomas Cook	Going Places	A.T.Mays	Independent
	800 shops	385 shops	713 shops	409 shops	
Airline	Britannia	Airworld	International	Caledonian	Air 2000
	28 aircraft	5 aircraft	21 aircraft	11 aircraft	no data
Cruise ships	MS *Sapphire*		MS *Carousel*		
			MS *Seawing*		
			MS *Sundream*		

1. In 1997, the UK package holiday industry had four organisations selling over a million packages a year. Thomson led the market with 4 million customers; Airtours sold 2.9 million, First Choice sold 2 million and Thomsan Cook sold 1.05 million holidays. Inspirations was ranked fifth with 411,600 sales.

2. Thomas Cook has a 14 per cent holding in First Choice.

- Horizontal integration occurs where two enterprises with the same output combine to increase the companies' control over output. It can occur through mergers, acquisitions, collaboration, franschising agreements and more complex contractual arrangements and may induce concentration in the same business.

- Vertical integration occurs when an enterprise with different interests and involvement in the supply chain acquires or merges with companies contributing inputs to its activities, or where output purchases provide a ready market for the service. This has the advantage of decreasing economic uncertainty in the supply system and the avoidance of problems related to contract breaking.

The significance of integration in the UK tourism industry is documented in Table 2.1 and the implications for tourists transport have been well documented by Sinclair (1991). It is evident that:

> The transport function is an important point in the exchange of rights in the tourism transaction chain. If this function is subcontracted to an independent operator this delicate and central function can go out of control; hence the close integration of transport with other facilities in the integrated multinational company to ensure a degree of control in the distribution system in the supply of transport services to tourists.

Buckley (1987) notes that integration in tourist transport operations, especially vertical ownership, may help to reduce cost where higher load factors can be guaranteed for associated companies. Transaction analysis highlights not only the driving force in the supply system but also raises questions which researchers may wish to address in relation to specific companies and their role in tourist transport.

Transaction analysis also provides an opportunity to consider the changing patterns and processes shaping the tourist transport system and the growing internationalisation of the supply chain. One of the growing issues in the globalisation of tourism supply is a reflection of the development of mass leisure tourism markets, which have been subject to the process of internationalisation. Williams argues that the internationalisation of tourism activity and investment has to be seen in the more general and increasingly rapid process of globalisation of international investment. As a result, transnational business interests have developed in the tourism industry, epitomised by some of the larger airlines such as BA, which aims to become a global carrier. Williams suggests that 'firms' competitive strategies are based on seeking cost leadership, product differentiation, and focusing on market niches; under certain circumstances these may dictate the inter-nationalisation of tourist activity and invest-ment'. Such research is underpinned by the earlier findings of Dunning that transnational development in sectors of the tourism industry such as transport is due to firms entering international markets for offensive and defensive reasons when using recognised brand names. They aim to establish location-specific advantages and to reduce risk by using the existing business advantages of an established company. Williams provides an interesting assessment of tansnationalism by seeking to apply theoretical constructs to the international aviation industry.

Transnationalism in the supply chain also raises important issues for service quality and service delivery. The implications for serviced quality are notable because integration raises a fundamental problem for the tourist transport operator: if an independent airline becomes vertically integrated, should the parent company manage its operation even if it has no experience of this specialised activity? If not, how can the parent company ensure it controls both continuity and quality in the service encounter throughout the supply chain? This has been referred to as *Total Supply Management*. In the area of corporate strategy, there is growing evidence that contractual arrangements are being used to ensure that service quality is a continuous process throughout the supply chain. For example, large companies such as Thomson Holidays are operated as independent organisations in the International Thomson Group of Companies which includes the sister company Britannia Airlines and their own travel agency chain, Lunn Poly. One option available to the group is to have a corporately administered system to ensure that a particular benchmark in service quality, for the tourist's experience is achieved throughout the supply chain. This would commence with the sale of a service via Lunn Poly, or direct through Thomson Holidays, and would include the flight and arrival in the destination, where a company representative meets tourists and travels with them on the airport transfer to

their accommodation. This is then followed by a welcome
where general information and a sales function is
undertaken by promoting tours with coach companies
endorsed by Thomson. During the holiday, the
representative is empowered to deal with consumer issues
in situ and to organise the return airport transfer for the
departure. During the return flight, a corporate customer
satisfaction questionnaire is administered by Thomson
Holidays to assess the level of satisfaction with the package
holiday, especially the transport element. This provides a
cheap form of market intelligence on corporate quality
standards and may highlight areas for attention to reduce
service interruptions and customer dissatisfaction.

Introducing a corporate quality control system may
help to minimise customer dissatisfaction, particularly if
the organisation employs and trains staff to deal with the
service encounter as an ongoing process, rather than viewing
the services as a series of discrete elements over which they
have only limited control. Yet even in a corporate quality
control system, employees have to recognise the limit of their
responsibiliti.: and be able to refer customers to the relevant
personnel empowered to deal with an interruption in the
service requested.

Where the tour operator and purchaser of the transport
service is unable to directly control the inputs and outputs
throughout the system, one option may be to develop a
contractually administered qualilty control system. Here all
parties involved in the supply chain may make a contractual
commitment to supply services to a certain standard to avoid
weak links in the system (e.g., poor quality food and service
on board an aircraft) which can affect the tourist's
impression of the entire service. All parties involved need
to agree on a paritcular quality principle (e.g., the British
Standard 5750 for service systems which some transport
operators, such as P&O Stena already employ) to implement
throughout the supply chain, using performance indicators
to ensure that the necessary standards are being reached.
One way of examining the supply chain in the case of tourist

transport operators which are public companies is to examine their annual report. For this reason, it is pertinent to consider the role of such data sources, their purpose and how they may be used.

Analysing Annual Reports: Company Accounts

An annual report is used by companies to provide a review of the year's activities and it contains company accounts which are prepared within accounting guidelines in force in the country where the head office is based. For example, in the case of SIA (Singapore International Airlines), the accounts must be deposited in Singapore.

Bird and Rutherford (1989) argue that company accounts contain message which use specialist jargon to deal with a complex situation. Once the specialist jargon is decoded by the reader, company accounts provide an insight into the financial performance of businesses. There are two key elements within company accounts:

- a balance sheet,
- a profit and loss account.

Within the balance sheet, items of value (assets) are listed and any claims against them are set out. A claim is a liability, such as an unpaid bill. Assets are divided into fixed assets, which are those acquired for use within the business, and current assets, comprising cash and other items which are to be converted into cash. Liabilities within the accounts are also divided into current liabilities, where settlement will be made within one year, and long-term liabilities to be settled after one year. It should be recognised that a balance sheet only provides a snapshot of an organisation's activities at one point in time. Therefore, analysts tend to consider company accounts over a three five-year period to give a more realistic assessment of an organisation's business performance.

There is a great deal of debate among accountants over the reliability of such documents, due to the degree of creative accounting which characterises them. In other words, critics argue that company accounts only record what a company wants to state publicity about its activities. In fact one can argue that the flexibility and vagueness of accounting rules in relation to the preparation of company accounts and financial results means that they are no longer an absolute measure of success. Manipulation of the profit and loss account and the balance sheet to report flattering results which meet corporate investors' and stock markets' expectations have contributed to the pressure for creative accounting. Notwithstanding these limitations associated with company accounts within published annual reports, they provide an important public relations function for companies and offer an insight into the organisation, operation and scale of a company's activities.

CASE STUDY : Singapore Airlines and the Supply of Tourist Transport Services

An interesting way to identify the extent to which integration exists within the tourist transport system is to consider one company and its activities. The case of Singapore Airlines (SIA) provides a useful example since it is based within one of the fastest-growing tourism markets in the 1990s —the Pacific Rim. SIA was also one of the most profitable international airlines in 1990/91 and this has continued throughout the mid-1990s. Its transformation from a state-owned enterprise (SOE) to a privatised company has been the focus of recent research. As a tourist transport operator, SIA has been widely regarded as Singapore's premier enterprise, formed in 1947, developing as the national flag carrier in 1972 and privatised after 1985. Its performance has been consistently profitable (Bowen 1997) and its close relationship with the government has meant it has developed a synergy with the Singapore Tourism Promotion Board to assist with the development of inbound tourism.

Sikorski provides a detailed analysis of how SIA was developed and financed as well as its route to privatisation. This case study focuses on SIA as an international transport operator, documenting its growth and then focusing on one data source—SIA's annual report to illustrate the scope and involvement of one company in the supply chain for transport and tourism services.

The Development of SIA and Aviation in Singapore

A recent study by Raguraman (1997) examines how civil aviation has contributed to the development of the nation and national identify in Malaysia and Singapore. Raguraman outlines the development of civil aviation in each country in three phases: 1930-57, during the era of British colonial rule; 1957-71, which was characterised by the development of regional air services; and post-1971, when each nation developed its own international airline service and national carrier. Prior to 1930, Imperial Airways, a British-subsidised airline, developed services and all-weather landing strips in Malaya. In April 1931, Imperial Airways made its maiden flight to Singapore on its mail service, *City of Cairo*. In 1934, Singapore established itself as a hub, linking the Imperial Airways flight from London to the flight operated by Qantas Empire Airways (QEA) to Darwin. The passage to Australia could be completed in $12\frac{1}{2}$ days. In 1937 Imperial Airways carried 70,000 passengers and flew in excess of 6 million miles; while in 1938, it was providing an extensive mail service using Empire flying boats to South Africa, New Zealand and Hong Kong. The airline fulfilled geographical objectives for the British government, seeking to sustain its sovereignty over the empire. In 1939, the British government nationalised and merged the newly formed British Airways with Imperial Airways to establish the British Overseas Airways Corporation (BOAC). The Second World War disru-pted aviation development in Singapore; services resumed in 1946 with BOAC and Qantas flights between England and Australia.

In 1947, Malaysian Airways Limited (MAL) began scheduled services on a Singapore-Kuala Lumpur-Ipoh-Penang route. The company was formed as a local joint venture between the Ocean Steamship Company, the Straits

Steamship Company and Mansfield Company. In 1948, BOAC acquired a 10 percent shareholding in the company. During this era of aviation development in Singapore, arrivals grew from 2,735 in 1937 at Kallang Airport to 183,023 in 1955 when the airport was closed and relocated to Paya Lebar. In 1957, Malaya became an independent nation while Singapore remained a colony and MAL became a public company with exclusive operation rights of air services between Malaya, Singapore and Borneo for a decade. Qantas and BOAC each acquired a 33 percent share of the new MAL since it removed the need for state investment in capital and human resources. Yet it also allowed outside interests to retain air rights.

In 1965 Singapore was separated from the Federation of Malaysia, and in 1966 an injection of S$15 million of capital from Malaysia and Singapore's governments provided them with majority control of MAL. This provided the national governments with a 33.74 per cent equity each, with 30AC and Qantas retaining a 13.2 per cent share and 6.12 percent being held by the Brunei government, private business interests and the public. In 1967, MAL underwent a name change to Malaysia-Singapore Airlines (MSA) and by 1970, the MSA network covered urban destinations in Asia, Oceania and Europe. Increased frequencies resulted from the introduction of Boeing 707 jet aircraft while the domestic network saw considerable development. MSA developed a profitable business.

A divergence of interests between the national objectives of Malaysia and Singapore towards MSA let to public and national dissatisfaction. While Malaysia privatised domestic services, Singapore was primarily concerned with international links. Despite the obvious commercial advantages of MSA (it made a small loss in 1966/67 and a pre-tax profit of M$42.46 million in 1971), the respective governments decided to split the airline in 1972. The assets were divided, minority shareholders were compensated, and new airlines (Singapore Airlines and Malaysian Airline System) were established.

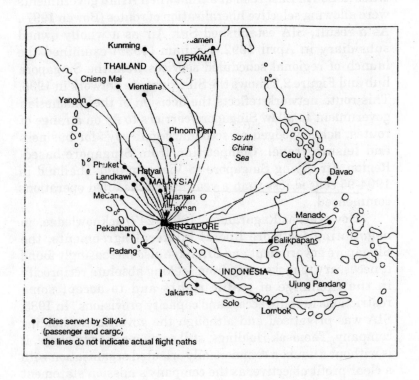

Fig. 2.2 : The Silk Air route network 1996 (redrawn from Singapore Airlines 1997).

During the early years of SIA, it did not receive the same level of government support as other Asian airlines, but being in a city-state removed its social obligation to provide unprofitable domestic services. Raguraman (1086) documents the early years of growth at SIA and acknowledges the numerous barriers it faced in gaining foreign market access. Through lobbying governments directly in the UK and Australia, SIA gained rights to fly to Manchester, Brisbane and Adelaide. The airline also recognised the growth potential of tourist flows to secondary cities in South East Asia at a time when Asian governments were allowing selective liberalisation of routes (Bowen 1997). As a result, SIA established Silk Air as a wholly owned subsidiary in April 1992. Graham (1995) examined the launch of regional scheduled services from the Singapore hub and Figure 2.2 shows the SilkAir route network in 1996. This route network reflects the decision of the Indonesian government to allow Singapore carriers to fly on a range of routes, acknowledged as secondary gateways for business and leisure travel. Competition from Singapore-based. Region Air, flying Singapore to Vietnam and Thailand in 1994-95 ceased less than a year after scheduled operations commenced.

However, as Raguraman (1997 : 247) acknowledge, 'in negotiating for more liberal bilateral agreements, the Singapore government and SIA have also increasingly found it necessary to move away from seeking absolute reciprocity in the exchange of traffic rights and to accept some restrictions in route access and capacity provisions'. In 1985, SIA was privatised and although the government holding company, Temasek Holdings, still owns a majority share, it is without a doubt a commercially oriented organisation with a clear profit objective, as the company's mission statement in 1997 states

Singapore Airlines is engaged in air transportation and related businesses. It operates worldwide as the flag carrier of the Republic of Singapore, aiming to provide services of the highest quality at reasonable prices for customers and a profit for the company.

Raguraman (1997 : 247) outlined the historical growth in traffic for SIA, where it achieved an annual growth rate of 10 percent between 1974 and 1994. Its network expanded from services to 24 cities in 1972 to 68 cities in 1994 and 76 cities in 41 countries in 1998 (including 3 serviced only by freighters (Figure 2.3). One immediate outcome of the success of SIA was the spillover effect for the development of Changi Airport as a hub and gateway to South East Asia.

Thus SIA is among Singapore's top three enterprises. By developing a large international route network, SIA can also achieve economies of scope (Sinclair and Stabler 1997), by increasing frequencies or points in its network through the use of SilkAir in South East Asia. Bowen (1997 : 136) recognises that companies such as SIA can gain benefits from economies of scope by:

- Developing a denser network of connections, through increasing efficiency in the use of resources, such as hub facilities at Changi, thereby reducing costs.

- Having a larger network gives an opportunity for price leadership.

- Deriving benefits from large-scale marketing that can offer a wide range of destinations.

Bowen (1997) also examines policy issues that could affect the future liberalisation of air travel in Asia, something which may yield additional benefits for established market leaders such as SIA. Having considered the growth of SIA and a range of issues affecting the airline in the 1980s and 1990s, we now turn our attention to the 1996/97 annual report.

The SIA annual report

The SIA annual report for 1996/97 comprises 80 pages compared to 139 pages in 1991/92 and some of the key themes are listed in Table 2.2. As a source of information on tourist transport, it contains a significant amount of public relations material which complements the statistical infor-mation on the airline. As an accessible data source for researchers, it is a baseline of information from which further research can be undertaken. The initial statistical highlights within the report provide an executive summary of the company accounts, but it is the discussion of the SIA group activities that is the most informative in terms of airline operations and integration within their business activities.

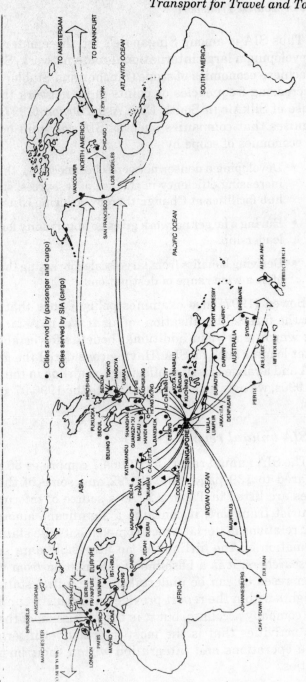

Fig. 2.3 : The Singapore Airlines route network 1993.

Table 2.2 : Key features of SIA annual report 1996/97.

- Mission statement
- Statistical highlights
- Chairman's statement
- Calendar of significant events
- The 50th anniversary
- General operational review
- Fleet and route development
- Cargo
- Our people
- Subsidiaries
- Finances
- Financial review
- Report by the board of directors
- Statement of the directors' profit and loss accounts
- Auditors' report
- Profit and loss accounts
- Balance sheets
- Cash flow statements
- Notes to the accounts
- Half-yearly reports of the group
- Five-year statistical record of the company
- SIA's flat
- Group corporate structure
- Information on shareholdings
- Share prices and turnover

The general operational review discusses the company's performance as SIA's group activities saw its operating profit decline by 14.3 percent in 1996/97 to S$896 million (including a S$174 million surplus from the sale of aircraft). The profit before tax dropped 0.6 percent to S$1,076 million. Passenger traffic increased by 9.8 percent on a capacity growth of 8.2 percent and the overall load factor increased by 1.1 percent to 70.5 percent. At the same time, yields declined by 4.6 percent. This meant that the break-even point rose from 62.6 percent to 65.9 per cent.

In terms of route performance, Table 2.3 highlights that North and South East Asia remains the major contributor to revenue generation by route in 1996/97, although it had declined by half a percentage point compared to 1995/96. In contrast, the contribution of American routes increased by 0.7 per cent on the 1995/96 result. European routes reported a 0.4 per cent decline in 1996/97 compared with 1995/96 while the South West Pacific routes experienced a 0.2 per cent increase in 1996/97. In the case of North and South East Asia, traffic grew by 8.9 percent and capacity growth resulted from increased frequently on services from Singapore to Hong Kong, Beijing, Manila, Nagoya, Ho Chi Minh City and Kuala Lumpur. However, SIA reported a 5.4 percent drop in its yield even though loadings increased by 0.8 per cent, due to a highly valued Singapore dollar and competition on the routes.

Table 2.3 : SIA route performance 1995/96 and 1996/97.

	Revenue ($ million)		Overall load factor (%)		Passenger seat factor (%)	
	1966/97	1995/96	1996/97	1995/96	1996/97	1995/96
North and South East Asia	2,167	2,103	61.5	60.7	70.5	69.6
Americas	1,482	1,372	73.4	71.7	77.8	75.8
Europe	1,342	1,305	76.6	74.6	77.7	73.7
South West Pacific	743	699	70.8	71.3	74.1	74.4
West Asia and Africa	589	559	63.6	64.3	68.3	70.8
Systemwide	6,323	6,038	70.5	69.4	74.4	73.0
Non-scheduled services and incidental revenue	196	214				
	6,519	6,252				

In the Americas, route performance saw traffic grow by 14.2 percent while capacity increased by 11.7 percent. An improvement in loadings by 1.7 percent in 1996/97 was a result of the provision of additional passenger services to San Franscisco and additional freighter services to New York and Chicago. However, the overall yield dropped by 5.4 percent, due of greater competition. In Europe, traffic grew by 7.3 percent in 1996/97, while capacity increased by 4.4 percent and the load factor rose by 2 percent. The rise in capacity was a result of greater frequency of services to Paris and Rome although the yield dropped by 4 percent, due to the strong Singapore dollar and competition. The South West Pacific, in contrast, saw traffic rise by 5.9 percent and capacity grew by 6.6 percent. At the same time, the load factor dropped by 0.5 percent in 1996/97. The main capacity increases resulted from additional service frequencies from Singapore to Adelaide, Sydney and Cairns, established in 1995/96. The overall yield increased by 0.3 percent, assisted by the strengthing of the Australian and New Zealand dollar against the Singapore dollar. In West Asia and Africa, traffic increased by 11.8 percent while capacity rose by 18.1 percent. Frequency increases in 1996/97 resulted from a growth in services to Male, johannesburg and Cape Town. However, the overall yield declined by 5.9 percent due to the strength of the Singapore dollar.

Aside from these operational issues, the annual report also provides information on new route developments. When this is compared with the existing route network, it is evident that SIA is an expansionist airline which seeks to grow its global influence as a major carrier. These developments comprise a strategy which includes code-sharing agreements, new air service agreements and an expansion of existing air service agreements.

Product and Service development

SIA's reputation as a global leader in the airline industry for product and service development saw the introduction in 1996/97 of the Krisworld in-flight entertainment system. This trend-setting innovation led to the introduction of an individual entertainment system with 22 video channels at the seat of every passenger. While other airlines have attempted to introduce such technology, it has been characterised by in-flight service breakdowns. Krisworld is a state-of-the-art technology which has proved popular with passangers, allowing customer choice in relieving the tedium

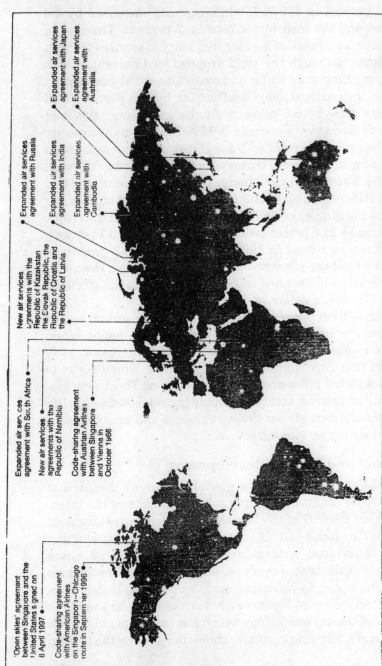

Fig. 2.4 : Singapore Airlines route expansion plans (redrawn from Singapore Airlines 1997).

of long-haul air travel. In 1996/97, 32 of the SIA fleet had this technology installed and the company's intention is to install it on all its Megatop-747s, Jubilee 777s and Celestar 340s in all classes. In contrast, airlines such as Air New Zealand have only introduced such technology in first class and business class, preferring to emphasis the comfort of their new ergonomically designed seating in economy class. SIA, however, has not stopped at Krisworld. For first class, it introduced active noise reducing (ANR) headphones in 1996, providing a high-quality sound system. For 1997/98, the airline is also planning the introduction of audio and video on demand (AVOD) in first class and business class (Raffles Class). This will allow travellers to choose a wide range of movies and music from SIAs CD music library.

Other innovations include Internet check-in for first class, business class and priority passengers departing from Singapore. Check-in formalities via e-mail or SIAs World Wide Web site will be followed by SIA confirming details by return e-mail.

At the airport, passengers can then collect their boarding passes from SIA check-in counters up to 45 minutes before departure and check in any luggage. Since 1997, first-class passengers departing from Changi Airport in Singapore on flights leaving between 2300 and 0000 hours can have their in-flight meal served at the Silver Kris (SIA lounge) prior to embarkation. This then enables passengers to rest upon boarding. While SIA continues to receive accolades for innovation in airline travel, its policy of continuous improvement to services and product development (including regular customer satisfaction surveys) indicates the competitiveness of international travel, particularly in the business and first-class market, making it a market leader.

Human resource issues

According to SIA, SIA's strategy for future success is firmly entrenched in attracting and developing staff who are highly qualified, trained and motivated to do their best'. In 1997, SIA employed 27,516 employees, of whom 10,334 were employed in the airline in Singapore and a further 2,973 by the airline overseas. One notable innovation, Towards Optimal Productivity (TOP), launched in 1996, encourages staff to contribute ideas on improving productivity and reducing waste. It is similar to schemes operated by other airlines, and in 1996 it reduced annual costs within the company by S\$22.9 million. The company also spends significant sums on staff training retraining and updating. For example, one of its subsidiaries, Singapore Airport Terminal Services (SATS), spent S\$3.7 million on staff training and development in 1996/97, involving extensive training for 600 staff on its Krischeck personal computer-based check-in system.

Integration in SIA group activities

The global scale and distribution of airline services has now become increasingly dependent upon computer reservation systems (CRSs) for marketing. These systems have been developed by airlines and account for the majority of airline bookings in North America and Europe. SIA has participated in this recent expansion in CRS technology (Archdale 1991, 1992) to extend its products to retail travel agents whilst encouraging other airlines to join its system to market their services. By January 1998, the following partners had joined SIA's Abacus CRS:

- SIA
- Dragonair
- Cathay Pacific
- China Airlines
- Malaysia Airlines
- Philippine Airlines
- Royal Brunei Airlines
- Vietnam Airlines
- Garuda Indonesia
- Eva Airways Corporation
- SilkAir (an SIA subsidiary)
- All Nippon Airways
- World Span (a CRS owned by Delta, Northwest and Transworld Airlines).

According to SIA, Abacus is the major CRS in Brunei, Hong Kong, Malaysia, the Philippines, Singapore and Taiwan, and is being extended to Korea and Australia to improve the distribution of airline services on a global basis.

The subsidiary and associated companies of the SIA group and their main activities are shown in Table 2.4, which highlights the involvement in the tourist transport system, particularly:

- Tour wholesaling (package holidays),
- Aviation insurance,
- Air transport (SilkAir),
- Airport services (catering, airport ownership, security services),
- Duty-free sales,
- Airport bus services,
- Aircraft leasing,
- CRS (Abacus Travel Systems),
- Airline software development,
- Aircraft engineering and maintenance,
- Hotel and property ownership (SIA Properties),
- Quality service training,
- Singapore Flying College,
- Cargo.

Table 2.4 : SIA subsidiary and associated companies at 31 March 1997.

	Activities	Country of incorporation & place of business	% Equity held by groups on 31.3.97
	1	2	3
Subsidiary companies			
Singapore Airport Terminal Services (Private) Ltd.	Investment holding company	Singapore	100
SATS Apron Services Pvt. Ltd.	Airport apron services (in voluntary liquidation)	Singapore	100
SATS Airport Services Pte. Pte Ltd (previously known as SATS Cargo services Pte Ltd)	Airport cargo, apron and passenger services	Singapore	100
SATS Catering Pte Ltd	Catering services	Singapore	100
SATS Security Services Pte Ltd	Security services	Singapore	100

	1	2	3
Silk Air (Singapore) Private Limited (Previously known as Tradewinds Private Limited)	Air tansportation	Singapore	100
Tradewinds Tours & Travel Private Limited	Tour wholesaling	Singapore	100
Singapore Aviation and General Insurance Company (Pte) Ltd	Aviation insurance	Singapore	100
SIA Engineering Company Private Limited (previously known as Singapore Engine Overhaul Centre Private Limited)	Engine overhaul and related services	Singapore	100
SIA Properties (Pte) Ltd	Provision of building management	Singapore	100
Singapore Airport Duty-Free Emporium (Private) Limited	Dormant company	Singapore	100
Singapore Flying College Pte Ltd	Training of pilots	Singapore	100
Abacus Travel Systems Pre Ltd	Marketing of Abacus reservation systems	Singapore	61
Singapore Jamco Private Limited	Manufacture of aircraft cabin equipment	Singapore	51
Aero Laundry & Linen Services Private Limited	Laundry services	Singapore	100
Cargo Community Network Pte Ltd	Provision and marketing Provision and marketing of Cargo Community systems	Singapore	51
Star Kindom investment Ltd	Real estate	Honkong	100
SATS (Curacao) N.V.	Catering services (in voluntary lilquidation)	Netherlands Aneilles	100
SH Tours Ltd.	Tour wholesealing	United Kingdom	100
Auspice Limited	Investment company	Channel Islands	100
Singapore Airlines (Mauritius) Ltd.	Air craft leasing	Mauritius	100
Airline software developments consultancy India (Pvt) Ltd.	Airlines software development	India	51
Associated company			
Island Cruises (S) Pte Ltd.	Dormant company	Singapore	50
Service Quality (SQ) centre Pte Ltd.	Quality service training	Singapore	50
Asian frequent Flyer Pte Ltd.	Provision and marketing of frequent flyer programme	Singapore	33.3
Combustor Airmotive Services Pte Ltd.	Repair of engine combustion chambers	Singapore	49

	1	2	3
Asian Surface Technologies Pte Ltd.	Fan blade repair & coatings	Singapore	29
Servair – SATS Holding company Pte Ltd.	Investment Holding company	Singapore	49
Maldives Inflight Catering Pvt. Ltd.	Catering Services	Maldives	40
Beijing Airport Inflight Kitchen Ltd	Catering Services	People's Republic of China	40
Beijing Aviation Ground Services Ltd.	Ground Handling	People's Republic of China	40
Asia Leasing Ltd.	Aircraft Leasing	Bermuda	21
PT Purosani Sri Lanka	Hotel ownership and management	Indonesia	20
PT Pantai Indah Tateli	Hotel ownership and management	Indonesia	20
Aviserv Ltd.	Catering services	Pakistan	49
Pan Asia Pacific Aviation Services Ltd.	Engineering services	Hong Kong	47.1
Asia Air Freight Terminal Company Ltd.	Cargo Handling Services	Hong Kong	24.5
Tan Son Nhat Cargo Services Ltd.	Cargo Hnadling Services	Vietnam	30
Taj Madras Flight Kitchen Pvt Ltd.	Catering services	India	30
DSS World Sourcing Ltd	Sourcing of supplies	Switzerland	33.3
Asian compressor Technology Services Company Ltd	Repair of aircraft engines & compressor	Taiwan	24.5

The activities of SIA's subsidiary companies are reported separately in the annual report, although the majority of the document focuses on SIA. For example, the financial review of SIA identifies revenue generated, expenditure (Table 2.5), the capacity and break-even load factor (the point at which an aircraft makes a profit), as well as detailed accounting information for the group (e.g., taxation, dividends, the financial position, balance sheet, liabilities and assests). SIA also produces an individual breakdown of the profitability of its three principal activities:

- Airline operations,
- Airport terminal services,
- Engineering services and others which are listed in Table 2.6.

Table 2.5 : Ten-year statistical review of SIA 1987/88 to 1996/97.

	1996/97	1995/96	1994/95	1993/94	1992/93	1991/92	1990/91	1989/90	1988/89	1987/88
Financial										
Total revenue ($ million)	6,519.3	6,252.4	5,940.7	5,560.5	5,134.6	5,012.7	4,601.7	4,730.7	4,271.8	3,778.2
Total expenditure ($ million)	5,866.0	5,496.5	5,124.2	5,026.4	4,479.6	4,149.0	3,760.2	3,601.8	3,406.7	3,301.6
Operating Profit ($ million)	653.3	755.9	816.5	534.1	655.0	863.7	841.5	1,128.9	865.1	476.6
Profit before tax ($ million)	933.8	903.3	950.5	733.0	794.2	1,085.2	1,124.2	1,397.8	1,025.4	608.7
Profit after tax ($ million)	901.8	875.9	939.0	722.6	741.1	920.7	886.8	1,176.8	928.4	569.9
Internally generated cash follow[1] ($ million)	2,163.8	1,779.2	1,942.3	1,695.5	1,366.4	1,604.7	1,814.2	1,703.8	1,834.4	1,493.9
Capital disbursments($ million)	2,365.9	1,395.1	1,790.7	1,835.4	1,619.0	1,620.2	1,077.3	1,140.0	912.6	723.7
Yield (c/ctk)	66.5	69.7	73.6	76.0	81.3	90.8	95.2	99.2	99.2	97.6
Unit cost (c/ctk.)	43.8	43.6	46.0	49.8	50.6	54.9	58.4	57.8	58.3	61.8
Break – even load factor (%)	65.9	62.6	62.5	65.5	62.2	60.5	61.3	58.3	58.8	63.3
Fleet										
Aircraft (numbers)	80	71	66	64	57	48	43	40	37	34
Average age (Months)	63	68	60	60	61	61	57	55	54	49
Production										
Destination cities (number)	77	77	75	73	70	67	63	57	57	55
Distance flown (Killion Km)	251.8	338.5	205.9	188.8	165.0	142.3	123.6	117.6	105.8	97.3
Time flown (hours)	325,085	294,880	264,096	241,346	211,435	180,744	157,039	149,355	136,632	124,175
Overall capacity (million tonne km)	13,501.1	12,481.3	11,167.3	10,155.6	8,982.3	7,624.4	6,644.3	6,280.3	5,682.7	5,136.5
Passenger capacity (millions seat – km)	73,507.3	68,529.4	64,074.0	59,290.4	53,077.6	47,454.3	41,701.2	39,236.4	36,461.6	34,438.0
Cargo capacity (million tonne-km)	6,203.9	5,585.1	4,773.6	4,231.3	3,630.0	2,898.3	2,494.5	2,380.7	2,080.8	1,736.1

	1	2	3	4	5	6	7	8	9	10
Traffic										
Passengers carried (000)	12,022	11,057	10,082	9,468	8,640	8,131	7,065	6,793	6,182	5,618
Passengers carried (million pax-km)	54,692.5	50,045.4	45,414.2	42,328.3	37,860.6	34,893.5	31,332.2	30,737.0	28,785.1	25,757.0
Passenger seat factor (%)	74.4	73.0	70.9	71.4	71.3	73.5	75.1	78.3	78.9	74.8
Cargo carried (million kg)	674.2	603.8	550.8	483.4	399.1	342.8	295.7	278.1	241.3	207.6
Cargo carried (million tonne-km)	4,249.4	3,820.1	3,389.4	2,973.4	2,411.5	1,954.8	1,705.7	1,679.4	1,448.6	1,284.8
Cargo load factor (%)	68.5	68.4	71.0	70.3	66.4	67.4	68.4	70.5	69.6	74.0
Mail carried (million tonne-km)	99.2	89.4	72.7	64.3	55.2	55.0	41.8	50.3	42.1	43.5
Overall load carried (million tonne-km)	9,512.0	8,662.0	7,789.3	7,058.8	6,086.3	5,331.2	4,715.0	4,643.5	4,223.3	3,770.5
Overall load factor (%)	70.5	69.4	69.8	69.5	67.8	69.9	71.0	73.9	74.3	73.4
Staff[2]										
Average strength	13,258	12,966	12,557	12,363	11,990	11,418	10,818	10,052	9,246	8,653
Capacity per employee (tonne-km)	1,081,336	962,618	889,329	821,451	749,149	667,753	614,189	624,781	614,612	593,609
Load carried per employee (tonne-km)	717,454	668,055	620,315	570,962	507,615	466,912	435,848	461,948	456,770	435,745
Revenue Per employee ($)	491,726	482,215	473,099	449,769	428,240	441,592	428,046	473,458	465,142	429,975
Value added per employee ($)	220,440	209,332	214,351	195,381	186,681	215,116	205,851	242,768	221,891	188,143

1 Internally generated cash flow comprises cash generated from operations, dividends from subsidies and associated companies, and proceeds from sale of aircraft and other fixed assests.

2 Figures for 1991/92 and prior years have been adjusted to exclude SIA engineering departments which became part of SIA Engineering Company from. 1 April 1992.

Table 2.6 : Revenue, profit and employee strength of SIA business type.

	Revenue ($ million)		Profit before tax ($ million)	
	1996/97	1995/96	1996/97	1995/96
Airline operations	6,627	6,337	827	783
Airport terminal services	308	283	120	139
Engineering services and others	287	270	129	160
Group	7,222	6,890	1,076	1,082
	Profit after tax ($ million)		Average number of employees	
	1996/97	1995/96	1996/97	1995/96
Airline operations	795	755	13,736	13,419
Airport terminal services	92	101	8,889	8,556
Engineering services and others	145	169	5,616	4,351
Group	1,032	1,025	27,241	26,326
	Total assets ($ million)		Capital expenditure ($ million)	
	31.3.1997	31.3.1996	1996/97	1995/96
Airline operations				
Aircraft, spares and spare engines	8,725	7,429	2,245	1,321
Others	4,594	3,964	95	77
Airport terminal services	918	860	77	152
Engineering services and others	284	942	33	23
Group	14,52	13,195	2,450	1,573

All inter-company balances and transactions have been eliminated upon consolidation.

SIA also lists its current fleet and aircraft orders (Table 2.7) which highlight the company policy to retain one of the most modern international airline fleets. The airline has increased its fleet from 48 aircraft in operation in 1992 to 80 in 1997, which is impressive by any standards.

It is evident that company annual reports can be a useful data source from which to examine not only integration in the tourist transport system but also the performance of individual companies. Annual reports are an accessible data source which can be obtained direct from public companies' head offices. Although the amount of detailed information contained within annual reports may be somewhat daunting and complex, analysis of such sources will yield important insights into the commercial, operational and supply aspects of different tourist transport operators. For example, Table 2.8 outlines the prevailing shareholdings in the airline and yet more detailed knowledge of the airline, its shareholders and reasons for investment are not evident from an annual report.

Table 2.7. SIA fleet and aircraft orders at 31 March 1997.[1]

Aircraft	Engine[2]	In Operation	On firm order	On lease to other operators	On option
B747-400 (Megatop)	PW 4056	36	8	1	10
B747-300 (Big Tcp)	PW JT9D-7R4G2	3	-	4	-
B747-300 Combi	PWJT9D-7R4G2	3	-	-	-
B747-400 Megaark	PW 4056	6	2	-	-
B747-200 Freighter	PWJT9D-7R4G2	1	-	-	-
B777	Rolls Royce Trent 800 series	-	36[3]	-	41[4]
A310-300	PW4152	17	-	-	-
A310-200	PWJT9D-7R4EI	6	-	-	-
A340-300 (Calester)	CFM 56-5C4	8	9	-	20
Total		80	55	5	71

[1] Average age of fleet 5 years 3 months (as at 31 March 1997).
[2] PW = Pratt and Whitney Engines; CFM = GEC/CFM Engines.
[3] Includes 6 aircraft intended for Singapore Aircraft Leasing Enterprise.
[4] Includes 10 aircraft intended for Singapore Aircraft Leasing Enterprise.

Summary

The analysis of tourist transport issues has attracted comparatively little research in contrast to the analysis of demand issues. The rise of transaction analysis is a useful way to view supply chain in tourist transport systems and the contractual relationships which exist between consumers and suppliers. However, more recent theoretical syntheses of tourism supply issues by economists (Sinclair and Stabler 1997) highlight the importance of understanding the competitive conditions and markets in which tourist transport businesses operate. It is this more theoretically derived analysis that begins to advance the supply side beyond simple descriptive studies. The discussion highlights the dominant influence of the tour operator sector in the supply of package holidays and the purchase of transport services on behalf of customers at discounted prices. The ability of tour wholesales to negotiate discounts with transport operators reflects the capital-intensive nature of the tourist transport business and the need to achieve high load factors to improve profitability. This reflects the indivisible nature of transport operations discussed in where airline companies cannot operate half an aircraft if it is only 50 percent full. The fixed costs of transport operations (e.g. repayments on loans to purchase capital equipment) mean that the incremental costs of selling existing capacity on a

Table 2.8 : Shareholders' investment in SIA in 1997.[1]

Major shareholders	Number of shares	%
1. Temasek Holdings (Private) Limited	690,055,172	53.80
2. DBS Nominees Pte Ltd	80,373,957	6.27
3. HSBC (Singapore) Nominees Pte Ltd	53,708,412	4.19
4. Chase Manhattan (S) Nominess Pte Ltd	52,047,811	4.06
5. Delta Air Lines Holdings, Inc.	35,186,330	2.74
6. Overseas-Chinese Bank Nominees Pte Ltd	30,690,354	2,39
7. United Overseas Bank Nominees Pte Ltd	28,499,641	2.22
8. Citibank Nominess Singapore Pte Ltd	24,419,947	1.90
9. Post Office Savings Bank of Singapore	21,507,200	1.68
10. Raffles Nominees Pte Ltd	21,384,066	1.67
11. The Great Eastern Life Assurance Co. Ltd	14,252,000	1.11
12. DB Nominees (S) Pte Ltd	13,809,329	1.08
13. NYUC Income Insurance Co-operative Limited	11,735,000	0.91
14. Swissair Swiss Air Transport Company Limited	8,000,000	0.62
15. Overseas Union Bank Nominees Pte Ltd	7,734,800	0.60
16. Prudential Assurance Company Singapore		
(Pte) Limited	7,334,000	0.57
17. Barclays Bank (Singapore Nominees) Pte Ltd	6,519,992	0.51
18. Chang Shyn Jin	4,256,000	0.33
19. ABN Amro Nominees Singapore Pte Ltd	3,871,830	0.31
20. Indosuez Singapore Nominees Pte Ltd	3,428,700	0.27
Total	1,118,814,541	87.23
Substantial shareholder (as shown in the Register		
of Substantial Shareholders)		
Temasek Holdings (Private) Limited	697,097,172[2]	54.35

transport service are low once it has reached its break-even point. This is one explanation of the reduced price of airline tickets and stand-by fares as it. Is more efficient to sell a reduced-priced ticket if the carrier has capacity than to underutilise the capacity. The contractual relationships associated with the supply of tourist transport are often negotiated up to six months in advance and a great deal of market planning goes into the provision of a service.

The provision of services which meet certain quality standards is one of the reasons why labour costs are so high in the supply of tourist transport services. It is a labour-intensive activity which requires staff contact with travellers to ensure their needs are met at each stage of travel. Employees cannot easily be substituted where a service is dependent on face-to-face contact with customers. Employee training and corporate human resource management policies (Baum 1993) are assuming an important role in ensuring that the supply of tourist transport services is based on a sound understanding of service quality, maximising customer satisfaction and developing programmes with incentives to foster customer loyalty. Analysis of company reports provides a useful source to assess both the role of the transport operator's involvement in the supply chain and their development of more sophisticated ways of serving the customer's needs.

The example of SIA highlights how important these issues are for a market leader in the tourist transport business. The degree of vertical and horizontal integration within a company such as SIA highlights the significance of annual company reports. SIA has certainly ensured that its involvement in the supply chain enables it to develop more sophisticated ways to meet the needs of its customers.

3

Managing Supply Issues in Tourist Transport

Introduction

The provision of tourist transport services by public and private sector organisations is a complex process, requiring a wide range of human resource skills and managerial abilities and a sound grasp of the transport business and how it operates. In recent years, meeting the needs of consumers (travellers) has also assumed a higher priority in the supply of services. In the conceptualisation and analysis of tourist transport supply issues highlighted the significance of understanding the broader strategic and contextual issues which affect the way different forms of transport supply perform in the market place. In this chapter, the emphasis is on a number of issues highlighted by the SIA case study, namely how successful transport providers can produce, manage and operate efficient supply systems to meet tourist needs. In particular, the chapter focuses on the mechanisms and tools used by operators to manage supply issues, together with the role of the public sector. This provides a comparison of the different objectives pursued by private sector operators, such as airlines, railway companies and cruise lines. Private sector operators, are motivated by the financial performance of the business, to ensure that an efficient operation delivers products to its customers. In contrast, the public sector agencies directly and indirectly associated with the provision of tourist transport services are often not motivated by profit. They frequently have a more strategic view and are concerned with planning, coordination and liaison functions to ensure tourist transport provision meets public policy objectives at various spatial scales. The chapter commences with a discussion of one of the most important tools used by transport providers in the late 1990s—information technology (IT). This is followed by a review of one important strategy used by airlines to improve supply issues and competitiveness - alliances. Next, the role of the state in regulating tourist transport supply issues is discussed in relation to airline deregulation in the USA. The supply of transport services in destination areas is then reviewed.

Information technology and supply issues in tourist transport: a role for logistics and IT?

It is widely acknowledged that society has entered the 'information age' and that this has had implications for transport provision. One of the immediate impacts for tourist transport providers is that up-to-date information flows are now vital when a supply chain exists, and the transport provider is just one component of the overall tourist product. As Christopher observes, the customer service explosion means there is a need for 'consistent provision of time and place utility. In other words, products do not have value until they are in the hands of the customer at the time and place required.' Christopher argues that logistics of service delivery are of paramount importance and enable organisations to add value and deliver a consistent product. Logistics is a vital concept to recognise, particularly when IT is also introduced, since IT and logistics enable transport providers to achieve their objectives in a competitive environment.

According to Quayle,

> Logistics is the process which seeks to provide for the management and co-ordination of all activities within the supply chain from sourcing and acquisition, through production where appropriate, and through distribution channels to the customer.

Logistics provides a competitive advantage by offering a strategic view of operational issues and an understanding of the links in the supply system. It also assists in the coordination of the service delivery function, and transport in its own right is a vital element of logistics in moving the customer nearer to the product in a tourism context. Logistics is documented in detail by Quayle (1993) and Christopher (1994) and performs a vital role in providing the link between the marketplace and operating activity of the business. Figure outlines the business functions which fall within the remit of logistics.

Within the literature on IT in tourism, the seminal study by Sheldon (1997) is fast becoming the key reference source, replacing the earlier work by Poon (1993). The tourist industry generates large volumes of information that needs to be processed and used within a logistics context. For example, Sheldon (1997) notes that each airline booking generates 25 transactions that need processing. In Sheldon's (1997) model of tourism information flows, there are three main agents involved: travellers, suppliers and travel intermediaries. For the purpose of the discussion here, it is the supplier's use of IT to handle, utilise and manage these information flows which is of interest. From a transport supplier's perspective, information is essential to allow the organisation to function and for different departments to make decisions about corporate objectives, their consumers and competitors. It can also be harnessed in the marketing function. Sheldon (1997) cites the example of the airline industry which makes extensive use of IT in a wide range of contexts, including:

- Global Distribution Systems (see WTO 1994).
- Frequent flyer databases

- Yield management programmes.
- Distribution and marketing of their products.
- The design, operation and maintenance of aircraft and luggage handling.
- Check-in systems at airport.

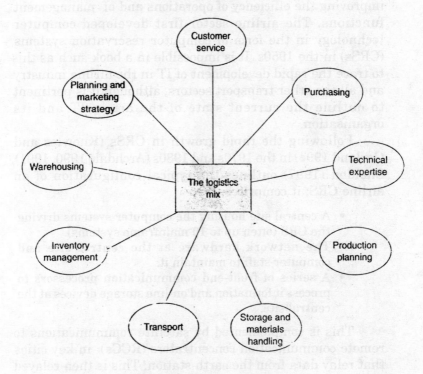

Fig. 3.1 : The scope of logistics.

Although other transport sectors involved in tourism also make use of IT (including train operators, car rental agencies and coach and cruise ship operators), it is probably most highly developed in the airline sector, due to large investment in capital and the highly competitive nature of the business. In that sense, IT is seen as integral to gaining a competitive edge, and in the case of SIA, in maintaining continuous product innovations. For example, on its Mega-top-747s, all passengers have access to an in-flight telephone to make credit card calls from air to ground, and the developments listed in the SIA case study, all enlist state-of-the-art IT.

Sheldon (1997) traces the development of IT in the airline industry, where it is primarily seen as a means of improving the efficiency of operations and of management functions. The airline sector first developed computer technology in the form of computer reservation systems (CRSs) in the 1950s. It is impossible in a book such as this to trace the rapid development of IT in the airline industry and all the other transport sectors, although it is pertinent to outline the current state of the art in IT and its organisation.

Following the rapid growth in CRSs (Knowles and Garland 1994) in the 1970s and 1980s (Archdale 1990, 1991), Sheldon (1997) outlines the typical configuration of an airline CRS; it comprises:

- A central site housing the computer systems driving the CRS (often up to 10 mainframe systems).
- The network hardware at the central site and computer staff to maintain it.
- A series of front-end communication processors to process information and on-line storage devices at the central site.

This is complemented by satellite communications to remote communication concentrators (RCCs) in key cities that relay data from the earth station. This is then relayed to reservation terminals and airports, providing rapid communications.

One of the major changes in the late 1980s and 1990s has been the move from CRSs which contained only airline information for the proprietary airline to systems containing data for multiple airlines. Sheldon (1997) traces the development of CRSs into what have now been called global distribution systems (World Tourism Organisation 1994), like the Asian GDS, Abacus, mentioned in the SIA case study (Chapter). Table outlines the principal developments contributing to the development of GDSs.

CDSs are CRSs which are affiliated with airlines. There has been a great deal of debate over the impact of airline affiliation on the competitiveness of air travel in North America, Sheldon (1997) argues that, following legislation, rules now exist to ensure all airlines are represented on GDS screens. According to Sheldon (1997), the significance of major GDSs in 1996 was:

• Sabre	US$1,500-2,000 million
• Apollo	US$1,100 + million
• Abacus	US$650 million
• Amadeus	US$600 million
• System One	US$500 million
• Worldspan	US$500 million
• Galileo	US$400 million

Table 3.1 : The development of GDSs

1976 Three North American airlines began to offer their systems - Apollo (United Airlines), Sabre (American Airlines) and PARS (Trans World Airlines) as well as offering US travel agents terminals to access their systems.

1981 Eastern Airlines established System One Direct Access (SODA).

1982 Delta Airlines launched its DATAS II.

1987 In Europe, Galileo and Amadeus were formed and offered to travel agents. In Asia, Abacus was formed and also offered to travel agents.

1988 Japan Airlines formed Axess.

1990 System One was purchased by a non airlines company - EDS. The merger of PARS and DATAS II resulted in the formation of Worldspan. In Japan, All Nippon Airways and Abacus formed Infini.

1993 Galileo and Apollo were merged to establish Galileo International.

1995 System One merged with Amadeus.

Although a CRS will only show one airline's schedules, a GDS has the advantage of showing data on multiple carriers, including:

• Flight schedules and availability.
• Passenger information.

- Fare quotes and rules for travel.
- Ticketing.

Since the advent of GDSs, airlines have also established 'a presence on the Internet and (are) using that as an important distribution channel especially to consumers. By accpeting payment by credit card, airlines have harnessed a developing technology to complement GDSs and traditional distribution channels.

Sheldon (1997) also discusses other airline IT applications which include:

- Baggage and cargo handling systems.
- Cabin automation (e.g., entertainment systems, visual route systems on in-flight screens using Geographical Positioning System equipment).
- Safety systems.
- Decision support systems.
- Flight scheduling and planning.
- Crew scheduling and management.
- Gate management and control.

In the the case of SIA, Sheldon (1997) discusses the current development of Krismax, a yield management system to assist with revenue and inventory control. The underlying principle behind Krismax is that the amount of space available on any flight segment can be controlled in relation to different classes of seats (as discussed in Chapter). The information is then fed into the CRS to control the availability of seats by segment. Sheldon (1997) observes that SIA's 'reservations from travel agents are taken care of with its major investment and involvement with Abacus, the Asian GDS, which has over 12,500 terminals in 5,000 travel agencies'.

Sheldon (1997) also examines the developments in IT which have been introduced into land transport operations to help the logistics of fleet management in relation to car rental and other innovations which improve the tourists' travel experience.

Having examined the significance of logistics and IT in managing tourist transport in a supply context, attention now turns to the way in which one part of the transport sector—airlines—has pursued strategies to improve supply issues through strategic alliances.

Airline Alliances

There is a very clear link between the use of IT in tourist transport sectors and the development and expansion of airline alliances. French argues that 'the development and exploitation of alliances on their current scale would not have been possible without the development from the early 1980s of immensely powerful global CRS systems, or without the parallel development of in-house computer programmes controlling the management of inventory, yield and revenue'. In fact, French implies that the rise of GDSs may prove critical to exploit the potential advantages global airline alliances may offer.

French argues that an airline alliance is 'any collaborative pooling of resources between two or more carriers, designed both to benefit all the partners in making their supply of capacity more efficient and in extending their market reach'. Bennett (1997) views such developments in the context of a growing globalisation of the tourist transport business, indicating that 60 per cent of alliances have been formed since 1992. This recent phenomenon within the aviation industry is not as new as Bennett implies, since French traces the development back to the 1970s. However, it is the speed of this development that is critical to the aviation industry worldwide and that has implications for tourist supply issues. French points to the principal data source for analysing airline alliances and their current status. This is the survey published each year in the June issue of *Airline Business*. It is therefore an important reference source to trace the evolution, changing status and dynamics of alliances. Based on the 1997 data in *Airline Business,* Table 3.2, documents the changes in alliance structure. It highlights two basic issues :

- The continued growth of alliances.
- A 'churn rate' (French 1997), indicating the formation and termination of agreements while the number has reached a critical mass.

Table 3.2 also highlights the need to explain the basic forms which alliances may take. Bennett (1997: 214) distinguishes between two types of alliance:

- *Tactical partnerships,* comprising a loose form of collaboration designed to derive marketing benefits, characterised by code sharing and exemplified by the hub-and-spoke system of air travel in the US domestic airline market. This is reflected in the smaller feeder and regional airlines being aligned with key hub-based carriers.

Table 3.2 : The development of airline alliances.

	1994	1995	1996	1997
Number of airlines	136	153	159	177
Number of alliances	280	324	389	363
with equity states	58	58	62	54
non-equity alliances	222	266	327	309
New alliances	-	51	71	72

- *Strategic partnerships,* where an investment or pooling of resources by partners aims to achieve a range of common objectives focused on the partners' strategic ambitions. Bennett describes strategic alliances as incorporating

Shared airport facilities (check-in lounges), improved connections (synchronised schedules), reciprocity on frequent flyer programmes, freight co-ordination and marketing agreements (code-sharing and block selling).

French by contrast, outlines ten principal features which may be included in strategic alliances developed by airlines:

- *Equity stake or equity exchange* may take two forms. First, a large carrier in an alliance may buy a share ownership in a smaller partner airline. If it is an overseas-based airline, this is likely to be a minority stake. Alternatively, if the airlines are located in the same country or region (e.g., the EU), it may lead to a majority shareholding. The second form in which the alliance may be developed is for two or more carriers to take part stakes in each other. A good example of this form is the Swissair, Delta Airlines and Singapore Airlines alliance established in 1989. Equity exchange or stakes are the strongest format an alliance may assume, given the investment and long-term commitment. However in 1997, only 54 of the 363 alliances were of this form.

- *Code sharing* is an agreement between two airlines, where one airline operates a single flight leg with its own flight code and that of its alliance partner. The advantage is that, aside from an airline expanding the flights it can offer, it can enhance its listing on CRSs. According to French, two-thirds of airline pacts involve code sharing. There is considerable debate about the effects of alliances on the structure of the airline industry (Alamdari and Morrell 1997), particularly in the USA (Hannegan and Mulvey 1995) and Europe. However, as Hannegan and Mulvey show, the alliance between KLM and Northwest, formed in 1992, led to an increase of 350,000 passengers per annum on its transatlantic routes. The added revenue enabled Northwest to post an operating profit of US$830 million in 1994 compared to a loss of US$60.1 million in 1991. Thus, regulatory authorities are monitoring code sharing because of its potentially anti-competitive effects on consumers (it may reduce choice and improve airline profitability), together with the effects on the industry.

- *Joint services* are offered within a code-sharing agreement, and occur when one 'airline supplies and operates the crew and aircraft, the revenue and profits of flights are shared...between two partner airlines'.

- *Block seat or block booking arrangements* occur where a partner airline reserves a block of seats on a connecting service for another airline so it is able to guarantee onward seats.

- *Joint marketing or a marketing agreement* is a collaboration on 'marketing, promotion and advertising of the flights of two or more partners. It generally recognises that some airlines have better local knowledge and experience in familiar markets, and can pass on the benefits of this to a partner airline through co-operation at the marketing level'.

- *Joint fares* occur (if regulatory authorities allow such collaboration) and may result in fare matching on routes and revenue pooling.

- *Franchise agreements* are contractual agreements which allow an airline to let its partner assume its brand image. This has the advantage of allowing the partner to extend its network while assuming the livery and service standards of the franchiser. Code sharing and schedule coordination occur normally and the franchisee can also buy into the franchiser's extensive resources, marketing and organisational framework.

- *Wet-leasing* is where one airline company hires the aircraft and crew from another airline on a fixed-fee basis. The hiring airline normally markets the airline using its own designator code.

- *Frequent flyer benefits, cooperation and reciprocity* indicates that 'two or more alliance partners may choose to link their loyalty programmes, allowing passengers to accumulate frequent flyer mileage awards on all alliance partner airlines'.

Bennett outlines the principal motivations which may explain why airlines enter into strategic alliances:

- To achieve economics of scale and learning, principally to improve profitability and perhaps also to benefit from economies of scope.

- To gain access to the benefits of the other airline's assets.
- To reduce risk by sharing it.
- To help share the market which may help reduce incapacity in mature markets and could reduce competition.
- Speed in reaching the market given the structural changes occurring in the airline industry.

According to French, 'airline alliances are now such a central part of strategy' that a period of consolidation appears to have been reached after the initial high 'churn rate'. In contrast, Bennett. Maintains that 'the success is poor...because there are a whole host of challenges of both a practical and political nature that need to be faced' relating to how the alliance is organised, particularly when a number of partner airlines are involved. In fact, while alliances become more important to the operation and management of the airline industry, Bennett reiterates the concerns that 'less competition equates with less choice, while improved economic circumstances for airlines are tantamount to higher prices'. Inevitably alliances are part of the trend towards a number of mega-carries dominating the airline industry as part of the globalisation process in tourism. However, attention now turns to another factor affecting the management and operation of tourism transport—deregulation and its impact on the domestic airline industry in the USA.

The State and the Supply of Tourist Transport: Airline Deregulation in the USA

Air travel is a major form of tourist transport since 30 per cent of international travellers use air as the main form of transport. International air travel provides an interesting example of how government policy has led to different upon the supply of transport services for tourists. Sealy identifies two approaches:

- A regulated transport system where a country exercises sovereignty over its airspace.

- A liberalised and unregulated system characterised by an open-skies policy.

It was clear that various historical and political factors may explain the aviation policy in a given country. The regulations governing airline operations by international bodies such as ICAO and IATA (see Holloway 1989; Mill 1992) and bilateral agreements were influential in shaping air travel in a regulated environment until the late 1970s (Table 3.3). In addition to IATA (the United Nations body which facilitates the international regulation of air travel), national governments play an active role in regulating air travel.

The experience of domestic airline deregulation in the USA in 1978 led to a complete re-evaluation of the supply of air travel in terms of its organisation, operation and regulation by the state. Deregulation in North America was also a testbed for aviation strategies subsequently developed in Australia and those planned for the EC (now the EU). The case of the US domestic airline market is also interesting because 'it is more highly developed and more extensively used in the United States than in any other part of the world'. For example, in 1988 air travel in the US exceeded 1.7 billion passenger kms and is set to increase to 2.2 billion by the year 2000. According to Button and Gillingwater (1991), the implications for the supply of tourist transport can be examined in relation to:

- The corporate response of airline companies to the new competitive environment for air travel.
- The effect on the functioning of the transport system
- The effect on consumers, service provision and service quality
- The impact upon complementary infrastructure (e.g., airports).

To understand the impact of deregulation of the domestic market for air travel in the USA, it is pertinent to examine the regulatory framework prior to and following deregulation as a context in which to consider the changes on the supply of air services.

Airline Regulation in the United States

In the USA, airline regulation can be dated to the passage of the 1938 Civil Aeronautics Act and the subsequent formation of the Civil Aeronautics Board (CAB) in 1946 which licensed routes and airline operations, regulated the pricing of fares and monitored safety issues.

Table 3.3 : International cooperation in air travel

International air travel requires countries to cooperate so that the movement of aircraft and people can occur in a reasonably flexible manner. To provide a degree of regulation and coherence in air travel, two important international agreements underpin present-day air travel; the *1944 Chicago Convention,* which established the principle of freedoms of the air and the *1946 Bermuda Agreement,* which provided a framework for bilateral agreements to implement freedoms of the air. A bilateral agreement is where two countries agree to provide air service on a reciprocal basis and it helps to facilitate and protect the rights of each country's airline irrespective of whether it is a profit or non-profit venture.

Consequently, the following 'Freedoms of the Air' can be observed:

Freedom 1: The right of an airline to fly over one country to get to another.

Freedom 2: The right of an airline to stop in another country for fuel/maintenance but not to pick up or drop off passengers.

Freedom 3: The right of an airline to drop off in a foreign country, traffic from the country in which it is registered, to a separate country.

Freedom 4: The right of an airline to carry back passengers from a foreign country to the country in which it is registered.

Freedom 5: The right of an airline to carry back passengers between two foreign countries as long as the flight originates or terminates in the country in which it is registered

Freedom 6: The right of an airline to carry passengers to a gateway in the country in which it is registered then on to a foreign country where neither the origin nor the ultimate destination is the country in which it is registered.

Freedom 7: The right of an airline to operate entirely outside of the country in which it is registered in carrying passengers between two other countries.

Freedom 8: The right of an airline, registered in a foreign country, to carry passengers between two points in the same foreign country.

Note: According to Mill the first *two* freedoms are accepted internationally while freedoms 3—6 are the subject of bilateral agreements and the last two freedoms are rarely accepted.

Federal regulation of civil aviation was firmly established within a government department. It also limited the number of domestic carriers until the 1970s to avoid excessive competition. Despite such measures, the postwar boom in domestic and international air travel in the USA was facilitated by a buoyant economy, innovation in aircraft design, reduced travel costs and stable fares maintained by the CAB. In addition, the CAB provided subsidies for local service carriers so that small communities could be connected to the emerging interurban trunk network of air routes, to achieve social equity in access to air travel. This also facilitated the development of major airlines as the CAB guaranteed loans for carriers who invested in new aircraft to serve such routes. To reduce subsidy payments, carriers were gradually awarded more lucrative longer-haul routes with a view to carriers cross-subsidising the shorter feeder routes from small communities to connect with trunk routes. These developments occurred against the background of pressure from the airline industry to increase fares in the 1970s, which appeared to place the consumer at a disadvantage. In 1975, the CAB began to relax some of its restrictions on the operation and pricing of charter aircraft to compete with scheduled flights, permitted discounted fares and licensed new transatlantic carriers prepared to offer low fares. This provided the background for the 1978 Airline Deregulation Act which established greater flexibility in route licensing and abolished the CAB in 1984. As Goetz and Sutton argue, 'the Act stripped the CAB of tis authority to control entry and exist, fares, subsidies and mergers'. As a result, some of the CAB functions were transferred to the Department of Transportation, including responsibility for:

- The negotiation of international air transport rights and licensing of US carriers to serve the airline market
- The monitoring of international fares
- The maintenance of air services to small communities
- Consumer affairs and complaints
- Airline mergers.

In contrast, the Federal Aviation Administration powers included:

- The promotion of air safety and use of navigable air space
- Regulations on the competence of pilots and airworthiness of aircraft
- The operation of air traffic control (ATC) systems.

From these regulatory responsibilities it is evident that the structure of the US airline business comprises:

- Airlines.
- Airports and ATC providers
- Aircraft manufacturers (e.g., Boeing and its recent acquisition, McDonnell Douglas)
- Consumers
- Third parties, such as government agencies (e.g., FAA and Department of Transportation).

In the case of the airline business in the USA, Shaw identifies the following structure for airline companies:

- The majors—earning in excess of $1 billion per annum
- The nationals—based on a regional network
- New entrants
- Small regional and commuter airlines which provide the short-haul link-ups with the majors to feed into the networks of their partner airlines.

The Effects of Deregulation on the Supply of Tourist Transport

Within the literature on the supply of tourist transport, one are which has been well researched is airline deregulation. This has focused on the controversy over the effect of such measures on the commercial environment for airline operations, and there is not space within this chapter to review the specialised range of papers generated by researchers on this topic. One approach is to consider a limited number of issues which are constantly referred to by researchers. According to the US Department of Transportation, following deregulation the number of carriers serving the USA increased from 36 in 1978 to 72 in 1980 and 86 in 1985, dropping to 60 by 1990 (including air cargo carriers); see Table 3.4. However, a range

Table 3.4 : Airlines providing interstate jet services during the deregulation era.

Origin and name	Began service[1]	Date	Status
1	*2*	*3*	*4*
Trunk carriers (11)			
American	pre-1978	1989	1st ranking carrier[2]
Braniff	pre-1978	1982	Ceased operation due to bankruptcy
		1984	Resumed limited service
		1989	Ceased operation due to bankruptcy
Continental	pre-1978	1989	6th ranking carrier (under Texas Air Corp)
Delta	pre-1978	1989	2nd ranking carrier
Eastern	pre-1978	1989	Declared bankruptcy; conducting limited operations (under Texas Air Corp)
National	pre-1978	1980	Acquired by Pan Am
Northwest	pre-1978	1989	5th ranking carrier
Pan Am			
TWA	pre-1978	1989	8th ranking carrier
United	pre-1978	1989	3rd ranking carrier

Western	pre-1978	1986	Acquired by Delta

Local service carriers (8)

frontier	pre-1978	1985	Acquired by People Express
Hughes Airwest	pre-1978	1980	Acquired by Republic
North Central	pre-1978	1979	Merged within Southern to form Republic
		1986	Republic acquired by Northwest
Ozark	pre-1978	1986	Acquired by TWA
Piedmont	pre-1978	1987	Acquired by US Air
Southern	pre-1978	1979	Merged with North Central of form Republic
		1986	Republic acquired by Northwest
Texas International	pre-1978	1982	Acquired by Continental
US Air	pre-1978	1989	4th ranking carrier

Intrastate carriers(5)

Alaska	pre-1978	1989	15th ranking carrier
AirCal	1979	1987	Acquired by American
Air Florida	1979	1984	Ceased operation due to bankruptcy
		1985	Acquired by Midway
PSA	1979	1987	Acquired by US Air
Southwest	1979	1989	9th ranking carrier

Charter carriers(2)

Capitol	1979	1984	Ceased operation due to bankruptcy
World	1979	1985	Ceased operation due to bankruptcy

Commuter carriers (3)

Air Wisconsin	1982	1989	18th ranking carrier
Empire	1980	1986	Acquired by Piedmont
Horizon	1983	1986	Acquired by Alaska

New carriers (17)

Air Atlanta	1984	1986	Ceased operation due to bankruptcy
Air One	1983	1984	Ceased operation due to bankruptcy
American International	1982	1984	Ceased operation due to bankruptcy
America West	1983	1989	11th ranking carrier
Florida Express	1984	1988	Acquired by Braniff
Frontier Horizon	1984	1985	Ceased operation due to bankruptcy
Hawaii Express	1982	1983	Ceased operation due to bankruptcy

Jet America	1982	1986	Acquired by Alaska
Midway	1979	1989	16th ranking carrier
Muse (Transtar)	1981	1985	Acquired by Southwest
New York Air	1980	1985	Acquired by Continental
Northeastern	1982	1984	Ceased operation due to bankruptcy
Pacific East	1982	1984	Ceased operation due to bankruptcy
Pacific Express	1982	1984	Ceased operation due to bankruptcy
People Express	1981	1986	Acquired by Continental
Presidential	1985	1987	Became feeder carrier for United
Sunworld	1983	1988	Ceased operation due to bankruptcy

[1]Date carrier began interstate service with jet aircraft.
[2]Size ranking based on passengers carried during 12 months ended September 1989.

of factors such as financial insolvency, mergers and acquisitions reduced the number of operators to 10 carriers of regional or national scale by 1988. This was followed by a period of consolidation, and by 1991 the situation had worsened, with both Pan Am and Eastern Airlines having faced bankruptcy: the existing carriers had either prospered or lost market share to competitors (Table 3.4).

Thus a 62 per cent increase in the number of domestic travellers carried on US airlines during 1978-90 has been followed by a greater degree of concentration and integration in the airline business Table 3.5 outlines the situation in the mid- 1990s, with the performance and passenger volumes for the main US airlines. Milman and Pope argue that in the late 1990s 'the US airline operates in an oligopolistic market structure...(and)...in recent years, access for airlines new to the industry has become more difficult due to the limited availability of terminal space and gates, a lack of departure and landing slots at major airports, and price competition from the dominant carriers' (Table 3.5). In terms of route structure, Table 3.6 outlines the ten most important domestic markets in the USA, highlighting the popularity of short-distance markets such as New York-Boston, Dallas-Houston and New York-Washington.

Table 3.5: Leading US airlines' statistics and performance, 1995/96.

	Passengers (million)			Revenue passenger miles(billion)			Employees		Number of aircraft		Aircraft departure (000s)	
	1995	1996	(%)change[1]	1995	1996	(%)change[1]	1995	1996	1995	1996	1995	1996
Delta	86.9	97.2	11.8	85.1	93.9	10.3	58,621	58,935	539	544	950	943
American	79.5	79.3	-1.2	102.7	104.5	1.8	84,915	82,571	635	642	823	787
United	78.8	81.9	4.1	111.5	116.6	4.5	75,634	79,205	558	564	780	785
US Airways(US Air)	56.7	56.6	-0.1	37.6	38.9	3.5	40,780	39,417	394	390	794	738
Southwest	50.0	55.4	10.7	23.3	27.1	16.1	18,816	21,863	224	243	685	748
Northwest	49.3	52.7	6.8	62.5	68.6	9.8	43,604	45,320	380	399	566	586
Continental	35.0	35.7	2.1	35.5	37.4	5.2	30,443	29,199	317	317	458	443
Trans World (TWA)	21.6	29.3	35.9	24.9	27.1	8.9	23,121	24,731	186	192	277	284
America West	16.8	18.1	7.9	13.3	15.3	15.1	9,402	9,357	93	99	195	207
Alaska	10.1	11.8	16.6	8.5	9.8	14.6	6,732	7,440	74	74	143	153
Total	484.6	518.0	6.9	504.9	539.2	6.8	392,068	398,038	3,400	3,464	5,671	5,674

[1]Calculated on unrounded data.

Table 3.6 : Top ten US domestic markets, 1995/96.

Makets		Passengers[1] 1995 (000s)	1996[2] (000s)
1. New York	Los Angeles	2,991.1	3,149.0
2. New York	Chicago	2,981.6	2,996.5
3. New York	Miami	2,675.6	2,777.6
4. Honolulu	Kahului, Maui	2,761.5	2,750.0
5. New York	Boston	2,491.4	2,400.9
6. New York	San Francisco	2,185.8	2,282.5
7. New York	Orlando	2,005.1	2,234.9
8. Dallas/Fort Worth	Houston	2,208.4	2,205.1
9. Los Angeles	Las Vegas	1,956.4	2,102.9
10. New York	Washington	2,118.2	2,087.4

[1] Outbound plus impound passengers.
[2] 12 months to end-September 1996.

Goetz and Sutton examine the effects of concentration in the airline industry post-deregulation in detail, noting that 200 carriers, were absorbed or went bankrupt in 1983-88, with the nine largest airlines (Ameri-can, United, Delta, Northwest, Continental, USAir, TWA, Pan Am and Eastern) responsible for 92 per cent of domestic revenue passenger miles. By 1995, 'the industry has been transformed from a regulated oligopoly of ten trunk carriers controlling 87 per cent of the market [in 1978] to an unregu-lated oligopoly of eight major carriers controlling 93 per cent in 1995'. This is an interesting situation given the rationale for deregulation: that it would lead to a situation of perfect competition with no major economies of scale or barriers to entry.

Goetz and Sutton's (1997) excellent synthesis of deregulation observes that while average air fares (in constant dollars) have declined since 1978, discount pricing and fare wars have also reduced fares. The result is that higher fares have been levelled for short-notice business travel; but under conditions of severe discounting, some fares have dropped below cost levels. However, airlines servicing more peripheral routes where one airline dominates have set fares 18-27 per cent higher on average than on trunk routes. Largely as a result of discount fares, domestic passenger volumes have increased dramatically under deregulation. In the period 1978-93, an 87 per cent growth occurred, with passengers increasing from 256 million to 478 million. Flight departures in the same period also grew from 5 million to 7.2 million. But between 1990 and 1993, airlines in the USA made record losses of US$13 billion—the largest losses ever in history. What has this meant for the structure and provision of services through American airline networks?

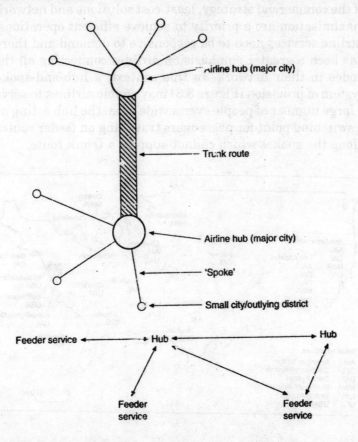

Fig. 3.2 : Schematic diagram of a hub-and-spoke system.

The Spatial Effects of Deregulation

From the transport geographer's perspective, a distinctive spatial structure in air travel has emerged in the USA, whereby the major US airlines have developed a hub-and-spoke structure as spatial and commercial strategies for organising airlines' operations in a deregulated environment. This contrasts with the CAB regulation era where interurban routes were often 805 km or more in length and little attention was given to integrating the route networks among operators. However, in a deregulated environment where cost reduc-tions are a central element of the commercial strategy, least-cost solutions and network maximisation are a priority to achieve efficient operations. Airline services need to be responsive to demand and there has been a greater emphasis on airlines connecting all the nodes in their network. In this context, a hub-and-spoke system of provision (Figure 3.3) may enable airlines to serve a large number of people over a wide area, the hub acting as a switching point for passengers travelling on feeder routes along the spokes which cannot support a trunk route.

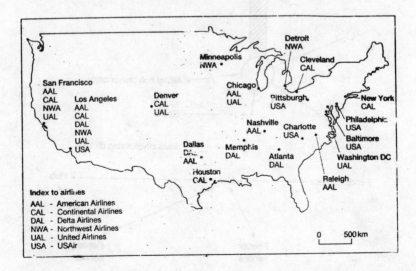

Fig. 3.3 : Distribution of major hubs in the USA.

According to O'Kelly hubs are least-cost solutions for airlines and may combine a range of airports in a region, assisting the airline in running a high-frequency service along trunk routes between hubs. Along the spokes, regional carriers, often code sharing under the major's identification, provide the feeder services. The result has been a geogra-phical concentration of airline hubs in major Us cities, based on historical ties with certain airports, airline mergers, the servicing of niche tourist markets and responses to competitors, so that major operators provide 100-200 departures each day from some of the key hubs. Thus, a spatial concentration has occurred among the six largest airlines, leading to the development of four major hub cities—Atlanta, Chicago, Dallas and Denver (Figure 3.4). This was illustrated in Shaw's (1993) recent analysis where the following national hubs emerged (with the regional hubs in parentheses).

• American Airlines	Dallas/Fort Worth, Chicago (Nashville, Raleigh/Durham)
• Delta Airlines	Atlanta, Cincinnati, Dallas/Fort Worth (Salt Lake City)
• US Air	Pittsburgh, Charlotte (Baltimore and Phila-delphia)
• United Airlines	Chicago (Washington DC, Denver)
• Northwest Airlines	Detroit, Memphis, Minneapolis/St Paul
• Continental Airlines	Houston, New York, Denver, Cleveland.

Figure 3.4 also incorporates two other hubs (Los Angeles and San Francisco) of lesser significance in the overall pattern of airline routes to illustrate the principal airports serving the western seaboard.

In spatial terms, Continental Airlines' network covers a wide area within the USA, while Delta Airlines' network is heavily concentrated in the southern states, with regional hubs serving the western seaboard. In contrast, Northwest Airlines serves the Mid West, while United Airlines has hubs located on an east-west axis across the USA, offering the best connections to cities on the western seaboard. US Air,

however, has four hubs in close proximity, due to its interest
in the East Coast market, Shaw (1993) observes that US
Air is unique as it operates many other nodes as smaller
hubs to serve other areas. This is one factor which has made
the airline attractive to foreign airlines such as British
Airways, which took a $200 million stake in the airline in
April 1993, providing it with a foothold in the lucrative North
American and transatlantic market.

Goetz and Sutton explain the spatial patterns of
deregulation in terms of coreperiphery concepts. They
distinguish between two types of hubs.

- domestic hubs
- international gateways.

They also expand upon Shaw's analysis as Table 3.7
shows. Goetz and Sutton identify the international gateway
as funnels for international services and connections to
domestic destinations but they do not function as domestic
hubs. The gateways are mainly located in coastal cities while
the domestic hubs are the focal point for the domestic system,
and Dresner and Windle raise a range of issues related to
such developments. In terms of the geographic concentration
in the airline industry which occurred post-regulation, Goetz
and Sutton (1997 : 244) argue that :

> Between 1978 and 1993, every domestic hub core except
> Cleveland experienced an increase in single carrier
> concen-tration. In 12 of the 22 hub cores as of 1993, one
> carrier accounted for more than 60 per cent of their
> traffic, and 9 hubs reported more than 70 per cent
> concentration. These high levels of concentration at hub
> cores reflect the increases in both hub and spoke
> operations and industrial consoli-dation. Once entry and
> exit regulations were removed and carriers adopted hub-
> based networks, carriers concentrated traffic, personnel,
> and infrastructure at key points in their systems. The
> development of 'fortress hubs'—cities where no other
> carriers were able to establish beachheads of operation-
> emerged as a key strategy for major airlines facing
> competitive threats from new entrants into the industry.

One key factor in hub dominance was CRSs, with CRS-owning airlines having a 13-18 per cent greater chance of selling airline tickets through travel agents. Williams (1993) also observed that travel agent use of CRSs became concentrated in hub cities, with Sabre processing 87 per cent of travel agent revenues in Dallas, and United's Apollo system handling over two-thirds of bookings in Denver.

Following deregulation, there has been a considerable debate amongst researchers over the effect on consumers (tourists and non-tourists). For example, Kihl (1988) argues that deregulation led to a decline in service quality as

Table 3.7: Domestic and international airline hubs in the USA.

Domestic hubs	Principal airline
Atlanta	Delta
Baltimore	US Air
Charlotte	US Air
Chicago	United American Airlines
Cincinnati	Delta
Cleveland	Continental
Dallas Fort Worth	American Airlines, Delta, Southwest
Denver	United
Detroit	Northwest
Houston	Continental, Southwest
Las Vegas	American West
Memphis	Northwest
Minneapolis	Northwest
Nashville	American Airlines
Newark	Continental
Philadelphia	US Air
Phoenix	American West
Pittsburth	US Air
Raleigh-Durham	American Airlines
St Louis	TWA
Salt Lake City	Delta
Washington	United, US Air
International gateways	
Boston	Delta, US Air, Northwest
Los Angeles	United, Delta, American Airlines, Northwest
Miami	American Airlines, Delta, USAir, TWA
San Francisco	United
Seattle	United, Alaska, Northwest

smallar communities not directly connected to trunk routes faced fare increases and less frequent services. Goetz and Sutton observe that 'smaller turboprop carriers' have replaced jet services and service quality has declined. It is clear that airline mergers may have led to a decline in the number of carriers serving some communities, but Jemiolo and Oster maintained that any changes in service provision to less-accessible communities were a result of recession and greater fuel costs rather than deregulation. Yet Goetz and Sutton argue that 'small communities overall have experienced frequent interrup-tions in service and many have been dropped from the air network altogether', a feature emphasised by Kihl. Of 514 non-hub communities with an air service in 1978, 167 had lost thier service by 1995, with only 26 communities gaining a new service. The Airline Deregulation Act did include provisions for Essential Air Service subsidies so that small communities were still served. In 1995, some 77 communities received such a subsidy.

Debate has also centred on the effect of deregulation on passenger safety (Moses and Savage 1990). Golich (1998) asserts that the development of hubbing operations led to a decline in safety as more services and takeoffs/landings were concentrated into specific areas, increasing the potential for accidents. However, the US civil aviation statistics for the period 1975-90 show that the number of fatalities actually dropped from 663 to 424, while the rate per million aircraft miles flown has remained constant at 0.001 for scheduled services. However, Golich's assessment may have a great deal of validity in view of the congested nature of many US airports which is discussed later.

Following deregulation and the growth in new entrants to the domestic airline market, consumer complaints increased to a peak of 40,985 in 1987 but dropped to 6,106 for 1991 and 4,629 in 1995 (US Bureau of the Census 1996). The most commonly reported sources of dissatisfaction in 1995 were:

- Flight problems, such as cancellations and delays (1,133)
- Baggage problems (628)
- Problems associated with refunds (576)
- Customer service issues such as unhelpful employees, inadequate meals and poor cabin service (667)
- Errors in ticketing and reservations (666)
- Incorrect or incomplete information about fares (185)
- The process of 'bumping' passengers off overbooked flights (by offering incentives not to travel on a specific flight) (263).

Airlines have exercised greater control over their workforces since deregulation, in pursuit of continued increases in productivity and greater economies of scale. Critics have also argued that deregulation has led to the larger carriers developing sophisticated marketing campaigns to foster customer loyalty to influence the choice of carrier through 'frequent flyer programmes' and the use of airline-controlled CRSs to promote their services via travel retailers, as noted by Goetz and Sutton. Investment in technology and marketing tools to shape the pattern of supply to potential customers has also been reinforced through the hub and spoking operations of the 'majors'. For new entrants to gain a foothold in the US domestic airline market, not only would they need to secure a slot at an airport but they would need to be able to offer services to compete with the existing frequencies and service available. This would require major capital investment and commercial nerve at a time of considerable flux in the aviation market. Furthermore, Graham identifies the influence which major carriers exercise on hub airports, particularly their ability to limit new competition. Ironically, this has meant that hub airports have become less financially secure in the US as restrictive practices such as 'majority-in-interest' may limit airport revenue generation through the airlines' power of veto on capacity improvements to encourage competition.

The changes brought about by deregulation have also had a pronounced effect on the US airport system as the demand for air travel has continued to grow despite constraints on the supply of airport capacity. Deregulation and the development of trunk routes and hubs have intensified congestion at major US airports. Sealy notes that 16 of the world's 25 leading airports handling in excess of 15 million passengers a year were in the USA.

Having examined the effect of deregulation on the supply of air transport, attention now turns to the interface of supply and demand issues in relation to land-based tourist transport systems. The example of Bermuda has been chosen to reflect some of the problems and management issues associated with the supply of tourist transport services in a small island where the available space for tourism and transport competes and conflicts with other land uses.

The supply of Tourist Transport in Destination Areas

The supply of tourist transport services in the destination area is one area neglected in Buckley's (1987) transaction analysis. Two studies which deal with this issue are Teye's study of Bermuda and Heraty's (1989) examination of supply-related problems which characterise less developed countries (LDCs). For this reason, the case of Bermuda is now considered, followed by an overview of the supply-related issues raised by Heraty.

Land-based Tourist Transport Systems: Bermuda

Tourism research on the Caribbean has generated a great deal of literature in learned journals such as *Tourism Management, Annals of Tourism Research* and more recently in publications by Gayle and Goodrich (1993) and Todd and Mather. The Caribbean is noteworthy as a major destination for over 10 million visitors from developed countries each year and is the focus of the world's cruise ship business. Therefore, it is an appropriate area on which to focus, particularly as tourist arrivals increased by 40.3 per cent in the period 1985-90, while world tourist arrivals only increased by 25 per cent. Tourist arrivals in the Caribbean generated $96 billion in gross expenditure for the region on 1990 (Gayle and Goodrich 1993). Research by Archer (1989, 1995) considers the economic impact and volume of tourism in the Caribbean basin and how international arrivals and cruise ship arrivals affect the economy of small islands (Table 3.8). The literature on small island tourism is still developing (Pearce 1987), but Wilkinson's (1989) analysis of such small island microstates provides a useful review into:

- Ways of classifying small islands.
- Why tourism has assumed such a prominent role.
- The problems related to scale and size on small islands.
- The impact of external influences seeking to control the supply chain (e.g. multi-national corporations and overseas investment companies).

Table 3.8 : Visitor arrivals and expenditure in Bermuda 1980-93.

	Visitor arrivals (000s)			Visitor expenditure[1] ($ million)		
	Air	Cruise	Total[2]	Air	Cruise	Total
1980	491.6	117.9	609.5	277.6	12.4	290.0
1981	429.8	104.7	534.5	275.0	13.3	288.3
1982	420.3	124.2	544.5	286.2	15.4	301.6
1983	446.9	120.8	567.7	319.3	16.2	335.5
1984	417.5	111.4	528.9	324.1	14.9	339.0
1985	406.7	142.0	549.6	335.6	21.9	357.5
1986	459.7	132.2	591.9	402.2	20.1	422.3
1987	477.9	153.4	631.3	439.6	25.0	464.6
1988	426.9	158.4	585.2	414.1	26.4	440.5
1989	418.3	131.3	549.7	426.5	24.3	450.8
1990	434.9	112.6	547.5	467.9	22.2	490.1
1991	386.2	128.1	514.3	423.9	31.7	455.6
1992	375.2	131.0	506.2	410.7	30.8	441.5
1993	413.1	153.9	567.1	465.2	39.3	504.5
1994	417.0	172.9	589.9	483.3	41.9	525.3

1 Within Bermuda, the Bermudan dollar exchangges almostt at par with US dollar.

2 Not all of the totals equal the sum of the figures included in the row because of rounding.

The effect of multinational corporations on microstates was reviewed by Britton (1982) in relation to tour operators, airlines and hotel corporations, which seize development and marketing opportunities to control the tourism economy through foreign ownership. Bermuda is an interesting example in this context. Wilkinson (1989) notes that its relatively strong economic and political will to restrict the large-scale expansion of tourism led to a moratorium on new hotels and limits on the number of cruise ships entering the harbour at any one time.

The development of tourism in microstates such as Bermuda has generated a requirement for a land-based tourist transport system to facilitate development and the movement of visitors around the island. Although infrastructure provision is not without environ-mental impacts, Bermuda is a good example where research into the role of tourist transport has led to a better understanding of the interface of transport and tourism and the conflicts they can cause.

Case Study : The Tourist Transport System in Bermuda

Bermuda comprises almost 150 small islands in the Caribbean, although only 20 are actually inhabited. A series to bridges and causeways connect the main islands where approximately 62,000 people live in an area of 55 km^2. Bermuda is unique within the Caribbean due to its high per capita income of $22,540 (1987) which is greater than both the USA and Switzerland (Teye 1992). Such prosperity derives from:
- International businesses in the islands.
- Military bases.
- Tourism, which is the largest contributor to the economy.

The high-spending markets (e.g., the North Americans) attracted to the islands require good quality air and sea transport links (Bertrand 1997) and a transport network which is coordinated and efficient. The reliance upon land transport for tourists within the destination to provide airport/port transfers to resorts, transport to tourist attractions and sightseeing has a major impact on the transport system on the islands.

One of the main concerns which Teye (1992) observes was the decline of the islands' railway system and the growth in car ownership which stimulated the development of the country's road network. As in many microstates, cars have become the symbol of economic prosperity, yet space constraints and the continued development of roads have contributed to high densities of car ownership (e.g., 220 vehicles per km^2 in Bermuda) with associated environmental impacts. Bermuda's government examined the problem posed by private car ownership in the 1970s and 1980s and the complex nature of transport planning for residents and tourism. The principal measures within Bermuda's transport policy have been to regulate ownership through licensing, speed controls and limits on vehicle replacement. The consequences for tourist transport are restrictions on car-hire, which have led to an expansion in motorcycle and moped use. This has led to conflicts between the use of mopeds by tourists (less than 50 cc engine size) for sightseeing and touring, and local traffic. For example, in 1970 there were 3,296 accidents and 24 fatalities, although a crash helmet law in 1977 and improved traffic education for tourists by moped hire companies led to a significant reduction in the number of accidents.

In common with many other small islands which have developed tourism, Bermuda has traffic problems related to non-tourist (commuting) and tourist travel to the capital city (Hamilton) and tourist travel within tourist zones and corridors along the south shore, where much of the tourist accommodation is located (Figure 3.5). Given the primary role of Hamilton as a commerical and entertainment centre and the hub of the island's bus services, congestion generated by resident and tourist transport use is virtually inevitable, unless these activities are decentralised to other areas.

Teye (1992) also notes the effect of seasonality in tourist movements on the islands (May-October) and the effect of cruise ships. The cruise ship business in the Caribbean in the 1980s is well documented by Lawton and Butler (1987) and there is widespread agreement that the arrival of such ships can swamp small islands when the visitors disembark. Table 3.6, outlines the growth of air and cruise ship arrivals to 1994. Unlike other cruise ship ports, Bermuda has attracted long-stay visits (up to four days) where the ships dock and remain rather than arriving in the morning and leaving that evening. As a result, Teye (1992) argues that 'cruise ships in Bermuda literally become docked resorts'. Yet prior to 1984, up to seven cruise ships a week were docking in Bermuda. The impact on the tourist transport system can be seen in traffic congestion due to visitors renting taxis for sightseeing.

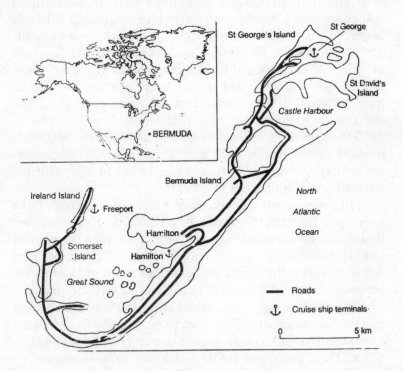

Fig. 3.4 : Bermuda: location and infrastructure.

One solution to the management of this problem was the introduction in 1988 of limitations on cruise ship passengers by restricting the number of ships to four in port at any one time and to attempt to restrict cruise ship visits. This deliberate policy by Bermuda's government eliminated weekend cruise ships from docking, thereby reducing overcrowding and temporary congestion on the island's transport network. This serves as a useful example of how the management of the supply of tourist transport infrastructure can induce a reduction in the demand. According to Peisley 'Bermuda remains the most tightly controlled of cruise ship destinations' in the Caribbean. In the 1990s, the number of ships which can operate in the area is limited to five of 4-star ranking or higher: two from the Celebrity Company, one from each of RCCL, NCL and Majesty. Cunard can make occasional visits with its three ships *OE2, Vistafjord* and *Royal Viking Sun*. the aim is not only to preserve the island's up-market image, but also to control visitor numbers and to ensure a relatively high onshore visitor expenditure.

One additional measure to manage tourist travel patterns in Bermuda, which was adopted as government policy in 1973, was the development of tourist-specific routes. Although little progress has been made in this direction, Teye argues that the severity of the traffic problems facing the islands may require a clear strategy to designate a road hierarchy to reduce the conflict between tourist and non-tourist use of roads. This would need to encourage the rational and managed touring of the islands' natural and man-made attractions and is preferable to further road building in a country already short of space. It is ironic that while tourism has generated prosperity for Bermudans, the symbol of success—the private car—is now posing major transport problems for the country, in common with many other microstates which have followed tourism as a route to economic development. As Teye readily acknowledges, 'most microstates have very few options if they allow poor transportation planning to destroy their tourist industry'.

Visitors expect good destination-specific transport systems and they form an important part of the tourist's overall experience of travel. For this reason, it is pertinent to focus on the issues raised by Heraty in the context of the LDCs in terms of how the supply of tourist transport needs to meet both the expectations and needs of visitors if the service encounter in the destination is to reach minimum standards. Although some of the problems Heraty examined are unique to LDCs, the general issues raised also have implications for developed countries. The issues which highlight tourists' expectations in the developed world and the maintenance of service quality, include:

- *Airport transfers* : Tourists arriving in a destination after a tiring flight, require convenient and comfortable transfer vehicles. The tendency to use a limited number of transfer vehicles to shuttle a large number of different tour groups to a dispersed range of hotels often adds to the inconvenience associated with long-haul travel in LDCs. The trend towards the use of baggage trucks to transport tourists' baggage to hotels due to the lack of space on old vehicles is disconcerting for tourists and can cause delays due to misdelivery.

- *Sightseeing tours* : For LDCs receiving high-spending tourists, one lucrative tourist transport service which offers potentially high profits to private operators is sightseeing tours. However, visitors from developed countries expect coaches with air-conditioning and a public address system, vehicles which are safe and give good all-round visibility. In many cases, the capital cost of such vehicles is prohibitively high for private operators in LDCs who are forced to import them. Yet where they are available, they significantly enhance the tourists' experience. Well-trained tour guides, able to provide commentaries and answer questions in a variety of languages, are also an important asset. Guides who are able to convey the local culture, history, customs and lifestyle to visitors will be able to contribute to the tourists' pleasant memories of their holiday and adequate stopping places at cafes, restaurants or clearings with toilets and refreshment facilities also have a part to play.

Independent Travel by Tourists

The more adventurous tourist often wishes to travel on local public transport systems and adequate information needs to be made available (e.g., timetables). The use of hire cars is also a major tourist service in LDCs which need to be supplied according to a code of good practice. According to Heraty, good practice should include:

- High-quality vehicle standards, insurance and contract conditions.
- Provision of tourist-oriented maps and leaflets.
- Signposting of routes to tourist attractions and sights.
- Training for the police in dealing with tourist drivers
- Action to address road-based and car-related crime affecting tourist hire cars.
- Safety standards for mopeds where governments permit tourists to hire such transport.
- Incentives to encourage short-stay visitors (e.g., cruise ship passengers) to venture away from the port to visit other locations.
- Licensing and regulation of taxi companies and drivers to prevent tourists being exploited.

From the transport policy makers' perspective, Heraty notes that in accommodating tourist transport needs, a range of problems need to be addressed at government level to facilitate tourist travel in destination areas, including:

- Import duties may need to be relaxed to facilitate the acquisition of new vehicles and to make them more affordable and able to absorb 'standing costs' (when the vehicle is off the road) as tourist use declines outside of the peak season.
- Roads and tourist transport infrastructure need to be maintained to reduce wear and tear on vehicles.

- Skilled mechanics and vehicle drivers need to be trained to ensure an adequate supply of labour to meet demands.
- Traffic congestion related to peaked seasonal demand by tourists needs to be managed.
- Sufficient transport operators need to be licensed to prevent limited competition and cartel-type operations resulting under prohibitively expensive situations.

A recent review by Grant et. al., (1997) also outlines the transport policies and strategies which local authorities need to develop to facilitate a more efficient supply of tourist transport services. They highlight the practical and organisational issues involved in the development of specific forms of tourist transport and in meeting the needs of users (e.g., car-based, coach-borne, pedestrians, people travelling on public transport) and needs of sightseers and the importance of integration. In a recent study of New Zealand's premier South Island destination, Milford Sound, congestion and inadequate road provision emerge as a potential threat to the area's tourism potential. The region's single-lane bridges and tight corners make it a difficult terrain for drivers. Since about 300,000 people travel to Milford Sound per annum, capacity problems may inhibit future growth. Research by Page and Meyer (1996) also illustrates the problem of foreign driver accidents on New Zealand's road system, where tight corners and driving conditions can raise safety issues for foreign visitors as Figure 3.6 shows.

Summary

The various issues facing transport providers in the 1990s in managing the supply of services and associated operational issues. In particular, it has emphasised how various transport providers, such as airlines, have used the two major tools, IT and logistics to improve the flow of information to assist in the management and delivery of services to customers. The growing importance of IT is demonstrated by the competition between international airlines (Oum and Yu 1998) and the greater use of IT to gain competitive advantage. This also applies to the role of infrastructure providers discussed in the next chapter, in optimising the use of the facilities to gain cost savings and optimal use of major

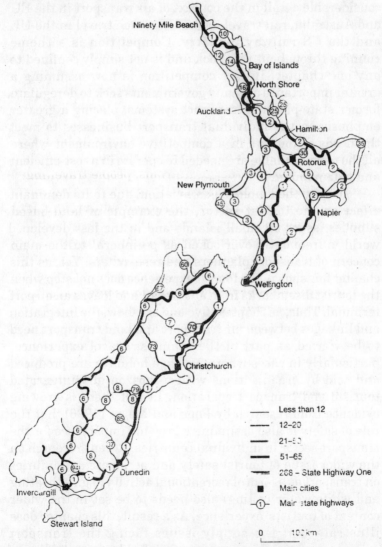

Fig. 3.5 : Tourist road accidents in New Zealand in 1994.

sunk costs in infrastructure. The oher tools now being harnessed in terms of strategic management by transport providers such as airlines, are the growing use of alliances and strategic partnerships. This is a function of enhanced competition in the marketplace, a feature discussed in considerable detail in the context of air transport in the EU and Australia, rail travel in the UK, coach travel in the UK and the US railway industry. Competition is a theme running throughout this book and is not simply confined to any one chapter. In fact competition is now assuming a greater importance as many governments seek to deregulate former state-planned transport systems, placing a greater emphasis on the individual transport businesses to meet the needs of tourists in a competitive environment where all the tools available are needed to operate in a cost-efficient and safe manner.

Despite the emphasis on aviation, due to its dominant effect on the tourist sector, the example of land-based supplies issues on small islands and in the less developed world is frequently overlooked as peripheral to the main concern of transport planners and researchers. Yet, as this chapter has shown, the tourist experience does not stop when the tourist disembarks from an aircraft and leaves an airport terminal. Thus, as chapters five and six show, the integration and linkages between air transport and land transport need to be viewed as part of the seamless travel experience, particularly in cases where package holidays are produced and sold by organisations with a horizontally integrated tourism and transport operation. In fact there is growing evidence from research by Page and Meyer (1996) that the role of safety is also assuming a growing importance for the transport sector in individual countries. Recent research on the wider issue of tourist safety and accidents and injuries on transport as a form of recreational activity (e.g., jetboating and white water rafting) also needs to be set in the wider context of tourists' experience. As a result, this chapter does illustrate that the supply issues facing the transport operator over a diverse range of fields from business operations, including IT and logistics, through to safety and management of the services provided to ensure the company operates in a profitable and sustainable manners.

The lessons of deregulation in the USA show that in a business environment free of state regulation, where profit is the motive for service provision, transport operators behave in the most efficient and restrictive manner in order to protect market share. The emergence of a hub-and-spoke structure may indicate how the European air line business will respond to a greater degree of deregulation in the 1990s. But as the discussion by Heraty (1989) suggests, the supply of tourist transport services in destination areas needs to be carefully targeted at the market to ensure both customer satisfaction and to maximise revenue generation for private sector transport operators. As the case of Bermuda shows, where there is a significant demand for a destination, government action may be taken to restrict the activities of tour operators and tourists without adversely affecting the tourism industry. Understanding the expectations and motives of visitors confirms the importance of setting the demand and supply for tourist transport services in a systematic framework where the wider issues and interrelationships can be understood. In this context, the next chapter considers the specific implications of supply and demand for infrastructure development.

4

Tourist Transport Infrastructure

Introduction

The development of tourism requires a transport infrastructure to facilitate the free movement of tourist traffic,
and much of the research in this context has focused on
modal forms of travel (e.g., rail travel, air travel and car-
based trips). One of the fundamental links that has been
overlooked in the tourist transport system is the way in
which demand and supply are brought together and
managed, and the infrastructure used to ensure the system
functions efficiently. In both the transport and tourism
literature, terminal facilities, which provide the context in
which the tourist embarks on the mode of transport, to
ensure the interaction of supply and demand takes place
smoothly, have been largely overlooked. Yet it is widely
recognised that the 'holiday experience' begins when the
tourist arrives at a terminal, ready to embark on a journey.
In fact some commentators even suggest that the experience
effectively begins when the traveller leaves their home
environment.

This chapter examines the challenge of managing the
interaction of supply and demand for tourist travel with
reference to one type of terminal facility - the airport.
Airports are probably the most complex environments and
systems in which this interaction occurs and yet they often

remain poorly understood in a tourism context. As Ashford et. al., (1991 : 1) argue, 'the airport forms an essential part of the air transport system, because it is the physical site at which a model transfer of transport is made from the air modes to land modes'. The chapter commences with a discussion of the management challenges posed by terminal facilities, emphasising the organisations involved in the management process. This is followed by a discussion of the locational and planning issues associated with airport development, particularly access to markets. Future development plans for world regions experiencing a rapid growth in tourist travel are then discussed, as arrivals are likely to outstrip existing airport capacity. But why focus on air travel rather than other types of terminal ? What literature does exist is airport-specific and ports, bus/coach terminals and railway terminals have not attracted much attention, with a notable exception being Bertolini and Spit. However, in Chapter the importance of the terminal environment for InterCity rail travel was discussed, albeit briefly, in relation to service quality and the travel experience. In addition, ATAG (1993) provided a convincing argument for a focus on air travel: in 1993, the volume of air travel worldwide was equivalent to one-fifth of the world's population travelling once a year. The air transport industry also generated 24 million jobs and US$??? billion in gross output. Therefore, while some of the principles and issues discussed in this chapter relate solely to air travel, some of the broader issues (i.e., developing a customer-focused approach) have a wide application to the management of the tourist-transport interface which occurs in transport terminal facilities.

The Management Challenge of Tourist Transport Terminals: Airports

To the uninitiated, occasional traveller, terminal facilities can be a bewildering, seemingly chaotic and unnerving experience. The semblance of chaos is conveyed by Barlay (1995):

The airport cavalcade can baffle or startle the inexperienced passenger...Laden with suitcases and packages, calm and rational people grow uptight, defensive with aggression, fail to allow themselves time to familiarise themselves with the layout or study the free guides to terminals.

The entire psychology of travel and the change in the behaviour of the traveller in airports (e.g., tunnel vision or airport syndrome) embraces a whole series of emotions among the diversity of passengers: 'joy, grief, anxiety, expectations, aggravation, yearning and fulfilment'. From a tourists' perspective, numerous factors affect their experience, according to Barlay (1995 : 49):

- Speed of check-in.

- Efficiency of passport control and customs clearance (the UK government is now placing the onus on airlines to check outbound travellers' passports in order to devote more resources to inbound travellers).

- Luggage retrieval.

- Availability of shops, duty-free goods and associated services.

- A spacious and relaxed environment in which to wait prior to boarding the aircraft.

From the airport's perspective, operational issues have dominated its work. The management challenge is to recognise the tourists' needs and to minimise likely problems while ensuring the terminal operates as a smooth series of complex systems. Doganis (1992) defines airports as complex industrial organisations that

...act as a forum in which disparate elements and activities are brought together to facilitate, for both passengers and freight, the interchange between air and surface transport.

In some countries, for a range of historical, legal and other reasons, the scope of airport activities can vary from the highly complex and all-embracing to the very limited. In physical terms, Doganis defines an airport as :

Essentially one or more runways for aircraft together with associated buildings or terminals where passengers... are processed...the majority of airport authorities own and operate their runways, terminals and associated facilities, such as taxiways or aprons.

Doganis distinguishes between the three principal activities of airports:

- Essential operational services and facilities.
- Traffic-handling services.
- Commercial activities.

although 'at most, if not all, airports, the major consideration must be passenger flows' and this in itself requires management measures to ensure smooth operation (e.g., pricing and flow management. This comprises a broad range of activities within any airport environment, whether in an international gateway airport, a regional or local airport:

- Ground handling.
- Baggage handling.
- Passenger terminal operations.
- Airport security.
- Cargo operations.
- Airport technical services.
- air traffic control.
- Aircraft scheduling (takeoff/landing slot allocation)
- Airport and aircraft emergency services.
- Airport access.

which are described in detail by Ashford et. al., (1991) in what remains the principal study on airport operations. Figure 4.1 highlights some of the relationships which need to be managed in the airport system so that the airport-airline-traveller interactions occur in a professional and smooth manner. Figures 4.2 and 4.3 also illustrate the spatial interactions in the airport system, indicating how the airport enables an aircraft to take off/land and to unload and load passengers. As part of these functions, it enables travellers to change their mode of transport and be processed efficiently (e.g., ticketing and documentation).

Each of these functions impinges upon the management of the tourists' experience of the terminal facilities. Table 4.1 outlines the weekly pattern of scheduled departures from the world's top 30 airports, which are only a fraction of the ICAO list of 1,012 airports worldwide. Of the top 30 airports, 19 are located in the USA, confirming a pattern similar to that observed by Sealy (1992). This is followed by Europe and Asia-Pacific.

At a global scale, the management of airports is affected by government policy which, in part, determines the pattern of ownership. As Doganis (1992) observes, there are four main types of ownership. These are:

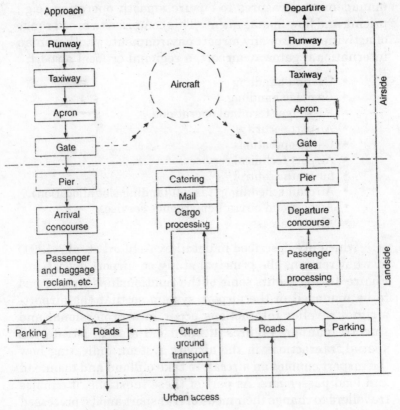

Fig. 4.1 : An airport system.

- *State ownership with direct government control,* characterised by a single government department (i.e., a Civil Aviation Department) which operates the country's airports. The alternative to a centralised government pattern of control and management is localised ownership such as municipal ownership.

- *Public ownership through an airport authority,* usually as a limited liability or private company. For example, the British Airports Authority (BAA) was one of the early examples of a national airport authority. Aer Rianta in the Republic of Ireland is another example of a national airport authority. There are also cases of regional airport authorities in the USA.

- *Mixed public and private ownership* is an organisational model adopted at larger Italian airports, where a company manages the airport, with public and private shareholders.

- *Private ownership* was a model of limited appeal prior to the wave of privatisation in the 1980s. One of the early examples in the UK was London City Airport in London Docklands, opened in 1987. However, Doganis (1992) points out that the major impetus to private ownership was the privatisation of BAA in 1987.

In generic terms, Doganis argues that a prime function of airport management is to determine the objective of any economic and management strategy for an airport by addressing four questions:

- Should airports be run as commercially oriented profitable concerns?
- How should one improve airport economic efficiency?
- Should profits from larger airports be used to cross-subsidise loss-making smaller airports?
- Should airports be privatised?

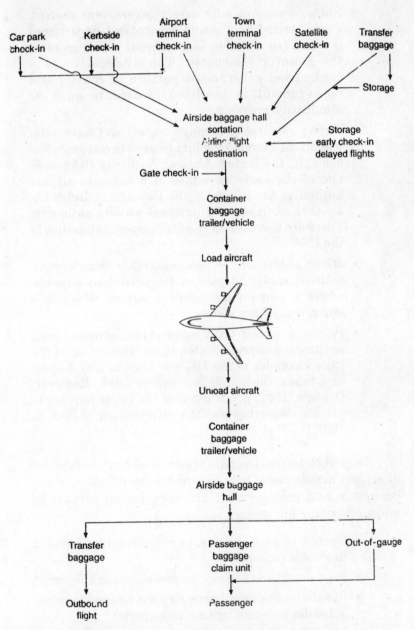

Fig. 4.2 : Luggage loading and unloading in the airport system.

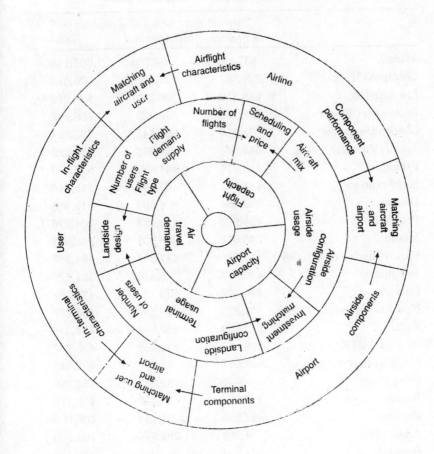

Fig. 4.3 : Airport relationships.

These four questions essentially raise the issue of what form of airport ownership a government deems important and the prime objectives which will affect the economic strategy each airport pursues. This in turn will require very different management strategies. For example, airlines and bodies such as IATA still argue that airports are public utilities when arguing against increased airport charges.

Table 4.1 : The world's top airports, January 1998.

	Aircraft seats (scheduled departures)[1]		
	Domestic	International	Total
Atlanta	937,414	68,725	1,006,139
Chicago/O'Hare	870,957	114,656	985,613
Los Angeles	688,819	206,210	895,029
Dallas-Fort Worth	788,265	70,723	858,988
London Heathrow	95,150	697,641	792,791
Tokyo (Maneda)	548,003	10,626	658,829
Frankfurt	113,771	444,882	559,593
San Francisco	461,281	87,065	548,346
Denver	509,794	6,594	516,388
Phoenix	486,953	17,323	504,276
Miami	243,010	256,202	498,212
Paris (Charles de Gaulle)	47,566	447,201	494,767
St Louis	483,087	8,440	491,527
Detroit	441,469	36,129	477,598
New York/Newark	372,380	90,890	463,270
Seoul	243,230	209,848	453,078
New York/JFK	208,331	242,458	450,787
Minneapolis-St Paul	401,973	30,976	432,948
Hong Kong	—	432,389	432,389
Boston	370,036	48,140	418,176
Houston	343,266	61,734	405,000
Amsterdam	4,292	391,610	395,902
Bangkok	101,192	289,998	388,188
Singapore	—	376,268	376,268
Las Vegas	370,425	3,672	374,097
Tokyo (Narita)	15,854	347,696	363,550
New York/La Guardia	334,881	28,089	362,970
Philadelphia	324,531	36,293	359,824
Rome	162,781	185,112	347,893
Seattle	322,408	25,430	347,838

[1]The statistics are based on services ending week of 12 January 1998
and code-shared flights have been removed where possible.

Table 4.2 : Operating costs at BBA airports in 1996 and 1997.

	1997 £ million	1997 £ million	% change 1996/9
Staff costs	238	246	3.4
Retail expenditure	166	176	6.0
Depreciation	100	110	10.0
Maintenance	64	72	12.5
Rent and rates	64	68	6.2
Cost of development			
Property sales	-	20	100
Utility costs	77	77	0
Police costs	39	38	−2.6
General expenses	62	75	21.0
Total	810	882	8.9

It is useful to examine a number of specific issues associated with airport management which will then be exemplified by a case study of BAA. As Doganis rightly argues, 'matching the provision of airport capacity with the demand while achieving and maintaining airport profitability and an adequate level of customer satisfaction is a difficult task'. One of the principal problems facing any airport manager is that of planning. The time lag between the decision to build and the opening of a new airport terminal is five to ten years, as the case of Heathrow Airport's planned Terminal 5 illustrates. In addition, planners also need to ensure forecasts of future growth are within realistic bounds so that terminal facilities can accommodate demand for at least another decade. However, for any airport development, probably the most fundamental issues to understand are :

- Costs.
- The economic features of airports.
- Sources of revenue.
- Methods of charging and pricing airport aeronautical services (see Forsyth 1997b; Reynolds-Feighan and Feighan 1997)

- The type of commercial strategy to adopt
- Potential sources of commercial revenue (see Zhang and Zhang 1997)
- The most appropriate management structure for an airport as a commercial/non-commercial organisation.
- Financial performance indicators (see Hooper and Hensher 1997; Gillen and Waters 1997)

Costs and Economic Characteristics of Airports

Research undertaken in the 1980s and reported by Doganis (1992) identified the following costs of airports based on an analysis of European airports:

- *Staffing* accounts for 42 per cent of costs; it is normally the major operational cost for most airports.
- *Capital* charges comprise 22 per cent of costs; they include interest payments on commercial loans and the cost of depreciation of capital assets.
- *Other operational items* (e.g., electricity, water and supplies) comprise 11 per cent of costs.
- *Maintenance* accounted for 9 per cent of costs while *Administration* resulted in 4 per cent of costs.

These costs are listed in Table 4.2 for the British Airports Authority for 1996/97. Doganis (1992) also draws attention to the differences between US and European airports; airport costs are reduced by airline rental or lease agreements on terminal facilities in the USA. Likewise, many US airports are not directly involved in baggage handling, which is left to airlines. But financing costs for US airports tend to be a major element of expenditure, often 44 per cent of total costs if depreciation is included, although staff costs tend to remain at approximately 22 per cent.

Table 4.3 shows the number of employees at the main airports in the UK in 1994/95 (CIPFA 1996); a total of 13,590 people were employed at national and regional airports, which indicates the significance of the direct employment-generating potential of such infrastructure. Three airports (London Heathrow, London Gatwick and Manchester) employed over half of the airport workers in 1994/95. In addition, Langley (1997) provides detailed data on UK airports from an operational and financial perspective.

Table 4.3 : Employment at UK airports 1994/95.

Airport	Number of employees
BAA owned airports	
Heathrow	3,562
Gatwick	1,857
Stansted	574
Glasgow	552
Edinburgh	315
Aberdeen	269
Southampton	133
Non-BAA airports	
Manchester	2,200
Birmingham	681
Newcastle	512
Belfast International	288
Luton	500
East Midlands	396
Bristol	308
Highlands and Islands	194
Cardiff	133
Leeds/Bradford	181
London City	166
Liverpool	54
Teesside	143
Humberside	80
Norwich	152
Exeter	121
Bournemouth	153
Total	13,590
Others	336

Two of the principal economic characteristics of airports are that :

- Economies of scale exist as the volume of traffic increases, though congestion can lead to increases in unit costs.

- Development programmes for airports increase unit costs, particularly when new terminals are opened and are operating below their design capacity.

Airport Revenue

According to Ashford and Moore (1992), airport revenue can be divided into two categories:

- *Operating revenues,* which are generated by directly running and operating the airport (e.g., the terminal area, leased areas and grounds)
- *Non-operating revenues,* which include income from activities not associated with the airport core business.

While Doganis (1992) divides it into aeronautic or traffic revenues and non-aeronautical or commerical revenues.

In terms of *aeronautical revenues,* a range of possible revenue sources exist (though not all airports necessarily collect or use the revenue in a set way):

- landing fees.
- Airport air traffic control charges
- Aircraft parking
- Passenger charges
- Freight charges
- Apron services and aircraft handling (where the airport provides such services).

In terms of *non-aeronautical revenue,* Doganis outlines the following sources :

- Rents or lease income from airport tenants.
- Recharges to tenants for utilities and services provided.
- Concession income (e.g., from duty-free and tax-free shops).
- Direct sales in shops operated by the airport authority.
- Revenue from car parking where it is airport-operated.
- Miscellaneous items.
- Non airport-related income (e.g., through land development or hotel development).

Within a European context, Doganis (1992) noted that aeronautical revenue accounted for 56 per cent of revenue and non-aeronautical revenue for 44 per cent of income. In the USA, the situation was slightly different, with airports generating more revenue from commercial sources (e.g. concessions 33 per cent; rents 23 per cent; car parking 4 per cent; other non-aeronautical sources 17 per cent and aeronautical fees 23 per cent). CIPFA (1996) provides a range of detailed data for all UK airports.

Pricing Aeronautical Services

According to Doganis, aeronautical fees (i.e. those costs commercial aircraft have to pay to land at an airport) will continue to remain a crucial element of airport finances since they can be adjusted to offset revenue losses. The impact of such fees on airlines varies from nearly 20 per cent of airline operating costs to less than 2 per cent. This directly affects the price the consumer pays for their ticket. Landing fees continue to be a key source of revenue and Ashford and Moore identify a range of approaches to charging fees, including :

- A fixed rate per tonne multiplied by a unit charge.
- A rate per tonne with weight-break points, with fees increasing in steps.
- Single fixed charges irrespective of size of aircraft, which are used to fund the following types of services:
  — air traffic control facilities,
  — landing facilities such as the runway and taxiways,
  — parking of the aircraft on a stand or apron for a specified time, after which a separate fee is levied,
  — use of aircraft gates, airbridges and terminal facilities (though increasingly airports are levying departure taxes to pay for the use of such facilities by travellers)
  — takeoff facilities.

CIPFA (1996) compared the landing charges for an international inbound flight using a Boeing 737-400 at various UK airports in 1994-95. A comparison of Cardiff and Gatwick indicates that the combined cost of the landing fee and passenger facility charge levied to land at Cardiff at

9.30 am in June was £2,589.00. This equates to a revenue per passenger of £17.26. The same flight would cost £1,814. 35 to land at Gatwick at the same time, with a revenue per passenger of £12.10. Such variations are marked within the airport system in the UK. However, as Doganis (1992) notes, each airports has in place its own levels of rebates/surcharges for flights and airlines, so these may not in fact be the true costs once such factors are taken into account.

In Europe, additional surcharges apply for the use of aircraft which do not meet noise requirements British Airways case study and research by Perl et al (1997) on pricing such impacts). Doganis outlines many of the issues associated with pricing airport charges and this should be read in conjunction with Toms.

Commercial Strategies for Airports

With the move towards privatisation in the UK and other countries, airport managers have had to adopt more commercially driven business principles when looking at the best strategy to adopt in managing airport infrastructures and services. Carter (1996), for example, points to the growing trend towards airport privatisation so airports can seek private sector finance to invest in the development strategy needed to compete in the new millennium. In fact Carter (1996) describes the move from a simple public utility view of airports towards a management-led approach which is more commercially driven. For example, O'Hare airport in the USA invested US$618 million in a new terminal facility in 1993 as well as a customs and baggage hall able to process 4,500 passengers an hour. Atlanta airport undertook a US$200 million refurbishment in the 1990s, resulting in an airport with 158 domestic departure gates. It has a daily average of 2,066 takeoffs and landings and 25,000 parking spaces (yielding US$50 million in revenue). From such an example, one can see the investment needs and importance of a commercial strategy to ensure airports maximise their revenue-generating potential and invest in the most judicious manner. As Skapinker argues, 'most of the world's airports...have barely begun to exploit their full commerical potential'. In many cases, seeking to generate additional revenue from non-aeronautical sources is far more attractive to many airport managers than resorting to increases in landing fees.

Doganis argues that, in establishing a commercial strategy for future development:

> Airport owners and operators have to make a choice between two alternative strategies. They can follow the *traditional airport model*...where airports see their primary task as being to meet the basic and essential needs of passengers, airlines, freight forwarders and other direct airport customers or users...The alternative strategic option is that of the *commercial airport model*.

In the commercial model, revenue maximisation from a wide range of customers offers the airport manager a greater flexibility in the finance available to invest in a demand-led approach to airport development. In many ways, the traditional model epitomises the government-managed approach, characterised by Athens airport in the late 1980s (Doganis 1992 : 113). In contrast, Frankfurt Airport exemplifies the commerical model, which requires airport managers to recognise a number of discrete markets amongst airport users:

- Passengers (departing, ariving and those transferring between flights).
- The airlines, which are major consumers of space for storage, maintenance, staff and catering.
- Airport employees.
- Airline crews.
- Meeters and greeters.
- Visitors to airports.
- Local residents.
- the local business community.

As a result of recognising the business opportunities afforded by these groups, there is potential to derive income from activities and services which these users require. Income can be derived from rents from service providers and concession aires which offer services on the airport premises as well as from involvement in those activities identified above (e.g., retailing, car parking and aircraft-related services). Developing the most appropriate organisational structure to manage the airport also needs to take into account the relationship with government bodies (i.e., should a commercial approach be developed?), ...the pressures for change, not least of which are those that relate to the personalities and abilities of individuals with directional responsibilities within the organisation...(and whether)...the airport authority assumes...a brokering function with minimal operational involvement in many on-airport activities (the US model) to direct operational involvement in many of the airports' functions (the European model).

For example, if a commercial model is pursued, it will require an organisational structure which is responsive to change. Ashford et al (1991) review the various management structures adopted by airports. Doganis (1992) and Ashford and Moore (1992) point to the preoccupation of airport managers with operational issues prior to the onset of the commercial model. As a result, airport management was traditionally organised into functional areas (e.g., security, finance, administration, human resource management, engineering and so forth). Each area was headed by a specialist manager reporting to the airport manager. The problem with such a structure was that commercial activities did not assume a clear focus, with different aspects of business dispersed across each of the airport's functional areas. The result was that no one assumed responsibility for pursing a commercial strategy. The commercial model therefore requires a greater focus on business and revenue-generation as a core activity of the airport and Doganis (1992) points to the BAA model at Gatwick Airport Ltd. Here the emphasis is on providing a service for external users and internal users within the organisation. Each department is headed by a director and the necessary business skills are drawn from within or from outside BAA. In 1989, the commercial director was responsible for the management of activities that yielded 59 per cent of the airport's revenue.

The development of commercial opportunities, most notably retailing and concessions, has been a major result of the more commercially driven model of development. Yet how can an airport evaluate the success of its management and business strategy? Ashford and Moore (1992) cite the earlier work of Doganis and Graham (1987) *Airport Management: The Role of Performance indicators* which evaluated the performance of 24 leading European airports based in 11 countries. They examined five key areas in airport management:

- costs,
- revenue,
- labour productivity,
- capital productivity,
- financial profitability.

The basic principle is to assess whether the resources being used at a given airport are effective, efficiently employed and able to achieve the desired outcome. Where measures are less satisfactory, it allows airport managers to address the issue.

Having examined the scope and issues confronting airport management, attention now turns to a case study of the British Airports Authority, which will provide more detail on the current operational issues and achievement of this airport operator. BAA also illustrates the progress one leading airport organisation has made through privatisation.

Case Study Airport Privatisation in the UK: the Role of BAA

In 1985 the British government produced its White Paper *Airport Policy* (HMSO 1985) which Doganis (1992 : 27) interpreted as stating:

(a) That airports should operate as commercial undertakings.

(b) That airports' policy should be directed towards encouraging enterprise and efficiency in the operation of major airports by providing for the introduction of private capital.

The ensuing 1986 Airports Act then turned BAA into a limited company, BAA Plc, which was floated on the Stock Exchange in 1987. This was then organised into a single company operating seven airports: London heathrow, London Gatwick, London Stansted, Southampton, Glasgow, Edinburgh and Aberdeen. The 1986 Act also led to the UK's largest regional airports (with a turnover exceeding £1 million) becoming public limited companies and being detached from their former local authority owners. In New Zealand, the three largest airports were also privatised in 1988 as individual corporations for an analysis of the costs, benefits and issues of airport privatisation), while in South Africa a semi-privatised model has been pursued (Prinz and Lombard 1995). Yet it is the BAA model which remains widely cited for its commercial success in the 1980s and 1990s.

BAA's Activities in the 1990s

One of the most accessible sources of current data on BAA is its annual report. In the BAA *Annual Report 1996 / 97,* the company mission statement identified its commercial focus:

> Our Mission is to make BAA the most successful airport company in the world. This means always focusing on our customers' needs and safety. Achieving continuous improvements in the costs and quality of our processes and services. Enabling our employees to give of their best.

The scale of operations at BAA is reflected in the following key statistics for 1996/97:

- A profit of £444 million (before tax and exceptional items).
- 98 million passengers passed through BAA airports.
- The total revenue from BAA airports was £1,373 million, comprising:

- airport traffic charges of £467 million (34 per cent)
- retailing revenue of £606 million (44.1 per cent)
- property services revenue of £252 million (18.4 per cent)
- other sources of £48 million (3.5 per cent)
- Capital expenditure at BAA airports was as follows:
- London Heathrow £321 million
- London Gatwick £60 million
- London Stansted £14 million
- Scottish airports £ 21 million
- Capitalised interest £51 million
- Other investment £29 million
- BAA airports handle 71 per cent of UK air passenger traffic.

The organisational abilities of BAA are also focused on a range of non-operational activities, including:

- Airport management at Melbourne Airport, Australia, and Indianpolis in the USA.
- Retail management.
- Property management.
- Project management.

In terms of airport management, BAA discusses various aspects of its activities, including:

- *Airport charges,* including the BAA's review of airport charges in which it ranked 16th (Heathrow) and 18th (Gatwick) among. European airports in terms of landing and takeoff charges.
- *Passenger traffic growth,* which recorded a 4.6 per cent increase in 1995-96 traffic volumes, with the strongest growth occurring in the North Atlantic (UK/USA) markets, which grew by 7 per cent. London Stansted represented an initial £400 million investment by BAA in 1991, and is now reported to be operating profitably. Following the lifting of restrictions on passenger volumes in 1996, London Stansted can now expand to 8 million passengers a year.
- *Meeting customer needs,* where the UK Monopolies and Mergers Commission (MMC) provided the means for

customers to express their views of BAA's activities. The MMC reported that 'BAA's quality of service is generally rated high by customers'. This is supported by BAA's ongoing Quality of Service Monitor (QSM) which has interviewed over 1 million travellers since its inception in 1990/91. The QSM interviews 150,000 passengers a year in relation to the airport experience and customer needs. The results for the 1996/97 QSM are reported in summary form in Table 4.4.

- *Safety and security,* where BAA reports that it has deve-loped 'the world's most advanced and effective hold baggage screening technology' (BAA 1997 : 13), to be introduced at all its airports at a cost of over £175 million.

- *Maximising employees' contribution to business success,* where employee empowerment measures have been intro-duced as part of BAA's commitment to quality. BAA also introduced a 'Freedom to Manage' initiative, where a greater emphasis on teamwork, simpler management structures and a greater commitment to customer service has been developed through centres of excellence. The improvements are reported in terms of airport employee productivity, where 1996/97 saw a 4.4 per cent increase in the number of passengers per employee handled at each UK airport.

In the field of non-aeronautical services, it is BAA's retail activities that have attracted a great deal of interest from analysts.

Airport Retailing

According to Skapinker, 'an airport is, in many respects, the ideal environment for retailers. The potential customers are affluent, or reasonably so, and are often on the lookout for presents for family or friends. Above all they are trapped.' This is the retailer's dream: a captive audience with disposable income and time to shop. BAA is a good example of an organisation which carefully assesses customer demand through a product market focus and this is reflected in its contrast to manage retailing at Pittsburgh Airport.

Table 4.4 : Quality of Service Monitor scores 1996/97[1].

Measures	Heathrow	Gatwick	Stansted	Southampton	Glasgow	Edinburgh	Aberdeen
Cleanliness	3.9	4.0	4.4	4.5	4.3	4.0	4.2
Mechanical assistance[2]	3.9	4.0	4.1	3.9	4.1	3.8	3.9
Procedures[3]	4.0	4.2	4.3	4.5	4.4	4.2	4.3
Comfort	3.9	4.0	4.3	4.5	4.2	4.1	4.1
Congestion	3.5	3.7	4.3	4.7	4.2	4.1	3.9
BAA staff	4.0	4.2	4.3	4.5	4.3	4.1	4.3
Value for money	3.5	3.7	3.6	3.7	3.6	3.7	3.5

[1]Scale: 1 = Extremely Poor; 2 = Poor; Average; 4= Good; 5= Excellent.

[2]This includes services such as luggage trolleys, aircraft access and flight information.

[3]This covers check-in procedures, security issues, baggage reclaim facilities and immigration procedures.

However, one of the criticisms which Skapinker reports is that 'some airline executives are unhappy about the way shops are taking over large areas of airport terminals... (which)...means there is less space for airline facilities, such as check-in desks...passengers become absorbed in their shopping, do not hear departure announcements, and arrive late at gates, delaying flights'. For airport operators such as BAA, such trends seem set to continue because of the returns on investment. In fact BAA and Amsterdam's Schiphol Airport have been shortlisted by the South African government to compete for a 20 per cent stake stake in the Airports Company of South Africa to provide new investment and private sector expertise, particularly in retailing.

In 1996/97, BAA generated a total of £425.2 million of net retail income, comprising:

- Duty-free and tax-free shops, £248.8 million (59 per cent).
- Bookshops, £21.2 million (5 per cent).
- Car parking, £64.1 million (15 per cent).
- Car rental, £17.8 million (4 per cent).
- Catering, £21.2 million (5 per cent).
- Bureaux de change, £27.6 million (6 per cent).
- Advertising, £11.7 million (3 per cent).
- Other, £12.8 million (3 per cent).

As BAA succinctly describe its position, 'a successful airport business without a successful retail operation is unthinkable' (BAA 1997 : 19). The BAA strategy for 1997/98 is to increase revenue by 9 per cent, double the rate of traffic growth. This does not seem unrealistic, given the fact that net retail income rose by 11 per cent in 1996/97. This reflects a focus on growing product markets as opposed to selling manufacturers' products. In 1996, BAA also intro-duced a bonus points customer loyalty scheme, yielding 170,000 members and a marketing database on regular customers using the airport. In physical terms, the £33 million redevelopment of Heathrow's Terminal 2 building created an additional 2,320 m² of retail space. In Pittsburgh, BAA has increased the number of retail outlets in its Airmall from 46 to

102, increasing sales per passenger from US$2.40 to US$7.10. Overall sales have risen from US$20 million to US$72 million.

In Europe, the possible loss in 1999 of duty-free sales for intra-European EU travel could affect BAA's retailing by £120 million, which is why Skapinker (1998:VI) argues that those airports 'with more advanced retailing skills will attempt to compensate by dreaming up more imaginative ways of parting passengers and their money'. In 1998, BAA was mounting a public awareness campaign at its major airports to highlight the effect of losing intra-European duty-free sales for passengers in terms of increased costs of travel. To maintain the cutting edge of its commercial acu-men and management skills, BAA also needs to invest in future projects to improve the airport environment. In 1996/97, BAA invested £496 million in its 10-year strategy which aims to invest a total of £4.4 billion in addition to the previous £3.3 billion in the first nine years of BAA's operation. The driving force is to meet the continued forecast growth in air travel and provide facilities to accommodate such growth. One of the largest investments is in the £440 million Heathrow Express rail link from Paddington in Central London to the airport. The rail link, operational in 1998, runs as a wholly owned subsidiary of BAA. Such investment also raises the broader issues associated with airport planning and development, since planning is a vital element of management.

Airport Planning and Development

According to O'Connor, 'airports are among the most important elements of modern cities...in many places, the traffic at the airport reflects the vitality of the tourist industry. For these reasons, airports are critical to the vitality of metropolitan areas', (Fig. 4.4), a feature observed in the seminal study by Hoare (1974) of London Heathrow as a growth pole. The significance of airport planning and development has been a feature often overlooked in many analyses of tourist transport. However, a number of UK (e.g., Sealy 1976) and North American texts have examined the theme of airport development indirectly (e.g., Wells 1989; Taneja 1988) and in a more focused manner (e.g., Ashford and Moore 1992; Smith et. al., 1984; Ashford et. al., 1991; Horonjeft and McKelvey 1983), although probably the most up-to-date and accessible source is French (1997a). O'Connor (1996) outlines the importance of locational factors in the development of airports in Asia-Pacific, notably:

- Physical and technical considerations (i.e. appropriate sites).
- Economic forces, where air traffic now is a vital element in the national economy of most countries
- The role of government in forward planning (e.g., Changi Airport in Singapore developed two parallel runways and has well-organised ground services and facilities to ensure the smooth passage of travellers, backed by high levels of investment).

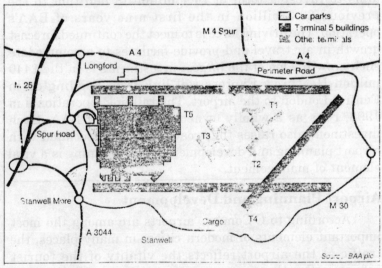

Fig. 4.4 : Proposed Terminal 5 extension for Heathrow Airport

In physical terms, locational factors are important (e.g. the availability of a large expanse of flat hand, access to urban centres which are the source of travellers and an environment able to accommodate the noise and physical pollution from airport operations). As the example of Kansai International

Airport in Japan shows, airport developers are having to seek new sites away from major population centres. Speak (1997) examines the example of Kai Tak, Hong Kong, which handled 21,370,000 passenger movements and 150,118 aircraft movements in 1995. The development and planning of the new Chek Lap Kok site was originally advocated in 1989, 25 km west of Hong Kong's central business district (CBD) (Figure 4.4). In 1996 an airport development authority was established to develop the project, and the airport opened in 1998. The physical development of the 1,248 ha site involved flattening a small island and land reclamation. The airport will be capable of accommodating 35 million passenger movements a year using the first runway; and it could expand to a capacity of 87 million once the second runway is completed. The need for access to Hong Kong's CBD required two bridges and a dedicated airport railway to be built (Figure 4.4) and has necessitated 10 associated infrastructure projects listed in Figure 4.5.

ATAG (1993) also acknowledged the importance of surface transport access to airports. Among the principal concerns of ATAG (1993) were:

- The needs and expectations of airport users that staff should be courteous and the prices charged should be compatible with the service provided.
- The provision of user-friendly airport terminal facilities.
- Provision of facilities which allow those with special needs or a disability to travel.
- Encouraging passengers to use public transport to journey to the airport to reduce environmental impacts.
- The development of interchange facilities that do not penalise public transport users financially or make access difficult through poorly designed interchanges.
- A well-planned network of roads and dedicated airport access routes.
- Adequate parking spaces which are well signposted to distinguish between short- and long-stay traffic.

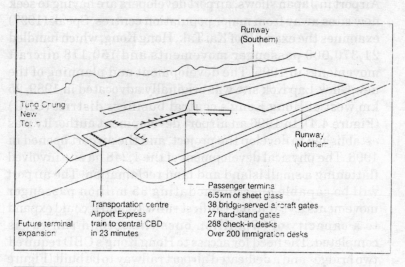

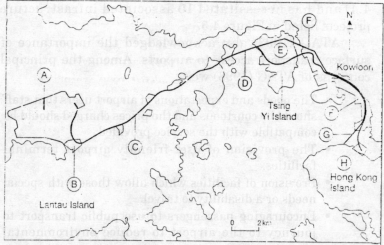

A. Chek Lap kok Aiprot 1,248 ha site built on a man-made platform from bedrock of
    2 islands and 938 ha of land reclaimed from the sea; cost $12.1 bn.
B. Tung Chung New Town; cost $1.38 bn.
C. North Lantau Expressway; cost $307 m.
D. Tsing Ma Bridge; cost $1.77 bn.
E. Tsing Yi Island; cost $5.6 bn.
F. Airport Railway; cost $8 bn.
G. Western Harbour Crossing Tunnel; cost $1.9bn.
H. Hong Kong Island land reclamation: cost $8.07bn. Airport Cost: $40 bn.

Fig. 4.5 : Chek Lap Kok airport.

- The development of rail-air services from major urban centres (e.g., London's rail-air services to Heathrow, Gatwick and Stansted and Schiphol's dedicated train service).

While not all of these access issues are important for every airport, it is evident from the BAA case study that improving access from urban centres consumes a significant element of capital budgets. For example, in 1997 Auckland International Airport in New Zealand was reported as requiring NZ$1 billion in capital expenditure over the next 15-20 years, a large proportion of which will be devoted to access issues and terminal design.

It is the process of physical planning of airports to which attention now turns. Through a focus on Denver International Airport, it is possible to understand the procedures and processes followed to build an airport.

Denver International Airport

According to Goetz and Szyliowicz (1997), Denver International Airport (DIA) opened five years late in 1995, mainly due to problems with its automated baggage system (de Neufville 1994). The cost overrun rose from US$1.7 billion to over US$5 billion, and though the airport was forecast to handle 56 million passengers by 1995, only 30 million used it in that year. It also received noise complaints from residents, despite seeking to minimise noise impacts. DIA is therefore an interesting example of how short-term problems in the planning process can emerge even where there is a systematic approach to development.

In the USA, the FAA has published guidelines on the approach towards airport development. Rycroft and Szyliowicz (1980) examine the limitations of the FAA approach where access to all forms of data is not possible, and argue that it overlooks the role of power and political variables. It also assumes that planning occurs in a rational manner, whereas there is all too often a lack of agreement on the principal goals of large projects such as these. Furthermore, this approach also assumes that it is possible to derive accurate forecast demand estimates. In the wider literature on transport planning, such problems remain intractable as traffic forecasts are notorious for their inaccuracy and inability to accommodate human travel behaviours. To overcome some of these problems, Maldonado (1990) and de Neufville (1991) have developed a strategic planning approach which recognises issues such as uncertainty and flexibility in future planning requirements.

The initial decision to expand airport capacity in Denver can be dated to 1974, when the political consensus was to expand the existing Stapleton International Airport. By the time deregulation occurred in the 1980s, expansion was not considered feasible, given the FAA's and Denver's consultants' forecasts for future traffic growth. Forecasts suggested that the existing traffic of 25 million passengers in 1983 would grow to 56 million by 1995. Runway capacity at Stapleton had already caused a bottleneck in the national air transport system during adverse weather conditions due to runway design. Goetz and Szyliowicz (1997) provide an interesting commentary on the politics of the decision to select a site for DIA. They also examine how the airline users exacted major concessions from the developer - the city of Denver. The most serious concession was exacted by United Airlines, which sought and gained an automated baggage system to service its concourse. This concession also contributed to major delays in the airport becoming operational. Delays to the airport's opening due to technological problems associated with the baggage system added to cost overruns. The airport traffic forecasts also assumed that Denver would emerge as a major hub. But in March 1994, Continental Airlines abandoned its hubbing operation at Denver, leaving United as the main hubbing operator while the FAA assumed that American Airlines might consider establishing a hub operation by 1995. The DIA project was downsized by reducing the number of run-ways from six to five and gates from 120 to 88—this was made possible by the modular design of the airport.

The airport also aimed to reduce noise impacts, being located 24 miles from Denver's CBD. But according to Goetz and Szyliowicz :

> In all of 1994, Stapleton received 431 noise complaints, but in the first twelve months since DIA opened the city received over 57,000 complaints. Much of this can be attributed to previously non-impacted populations now receiving some amount of aircraft noise. But it remained unclear whether these complaints indicate that the original noise contours developed in the Environmental Impact Statement are still accurate.

Goetz and Szyliowicz (1997) view the DIA example as highlighting the airlines' role as something which could not have been foreseen in the rational comprehensive planning model advocated by the FAA. The goals of each airline were not in sympathy with those of the city of Denver and the FAA, and the political system affected both the decision-making and implementation phases of planning. As Szyliowicz and Goetz (1995) argued, a range of actors with different strategies, agendas and purposes ensured that no one unitary actor drove the project forward. As a result, poliical and cognitive factors were powerful in shaping the airport development process. The ability to accommodate future risk and uncertainty also assumes a much greater role given the 'critical nature of aviation forecasts for airport planning and design and of demand forecasts'. This means that the planning process needs to be able to accommodate likely errors in forecasts. Goetz and Szyliowicz (1997) also point to the need for decision makers and planners to adapt to new business situations with flexibility rather than remaining locked into a project that may not be suitable on completion. Vested interests, political careers and an unwillingness to admit that earlier decisions may have been made on inaccurate information still affect mega-projects such as airports. A similar problem can be seen in the CAA's Swanwick air traffic system being developed for the UK. This is a mega-IT project which has so far revealed 15,000 errors in the computer software and is expected to be £100 million over budget and several years late. It was envisaged that it would replace the ageing West Drayton air traffic control centre, although some critics believe it may even be abandoned if it cannot be made operational. Both DIA and the Swanwick example highlight overoptimistic expectations that technology which is not tried and tested can be put into practice immediately. What emerge is a need for flexibility and constant monitoring once the decision has been taken to implement a project and a willingness to halt the project if technical problems cannot be solved.

Global Airport Development

French (1996a) reviews the environmental constraints which now affect airport expansion, notably community objections to aircraft noise and emissions. These have resulted in a range of state-of-the-art airport development projects which can meet future demand on new sites while mitigating environmental concerns. A significant number of these new projects are located in Asia-Pacific. Nevertheless, French (1996a) argues that planners are not keeping pace with demand. In late 1995, there were only 11 new airports under construction:

- In Europe: Oslo, Athens and Berlin.
- In Asia-Pacific: Sydney, Hong Kong, Seoul, Bangkok, Kuala Lumpur and three sites in China (Shanghai, Guangzhou and Shuhai).
- In the Middle East: three new airports.

In Japan, government agencies are currently identifying sites for Tokyo's third airport, likely to cost US$32 billion, with construction starting in the year 2000. Japan also has a US$500 million plan for a domestic airport at Kobe, to be operational by 2003 and a five-year US$40 billion programme for other airports. In India, a feasibility study is considering a new US$3.2 billion airport for Bombay, to open in 2005. A large number of airport enhancement projects are also under way in Asia-Pacific to upgrade terminal buildings and to construct new runways. French points to concerns that by 1995 half the airports in Asia-

Pacific are capacity-constrained. A number of efficiency gains at Asia-Pacific airports may reduce pressure at some airports (e.g., improvements to surface transport access and customs procedures).

French points to the improvements achieved in European air travel by new air traffic control systems. The cost of congestion was estimated at US$6 billion for European airports to the year 2000, based on estimates by ATAG. Among the most pressing problems are airport congestion at peak times and runway capacity constraints. The Association of European Airlines argued that 26 of Europe's 29 larges airports would need additional terminal capacity in 1995, and 25 will need extra runway capacity by the year 2005. These airports are forecast to handle 1.2 billion passenger movements and 16 million aircraft movements. Those airports which the Asso-ciation of European Airlines believe will be worst affected are the following hubs:

- London Heathrow and Gatwick,
- Frankfurt,
- Paris (Charles de Gaulle),
- Schiphol Airport, Amsterdam,
- Rome,
- Madrid,
- Zurich.

As French observes, 'by around 2000 most of the world's major city airports will be faced with critical decisions on how to ensure that their status as leading traffic hubs is maintained, both for their own economic benefit and for the ... the air transport industry itself'.

Conclusion

There is no doubt that 'airports are complex business with functions that extend substantially beyond the airfield or traffic side of operations'. Airports provide the vital infrastructure which links:

- the airline,
- the traveller,
- air and surface transport.

and they are complex systems which require clear management guidelines and structures to ensure they operate efficiently.

The late 1980s and 1990s have been the process of privatisation sweep across many of the world's airport organisations, as the public sector is unable to provide access to large sources of capital to invest in upgrading schemes. The full or partial privatisation of airport companies has also changed the airport as a travel terminal. Under privatisation, a greater focus on non-traffic revenue sources and a broad revenue strategy have transformed the airport from a waiting area and functional environment. The transformation, which has been inspired by business principles to generate revenue from retailing, has generated the airport mall as a cultural icon. The airport is often viewed as a post-modernist expression of the conspicuous consumption now pervading many developed societies, epitomised by leisure travel. In this new environment where marketers have seized the initiative to develop products and services for a wide range of target groups (including the traveller) the airport is now firmly part of the broad travel experience. The example of BAA and its QSM embodies the current concern with customer needs in a market characterised by high-volume business and a captive clientele. The consumer's interests are also represented by the UK Consumers' Association publication, *Holiday Which,* 1st Winter 1998 survey, *Which Airport,* undertakes a qualitative review of UK airports and compares value for money, access, areas in need of improvement (e.g., catering) and the best departure lounges as well as the range of shops available. Such surveys illustrate how important the airport is now becoming in the wider travel experience.

The case study of BAA also illustrated the diverse range of activities associated with airport management, the sheer scale and volume of their operations, and the fact that they now have a customer-driven focus to improve the traveller's experience. Even so, large organisations such as airports cannot necessarily respond to issues as quickly as the customer would like. For example, on a flight from Scotland to London in March 1998, the author experienced an incident which highlights this issue: the ground staff held the departure up to allow an inebriated passenger on board, who was served additional alcohol during the flight and who then created difficulties during and after the flight. At the destination, ground crew were faced with this situation and it took an inordinate time for the airport security staff to be called. While this reveals total ineptitude by the airline staff for allowing a passenger on board who was unfit for travel, it also illustrates the unexpected events with which airport staff have to deal and the time delay in putting the appropriate system and action in place. It was also the airport staff who had to deal with the outcome of the airline staff's inexperience and lack of understanding of the situation. Thus, airport management embraces a wide range of operational and human interactions which affect the way travellers perceive the airport environment.

In terms of development strategies for airport growth, the example of DIA illustrates the complex interaction of factors that can affect the final outcome. Airport development involves extremely large funding, increasingly from the private sector, to meet the complex needs of airlines and travellers as well as the airport operator. To describe such entities as mega-projects is a good description, given their scale and vastness. Managing such entities once they are fully operational and meeting a broad range of customers' needs in the fast-changing world of domestic and international travel is a key challenge.

5

The Human and Environmental
Impact of Tourist Transport

Introduction

The international expansion of tourism and the development of transport systems to meet this demand have had a range of direct and indirect social, cultural, economic and physical impacts on both host populations affected by the operation of tourist transport and destination areas. In the 1970s and 1980s this led to a growing concerns about the impact of tourist travel on the environment, but little attention has been given to the experiences for tourists whilst in transit. This chapter examines the effect and impact of tourist transport from two perspectives : the effect of travelling on the tourist's experience and the impact of transport system an the environment. The concept of the service encounter was discussed (by using Bitner et. al., 1990), which recognise that dissatisfaction with tourism services is associated with three types of incident: employee failure to respond adequately to customer needs; unprompted and unsolicited employee actions and service delivery failure. The first part of this chapter focuses on service delivery failure, particularly how travel delays and service interruptions may contribute to the stress of tourist travel, and some of the measures taken by transport operators to address such problems. This is followed by a discussion of environmental issues from the transport provider's perspective, including the role of Environmental Auditing and Environmental Assessment to address the long-term implications of new tourist transport projects for the environment. The chapter concludes by considering the extent to which sustainable tourist travel may assist in identifying ways of reducing transport's impact on the environment. A landmark study in this area is Banister.

The Human Consequences of Modern Tourist Travel

Previous chapters have shown that the tourist travel experience in complex phenomenon to understand. Social psychologists (Peace 1982) and marketers are continually trying to understand the relationship between consumer behaviour (Qaiters and Bergiel 1989; Schiffman and Kauk 1991) and tourist travel (Goodall 1991), tourists' degree of satisfaction which travel services and their propensity to revisit destinations in the future. One area which has really lacked serious academic research is the tourists' feelings and the traurma sometimes associated with international travel; a more detailed discussion of tourist health can be found in Clift and Page (1996). In terms of foreign travel, stress is a feature often overlooked since tour operators and travel agents often extol the virtues of taking a holiday to fulfil a deep psychological need. Ryan (1991) notes that tourist travel experiences offer many potential avenues of research.

The stress associated with international and to a lesser degree, domestic travel is the result of various psychological factors which are compounded by the effect of congestion on transport systems. For example, in March 1998, a British Airways jet in Florida experienced technical problems and after two days and two attempts to repair the aircraft, a replacement was sent to Florida to ferry passengers back to the UK. BA offered full refunds as compensation but the stress and anxiety such events can cause for certain passengers on holiday cannot be underestimated (Barley 1995 for a range of interesting insights into the delights of air travel). McIntosh (1990a) argues that the stress of travel could be attributed to :

- preflight anxieties
- airside problems
- transmeridian disturbance
- fears and phobias
- psychological concerns

while in-flight health problems can also be added to the stress involved in modern-day long-haul travel (Harding 1994).

Preflight anxieties emerge when tourists commence their journey by travelling to the place of departure, often to meet schedules imposed by airlines. McIntosh (1990a : 118) suggests that the marketing of travel insurance to cover eventualities such as missed departures can also heighten the inexperienced traveller's sense of anxiety. Once at the departure point, the preflight check-in and the complex array of security checks associated with luggage can subject the traveller to a significant amount of stress in an unfamiliar environment. In addition to this is 'the apprehension...initially generated by preflight security... searches ...(which are)...a reminder of the risk of hijack and in-flight explosion' (McIntosh 1990s : 118). Overscrowding in terminal buildings associated with the throughput of passengers at peak times can overwhelm and disorientate travellers, whereas seasoned travellers (e.g. business travellers) often have access to executive lounges and a more relaxed and welcoming environment free from some of these stressors. In fact Air New Zealand's Kour Club membership scheme is an excellent example of one such marketing tool to help relieve preflight stress.

Airside problems, including the design and layout of holding areas for passengers travelling economy class, may contribute to an impersonal and dehumanising process prier to departure, which is exacerbated by an absence of information about the nature and duration of delays. As Ryan

(1991 : 43) argues '...passengers delayed in air terminals might be observed as passing through a process of arousal to anxiety, to worry, to apathy, as they become initially frustrated by delays (and) eventually reach apathy because of an inability to control events.'

Transmeridian disturbance associated with time zone changes during longhaul travel is a major problem for some travellers (Petrie and Dawson 1994). The condition is often associated with a lack of sleep on long-haul flights and a sleep-wake cycle which can cause exhaustion, commonly referred to as 'jetlag'. Travel agents may need to be sensitive in their advice to some clients as to the effect of transmeridian disturbance on those suffering from depression. Taking a long-haul holiday to forget their problems may heighten their sense of depression on east-west travel across the world's main time zons. One solution which Barlay (1995) identifies is the use of mild sleeping pills or use of melatonin. Melatonin is a 'naturally occurring neuro-hormone secreted by the pineal gland, a small pea-like organ at the back of the brain. Its rate of secretion in increased by darkness, causing the individual to feel sleepy' (Barely 1995: 166). However, there is a medical debate on the possible side-effects of such a drug and in New Zealand it is now only available on prescription.

Fears and phobias associated with the likelihood of political insurrections, how hospitable the host population will be and potential language difficulties in the destination region all contribute to the traveller's apprehension in transit. This stress can be alleviated by in-flight entertainment and public relations campaigns by national tourism organisations to reduce travellers' fears. The threat of terrorism or hijack is also an underlying worry for some travellers. Travellers' anxiety appear to follow a cyclical pattern, being heightened after an incident and then subsiding in response to the ensuing public relations exercises by airlines to reassure passengers of the increased security measures which are in place. Yet in extreme case, terrorism may pose a major threat to travel. For example, terrorist activity and threats in Europe actually deterred North American visitors from travelling to popular destinations such as London in the 1980s.

Psychological concerns, such as loneliness and a sense of isolation can also contribute to the traveller's feelings of anonymity during their journey, particularly if travelling alone (McIntosh 1995). The experience is often heightened on a busy jumbo jet carrying approximately 450 passengers, where an individual feels a sense of anonymity and of being confined in a strange environment 10,000 m up in the sky. Safety issues also induce a sense of imease amongst travellers following an incident such as an air crash. Although air crashes are rare occurrences (Steward 1986) in term of the volume of passengers carried and the number of takeoffs and landings undertaken, they do assume a prominent role in the psychology of tourist travel. According to Barlay (1995 : 7) 'the worst pterophobia sufferers confess their debilitating fear' But as many as 80 per cent of regular fliers have apprehension when boarding an aircraft. Although few people experience outright panic, mild pterophobia can affect many passengers. On a boat, travellers reason that they could potentially swim to safety in the event of an accident. It a car or train, they feel a greater degree of control. However, travellers can choose which airline they fly with, based on their safety record, which may help overcome some of the worst effects of pterophobia. While claustrophobia in the aircraft cabin may also exacerbate the anxiety passengers feel, airlines such as SIA have recognised that gadgets such as Krisworld and high-quality catering (Frapin-Beange et. al., 1995) can assist in passing the time and breaking the monotony on long-haul flights. At the destination, tourists may need reassurance when using local transport systems where operators gives the impression of being blase or unconcerned about safety issues and passenger welfare.

In-flight health-related problems may also affect passengers on long-haul flights where immobility, reduced air pressure within the flight cabine and dehydration may occur due to the recirculation of dry air within the aircraft. Barlay (1995) shows that most airlines use a mix of recycled and fresh air, leading to a build-up of CO_2 that can exacerbate jet lag, nausea and the onset of migraine. There is also growing concern over the effect of smoking on long-haul flights as recirculated air may lead to passive smoking risks when air filters are not adequately maintained.

Barlay (1995 : 164-168 also lists a number of measures for passengers to consider to ensure a comfortable flight :

- *air pressure*—mild flu can cause extreme pressure in the ears which may be relieved by pinching the nose and swallowing, sucking a sweet or in extreme situations, some airlines carry a decongestant which may be inhaled.
- *shoes*—comfortable footwear and regular exercise on the aircraft are essential to help prevent swollen ankles.
- *clothing*—layers of loose, roomy clothing are ideal for flying and can be adjusted depending on the changing cabin temperatures.
- *Spin dehydration*—frequent application of moisturising creams is highly recommended.
- *liquids and alcohol*—dehydration is a major problem on long-haul flights as eyes can become dry and sore. Consumption of alcohol exacerbates dehydration, compounded by high-altitude flights. Mixing drinks (tea, coffee, non-carbonated water and fruit juice) are recommended by the British Airline Pilots Association to keep the body topped up with fluids.
- *food*—eating with moderation, especially in business class and first class, in strongly recommended to avoid indigestion and feelings of being bloated.
- *exercise*—gentle body movements can assist in avoiding the effects of tiredness and aching limbs on long-haul flights, together with walking up and down the aisles.

There are also a range of other more persistent physical problems that affect the tourist's experience in transit, most notably *motion sickness*.

McIntosh (1990b : 80) provides a useful overview of motion sickness as a 'debilitating but relatively short-lived illness which indiscriminately affects air, land and sea travellers'. Yardley (1992) examines the literature associated with the concept of motion sickness, casting doubtover previous explanations of its cause and the tourist's susceptibility. It is clear from the existing literature on travellers' health that this affliction is not fully understood (Oosterveld 1995). Some researchers believe it is associated with the way in which different modes of transport stimulate an alteration in the perceived stability of the travel environment (i.e.. motion changes such as swaying from side to side or violent changes in altitude due to turbulence in air travel) and this affects one's sensory system. This tends to overestimulate the sensory preceptors. It may affect the traveller's perception of the environment and causes various symptoms such as drowsiness, vomiting, increased pulse rate, yawning, cold sweats, nausea and impaired digestion. Although some drug therapy may attempt to block the effects of motion sickness, no comprehensive cure exists and McIntosh (1990b : 82–83) reviews measures to assist the traveller in overcoming sea, car and air-sickness. However, Barlay (1995) argues that motion sickness is now a rare event in modern passenger transport, though Barlay has obviously not experienced some of the challenging weather conditions in which airlines fly.

The experience of travel stressors and health-related problems may be severe among certain groups such as the elderly. McIntorsh (1989) reviews the range of problems which the elderly may experience on tourist transport systems such as immobility and confusion when a number of time zones are crossed during a journey. In view of the increasingly aged structure of tourism markets in developed countries (Viant 1993; Smith and Jenner 1997), the welfare of elderly travellers and their service experience in transit is assuming a greater significance (McIntosh 1998) among the more innovative transport carriers. According to Viant (1993), the 'senior travel market' (those over 55 years of age) in Europe accounts for 20 per cent of domestic and international tourist trips and is forecast to increase from 142.1 million trips in 1990 to 255.2 million by the year 2000, an increase of 79.6 per cent. As growing numbers of senior travellers experience excellent health, it is evident that this niche market will present many opportunities for the tourist transport system.

There is a growing concern for disabled travellers in the transport literature (Oxley and Richards 1995). A recent study by Abeyratne (1995) considers a range of international and national regulatory measures for the carriage of elderly and disabled persons by air. Abeyratne (1995) examines the scope of the issues for airlines and airports in terms of:

- Contacts with airline reservations and ticket sales agents who can advise travellers.
- Specific fares, charges and related travel conditions, since some airlines require some elderly and disabled passengers to be escorted.
- Accessibility of aircraft, via wheelchair or airbridges for incapacitated travellers.
- Movement, facilities and services on board aircraft to ensure that the passengers' carriage can be undertaken in a way that provides a safe and comfortable environment.

In the context of the USA, Abeyratne (1995) produced a set of detailed guidelines to facilitate further the 'passage of elderly and disabled persons'. These guidelines highest a range of policy issues for airports and airlines and the practical measures needed to faciliate the further growth in travel by disabled and elderly tourists.

With these guidelines in mind, it pertinent to consider the measures transport operators can take to reduce the stressful experience associated with different aspects of tourist travel:

- Provision of special assistance at airports for senior travellers and disabled tourists, building on Thomes Cook's innovative Airport Travel Services for group travel to reduce the stress for group organisers taking larger parties of tourists abroad.

- Development of 'fear of travelling' programmes for different modern of transport, especially air travel (e.g., Thomson Holidays in the UK offers such a scheme through its own airline Britannia and British Airways also offer a one-day fear-of-flying programme—Barlay (1995) for humorous review).

- Planners and designers can impreye the structure and appearance of terminal buildings so that they are built with the customer in mind, reducing the stress of being in an unfamiliar environment. The award-winning design of the Stansted Airport terminal building (London) is one example of how to incorporate these principles into new terminal buildings. The contrasts markedly with smaller '1930s-style' regional airports, e.g., Jersey in the Channel Islands (Perks 1993), which has inadequate space to accommodate departing tourists in its check-in area, an absence of air-conditioning in the departure area and too few seats at the departure gates, requiring passengers to sit on the floor in the height of the summer season. This was one result of banching charter flights on a Saturday in the 1993 season rather than distributing them across the week. The overcrowding and unnecessary queuing induced through poor planning and inadequate staffing levels undoubtedly contribute to the stress of tourist travel. It is apparent that many of the first-generations '1930s airports' are now too small and not designed with the 1990s tourist-traveller in mind

- Provision of accurate and up-to-date information when travel delays occur

- Airline staff should inform travellers prior to takeoff about the aircraft sounds they will hear (e.g. as wheels are retracted and the change in engine sound at the cruising altiude) to allay any fears

- Provision of accurate in-flight advice for travellers, such as KLM Royal Dutch Airlines' *Comfort in Flight* brochure (Leggat 1997 for more detail on the 15 airlines surveyed)

- Replacement of 'anxiety-provoking intensive security screening' (McIntosh 1990a: 120) with low-profile security checks at ports of departure to reduce the potential for passenger stress
- In extreme case, general practitioners may prescibe mile medication (e.g., diazepam to relax the traveller in-flight, but this is often a last resort

To date, research on tourists' experience of travel has focused on travellers' health, health precautions prior to departure and problems encountered at the destination (see the journal *Travel Medicine International* and the *Journal of Travel Medicien*). This discussion, however, has shown that throughout the transport system, greater attention needs to be paid to the tourist's experience in transit, due to the range of problems that travel may engender. As Gunn (1988 : 163) suggests :

> Tourists seek several personal travel factors and will opt for the best combination...[of] comfort (freedom form fatigue, discomfort, poor reliability), convenience (absence of delays, cumbersome systems, roundabout routines), safety (freedom from risk. Eight from the equipment or other people), dependability (reliable schedules and conditions of travel), price (reasonable, competitive) and speed'.

Thus tourist 'transportation is more than movement—it is an experience' (Gunn 1988 : 167). The operator needs to recognise this so that the total travel experience is as free from incongruence and stress as possible.

Tourist transport not only has an impact on the traveller, but also affects the environment. For this reason the second part of the chapter considers some of the issues associated with the environmental effects of tourist transport.

The Environmental Impact of Tourist Transport

During the 1980s, there was increasing concern with environmental issues and the impact of different forms of economic development, particularly tourism. This international growth in *environmentalism* has meant that there is a greater emphasis on the protection, conservation and management of the environment as a natural and finite resource. Within the tourism and transport business, this concern has emerged in the form of the concept of *sustainable* tourism which highlights the vulnerability of the environment to human impacts from tourism and the need to consider its long-term maintence (Hall and Lew 1998). Much of the work on sustainability can be dated to the influential 1987 World Commission on Environment and Development report *Our Common Future* (Brundtland 1987) which asserts that 'we have not inherited the earth from our parents but borrowed it form out children'. In other words, sustainable development is based on the principle of 'meeting the needs of the present without compromising the ability of future generations to meet their own needs' (Brundtland 1987). This requires some understanding of the natural environment's ability to sustain certain types of economic activities such as transport and tourism. However, research on transport and tourism has often been considered in isolation, as the following discussion will show, although the use of research techniques such as Environmental Auditing and Environmental Assessment may help to bridge this gap and, to recognise the specific impacts of tourist transport systems.

Transport and the Environment

Tourist transport is one component of a much wider concern for more sustainable forms of development as problems relating to the impact of transport on the environment are symptomatic of the need for more environmentally sensitive forms of development (Banister and Button 1992). Within the context of transport planning, there has also been a greater understanding of the complex and sometimes detrimental impact of certain forms of transport on the environment (Carpenter 1994 offers a detailed insight in relation to railways). The emerging environmental research on the impact of different modes of transport (TEST 1991) has focused on the implications for transport and policy making (Department of the Environment 1991; HMSO 1997b) in relation to controversial new tourist and non-tourist infrastructure projects. This interest in the impact of infrastructure projects has led to measures for environmental mitigation. The emphasis on the environment has also led to detailed research on specific components of environmental problems induced by transport such as :

- health and safety.
- air pollution.
- noise pollution.
- ecological impacts.
- the environmental effects of different modes of transport.

One consequence of such research is that policy makers have focused on the direct costs and problems associated with the development of new transport infrastructure, which is now subject to more rigorous environmental safeguards to minimise the detrimental impacts. This concern for the environmental dimension has also been mirrored in tourism research.

Tourism and the Environment

The increasing sophistication among tourists has been reflected in the development of a 'new tourism' (Poon 1989), accompanied by a greater emphasis on the consumer requirements of tourists in terms of their search for more authentic holiday experiences and individualised tourism services. One consequence of this 'new tourism' phenomenon is a greater concern for the natural and built enviornment in which tourism activities are undertaken and their impact in different localities. This greater awareness of environmental issues related to tourism is reflected in the rapid expansion and diversity of research is 'sustainable tourism' (Smith and Eadington 1992), which emphasises the need for a more holistic assessment of how touristrelated activities (e.g., tourist transport) affect the environemnt.

Recent reviews of research on the environmental dimension is tourism have identified the scope and nature of this growing body of knowledge as well as the existing weaknesses in the structure and form of such studies (Pearce 1985). The recognition of the sysmbiotic relationship between conservation and tourism (Romeril 1985) has led to the need for a greater integration of interdiciplinary and mutidisciplinary approaches to research on tourism and the environment in order to achieve sustainable tourism development, of which transport is an integral component. Central to sustainable tourism development in the need to overcome tourism's tendency on occasions to destroy the very resources on which it depends. This is the focus of the *Tourism and the Environment* report (Department of Employment/English Tourist Board 1991) aimed at enccouraging the UK tourism industry to recognise that the environment is its life-blood and that it needs to consider the long-term consequences of tourism activity and development. Although Romeril (1989) argues that appropriate strategies and methodologies are required to understand the complex inter-relationships between tourism and the environment, no universal environmental methodology appears to have been adopted by researchers in their assessment of tourism and the role of transport in affecting the environment.

It is evident from the discussion so far that tourism and tourist transport systems are consumers of the environment, (Goodall 1992) since the provision of tourist infrastructure has a direct impact on the environment, particularly in destination areas. Selman (1992) and Newson (1992) discuss the concept of Environmental Auditing as one way of examining the extent to which tourist transport system and their activities are environmentally acceptable. Does tourist transport cause unnecessary pollution? Can meansures be taken to mitigate and reduce the harmful effects on the environment without compromising the commercial objectives of the tourist transport operator? According to Goodall (1992 : 62) one needs to distinguish between the existing and the future impacts of tourist transport. Two type of research methodology can be used here:

- Enviornmental Auditing of existing transport systems and their performance and effect on the natural and built enviornment.
- Environmental Assessment to consider the impact of proposed developments in the tourist transport system.

Each methodology has been developed as a multidisciplinary technique requiring an input from disciplines such as economics, atmospheric science, environmental science, geography, management studies and planning. Within these techniques, a systems approach is often used as method of examining how different tourist transport impute affect the enviornment and how to mitigate the effects of outputs which contribute to environmental degradation (Wathers 1990).

Environmental Auditing and Tourist Transport

Within tourism and transport studies the two most notable studies published on Environmental Auditing are Goodall (1992), Goodall and Stabler (1997) and Sommerville (1992), which illustrate how this research technique is used as a response to the growing interest in sustainable development (Banister and Button 1992). Environmental Auditing is a voluntary exercise which tourist transport operators and tour operators, who contract transport services for clients, may undertake to assess how their activities affect the environment and how they can reduce this impact by making modifications to existing business practices. Newson (1992 : 100) notes that 'the term auditing, borrowed from finance, implies a thoroughness and openness which is essential in a meaningful desire to reform commercial practices' but few Environmental Audits have been publicised. Some examples from the field of consumer products (e.g. the Body Shop and Proctor and Gamble in the UK) have followed the lead of North America in terms of consumer demand for more 'green products' (Selman 1992). Critics argue that such companies have harnessed new-found environmental awareness to gain competitive advantage and increase market share by offering environmentally friendly services and products as part of the move towards total quality management with in their organisation.

Research by Forsyth (1997) raises a wider debate on tourism and environmental regulation, since auditing is a voluntary process. Forsyth surveyed 69 UK-based companies involved in tourism (e.g., tour operators, travel agents, hotels passenger carriers, tourism associations, national tourist offices and consultancies advising companies sending tourists overseas). Forsyth argues that self-regulation is viewed as preferable in the tourism-environment debate because environmentally responsible practices can be harnessed to increase competitive advantage. Forsyth's survey was sponsored by the World Wide Fund for Nature (UK) and Tourism Concern and prior to any interviews, respondents were sent a copy of *Beyond the Green Horizon: A Discussion Paper on Principles for Sustainable Tourism* (Tourism Concern and World Wildlife Fund 1992). Forsyth's (1997) results identify four main types of practice:

- Cost-cutting measures (e.g. paper recycline),
- Adding value to the product (e.g. information of destinations on destinations as sympathy booklets,
- Long-term investment (e.g. staff training),
- Legislation (e.g. tourist taxes–see Abeyratne 1993 for a fuller discussion of air transport taxes).

Businesses, however, saw themselves as powerless to effect change, given the threat of competitors who did not adopt similar measures. The main obstacles businesses perceived to developing practices compatible with sustainable tourism principles were :

- It is the responsibility of government to initiate sustainable tourism.
- It may leave businesses at a disadvantage if competitors do not embrace similar practices.
- Operators are powerless to produce change.
- a potential lack of interest among customers in sustainable tourism.

The potential for businesses was in 'labelling green to sustainable tourism as quality tourism and by acknowledging that populist market demand way lead to stereotypical approaches to minorities or ecotouism not helpful to equitable development (Forsyth 1997 : 270).

For those businesses which view environmental self regulation as offering benefits to their image and product, there is evidence that if committed transports operators undertake an Environment Audit, it may prompt other companies to follow suit, thereby improving the awareness of environmental issues within their sector of the tourism business. The establishment of the British Standards Institution's (BSI) new Environmental Management System, mirroring the BS 5750 quality system for service providers is evidence of the significance of Environmental Auditing as a potent force in the 1990s which will encourage companies to establish a benchmark of acceptable standards of environmental management in commercial activities. Tourist transport system are on exception to this environmental awareness and it is likely to increase in the 1990s and in the new millennium. For example, P&O European Ferries have undertaken a comprehensive environmental review and implementing environmental policies to reduce the company's impact on the atmospheres, marine environment and on shore.

Goodall (1992) identifies the role of Environmentla Auditing in corpora ate policy making among tourism enterprises (e.g. transport providers) which includes:

- A *consideration stage,* where the legislation and scope of environmental issues are considered.
- A *formulation stage,* where an environmental policy is developed.
- An *implementation stage* where both existing and proposed activities can be considered.
- A *decision stage* where transport operations are either modified or left unchanged in pursuit of a corporate environmental policy.

More specifically, Goodall (1992 : 46) recognises that policy statements and action to minimise environmental impacts need to consider:

Table 5.1 Types of Environmental Audit.

Audit	Description
Activity	An overview of an activity or process which crosses business boundaries in a company, e.g., staff travel by employees of a hotel chain.

Associate   Auditing of firms which act as agents, subcontractors
              or suppliers of inputs, e.g., tour operators using only
              hotels which have adequate waste water and sewage
              treatment or disposal facilities and which are in
              keeping with the character of a destination.

Compliance   Relatively simple, regular checks to ensure the firm
              complies with any current environmental regulations
              affecting its operations, e.g., airline checking on notes
              levels cf its aircraft at takeoff.

Corporate   Typically can audit of an entire company, especially
              a transactional one, to ensure that agreed
              environment policy is understood an followed
              throughout the firm.

Issues   Concentration upon a key issue, e.g., ozone depletion
              and evaluation of company operations in relation to
              that issues, e.g., noted chain checks aerosols used are
              CFC-free, uses only alternatives to CFC-blown plastic
              foamss for insulation and retrieves any CFCs used in
              air-conditioning plant for controlled disposal.

Product   Ensuring that existing products and proposed product
              developments meet the firm's environmental policy
              criteria, e.g., tour operator designs holiday based of
              walking once destination reached, using locally owned
              vernacular accommodation and services.

Site   Audit directed at spot checks of buildings, plant and
              processes known to have actual or potential problems,
              e.g. hotel checking energy efficiency of its heating
              and lighting systems, airport authority checking aircraft
              noise levels near to landing and takeoff fight paths.

- The extent to which transport operations and associated activities comply with environmental legislation
  through company regulations
- Ways of reducing negative environmental impacts
  such as polluting emissions and use of energy-efficient
  modes of transport and equipment based on state-of-
  the art technology
- The development of environmentally friendly products
- How to encourage a greater understanding of
  environmental issues among staff, customers and
  people affected by tourist transport.

Translating these principles into commercial practice
is a complex process even though organisation such as the

World Travel and Tourism Council recommend that such audits should be undetaken annually to foster more responsible forms of development (Goodall 1992). As Table 8.1 shows, the nature and scope of Environmental Auditing in the tourist transport system may be determined by the objectives, commitment of senior management and the size of their organisation to resource such an exercise. One tourist transport operator which has developed a corporate audit is British Airways.

Case Study—British Airways and environmental management

Consumer interest in environmental issues in the late 1980s prompted tourist transport operators in the UK to undertake Environmental Audits to provide a public image of 'environmentally conscious' companies. Purchasers of tourist transport services (e.g., tour operators such as Thomson Holiday) also undertook Environmental Audits to respond to this trend as previously mentioned with reference to Forsyth (1997). This case study focuses on the extent of environmental management by one of the world's largest tourist transport operators—British Airways. The significance of British Airways (hereafter BA) as a tourist transport company has been documented elsewhere and need not be reiterated here. Commercial aviation dominates the world's communications infrastructure since over '8,800 subsonic jet aircraft...flew over 1.7 billion passenger kilometres in 1990' (Sommerville 1992 : 161). BA's role in the world airline industry is reflected in its £8.37 billion turnover in 1996/97, having carried 38 million passengers on its fleet on 258 aircraft (British Airways 1997). Air travel is a useful example to focus on as airline operation has a variety of impacts on the environment. These can be dealt with under the following headings.

Noise

Early tourist travel on turbe-prop and jet-propelled aircraft generated a significant noise impact during takeoff, in flight and on landing (Farrington 1992 for a discussion of the technical issues). Modern aircraft technology has reduced the level of noise impact in response to international conventions and legal requirements at specific airports which aim to reduce noise impacts for local communities. For example, Air New Zealand's ageing fleet of Boeing 737s had to be hush-kitted to operate at certain New Zealand airports. The sheer volume of air travel creates a persistent problem for those affected by airlines' flight parths. As sommerville (1992) notes, since the 1970s, the number of people affected by noise nuisance at Heathrow within a 35 Noise Index Number contour has dropped by almost 75 per cent, but this was accompanied by a dramatic increase in the volume of air travel. Increasingly airports are monitoring individual aircraft (e.g., their noise footprint) to ensure they meet noise regulations (M. Smith 1989 for further information). The phasing out of older aircraft is one way of reducing the noise impact in line with recent guide lines issued by countries abiding by ICAO recommendations. From April 1995, air craft over 25 years old are to be replaced in countries observing ICAO guidelines, while additional regulation will apply in European airspace.

BA's (1997) Annual Environmental Report lists its fleet compensation and it plans to replace its aircraft in advance of the ICAO guidelines and introduction of Chapter three aircraft by 1 April, 2002 in Europe and 31 December 1999 and in the USA. As Table 5.2 shows, BA's aircraft are progressively being updated to meet the Chapter Three requirements for European and transatlantic operation. As at 31 March 1996, 18.6 per cent of BA's fleet were Chapter two aircraft. In terms of the impact of noise on residents at Heathrow, the number affected by the 57 Leq contour (noise threshold) had dropped by 6.5 per cent in 1994. In the UK, London. Heathrow and London Gatwick and Manchester International Airport use aircraft noise monitoring system; more detailed measurements and data can be found in BA's *Report of Additional Environmental Data* (BA Report No. 6/97) which accompanies its 1997 environmental report (BA

1997). BA also lists its day and night noise infringements at a range of airports, together with the noise cost of BA's Chapter Two aircraft at airpots around the world. BA (1997) also discusses how to reduce the noise impacts and records its progress towards targets it established to improve its environmental impact. Table 5.3 highlights the noise targets.

Table 5.2 : British Airways fleet composition as at 31 March, 1997.

Aircraft type	Engine type	ICAO Annex 16 Chapter / FAR Part 36 stage	Number of aircraft	Average Age of aircraft (years)
Concorde	Olympus 593	Exempt	7	20.3
Boeing 747-100	JT9D 7/7A	2	15	24.9
Boeing 747-200	RB211-524D4X	3	16	16.4
Boeing 747-200	RB211-524G/H2	3	22	5.1
Boeing 777-200	GE90-76B	3	5	1.4
Boeing 777-200/GW 777-200	GE90-85B	3	4	0.2
McDonell Douglas DC 10-30	CF6-50C2	3	8	17.8
Boeing 767-300	RB211-524H	3	16	5.4
Boeing 757-200	RB211-535C/E4	3	37	10.2
Airbus A320 100/200	CFM56-5AI	3	10	8.1
Boeing 737-200	JT8D-15A	2	41	14.9
Boeing 737-400	CFM56-3CI	3	13	5.1
BAe ATP	PW 126[1]	5/Stage 3	13	7.4
DHC7-100	PT6A-50	5/Stage 3	2	13.0
DHC8-300	PW123	5/Stage 3	8	5.2
Total			230	10.0

Table 5.3 British Airway noise objective 1996/97.

Last year's objectives / targets	Status
To work with airport and other bodies to reduce the operational noise impact of aircraft.	Representation of Noise and Trak Keeping Groups and repressenting the industry on appropriate consultive groups. No scheduling of aircraft in the half-hour prior to night quouta period. Simulator trials to test steeper angles of approach. (Ongoing)
To have aircraft at Heathrow by the summer of 2000 with an overall phase out ahead of the compliance deadline.	Increase of 0.9% in British Airways aircraft to Chapter 3. Over. 92% of the Heathrow fleet (at 31/3/79) were Chapter 3. (Restated)
At Heathrow and Gatwick, the number of flights and their noise impact to stay within the current movement and noise quota limits.	Night movement quotas not exceeded. British Airways has a voluntary restriction of only using QC2 aircraft in the night uota period. (Ongoing).
Aircraft noise infringements at Hearthrow and Gatwick not to exceed the base year of 1995 (assuming no change in the regulatery standard).	Reduction of 50% in noise inferngements at Heathrow. Noise infringements at Gatwick increaseed threefold as result of additional operations. Overall total increased 2.4%. (Remains target but regulatory regime likely to change)
To use fixed electrical ground power supply for aircraft on all stands where it is available, subject to requirements for start-up and shutdown of aircraft systems and for short turnarounds.	Operation of GPUs in the night period monitored by HAL. British Airways charged £4,500 for operating GPUs at night on stands with serviceable FEGP (Jan-Mar. 97). (Restated)
To have modified or replaced all ground power units at Heathrow and Gatwick to meet the improved noise standard by the end of 1999.	Programme of replacement proceding according to plan. (Ongoing)
Testing tonight of aircraft engines in the noise enclosure of No. 1 maintenance base at Heathrow not to exceed an average of three runs per night at high thrust setting with a maximum of 30 minutes duration for any single night at high thrust.	New procedure developed with HAL to reflect reduced need for engine ground running time reduced from 240 miniutes to 150 minutes per night. Survey of engine ground running carried out. (Met)
To develop a long-term strategy for the central location of engine ground run facilities at Heathrow, in order to reduce further noise impact on our neighbours.	Strategy now settled. It depends on planning approval of new centrally located engine ground run pens on British Airways West Base and at Terminal 5 Forward Maintenance Unit. (Ongoing) Project manager appointed to carry out research on potential improvements (Ongoing)

To improve the operational noise performance of the Heathrow East Maintenance Base engine ground run facility and the impact of night testing of engines at Heathrow over the next 12 months. It is an objective that the Forward Maintenance Unit ground run pen, planned as part of the proposed Terminal 5 at Heathrow, will meet recognised standards for noise impact.

Engine runs at the Forward Maintenance Unit ground pen will not exceed 65 dB(a) at the nearest residential property, meeting criteria which avoid sleep disturbance. British Airways will accept planning conditions on this basis if permission is granted. (Ongoing)

New or restated objectives/targets

To have no aircraft at Heathrow and no Chapter 2 Boeing 747 aircraft by the summer of 2000 with an overall phase-out ahead of the compliance deadline.

To review by August 1997 opportunities for the earlier scheduling of the service to Nairobi/Entebbe/Dar es Salaam in order to reduce noise infringements at Gatwick.

To reduce to zero the number of GPUs used on stands with serviceable FEGP and to prevent the unnecessary use of APUs on stand.

To establish a record keeping system for engine ground running at Gatwick by the end of 1997.

Table 5.4 : Airline emissions[1]

Emission	Environmental effects	Approximate emission (millions of tonnes) Commercial aviation	Worldwide (fossil fuels)
Oxides of nitrogen	Acid rain. Ozone formation at cruise altitudes and smog ozone at low levels	1.6	69[2]
Hydro-carbons	Ozone and smog formation at low levels	0.4	57[2]
Carbon monoxide	Toxic	0.9	193[2]
Carbon dioxide	Stable–contributes to greenhouse effect by absorption and rejection of infrated radiation	500-600	20,000[2]
Sulphur dioxide	Acid main	1.1	110[2]
Water vapour	Greenhouse effect by absorption and reflection of inferred radiation	200-300	7,900[3]
Smoke	Nuisance-effects depend on composition	negligible	N/A

1 Other emissions, mainly from paints and cleaning solvents are associated with aircraft maintainance and also from ground transport supporting the airline's operation.

2 OECD Secretariat estimates (for 1980), from OECD Environmental Data 1989.

3 Derived from BP Statistical Review of Energy 1991.

Emissions, Fuel Efficiency and Energy

The growing concern over global warming and 'greenhouse gases' (e.g., CFCs, CO_2, NO_x and methane) has meant that atmospheric pollution from aircraft has come under increasing scrutiny, BA (1992) identified the range of emissions from aviation (Table 5.4). At a global level, BA (1997) estimated that civil aviation accounts for 400-500 million tonnes of carbon dioxide from 20,000 million tonnes of fossil fuels. This recognises that almost 50 per cent of global warming may be a consequence of man's activities, with civil aviations's contribution accounting for 3 per cent of the total effect of global warming. Table 5.5 shows that BA's fuel consumption increased in 1995/96 and 1996/97, due to increased loads and a greater amount of operational activity. Table 5.6 is interesting since it shows the approximate fuel consumption of specific types of aircraft in kilograms of fuel per 100 available tonne Kilometres (ATKs) flown which is the number of tonnes of capacity available for the carriage of revenue load multiplied by the distance flown (BA 1997 : 52). Table 5.6 illustrates the relative efficiency of long-haul aircraft, while the use of boeing 757s on shorthop 'shuttle' services explains why their consumption is relatively high.

Wastwater, Energy and Materials

In 1990, BA's expenditure on waste disposal was £1.5 million and it has pursued a corporate 'reduce, reuse and recycle' philosophy since then. Recycling of aircraft materials (e.g. waste oil, tyres, batteries and metals) has been in place since the 1950s and aluminium and paper recycling occurs, while water and effluent management schemes have been reviewed to ensure the quality of waste management is improved. In 1996/97, BA generated £97,860 in recycling revenue, a 54 per cent increase on 1995/96 and £25,000 of the revenue was donated to 81 charities (compared to £10,000 given to 60 charities in 1995/96). Complex energy efficiency monitoring is also undertaken to identify energy savings. BA's use of CFCs and chlorcaibon (CC) in its enquineering operations for cleaning purposes has been reviewed and alternatives are being sought, with aerosol use replaced wherever possible by trigger sprays. Deicing fluid used in BA's airport operations is biodegradable and there is evidence of a decline in its use between 1989 and 1997 (except in 1995/96). The annual environmental report also provides a range of detailed tables of data associated with the chemicals BA uses in its airline operations and documents a gradual reduction since 1993/94.

Table 5.5 : British Airways emissions from worldwide flying operations (mainline).

	Tonnes 1995/96	Tonnes 1996/97	(%) Change
Fuel consumption	4,468,051	4,880,000	9.2
Carbon dioxide	14,063,701	15,392,000	9.4
Water	5,524,582	6,046,000	9.4
Unburned hydrocarbons	5,175	5,400	4.6
Carbon monoxide	14,511	16,000	10.1
Nitrogen oxides	54,399	59,400	9.2
Sulphur dioxide	4,113	4,500	9.2

Table 5.6 : Birtish Airways approximate fuel consumption by aircraft type 1996/97

Aircraft type	Consumption (kg/100 ATK)
A 320-111/211	286
BAe ATP	327
B737-200/400	357
B747-100	265
B747-200	255
B747-400	239
B757-200	331
B757-200 (F4)	358
B767-300	221
B777-200 (GE90/76B)	203
B777-200 (GE90/85B)	206
DC-10-30	281

Source: BA (1997 : 29) based on data calculated from air craft flight recorder. Reproduced courtesy of British Airways.

Table 5.7 : Estimates of additional fuel burned due to congestion at London Heathrow and London Gatwick airports 1995/96 and 1996/97.

Quantities and costs	Location	1995/96	1996/97
Fuel burned due to carrying	Heathrow	13,800	15,800
extra fuel (tonnes)	Gatwick	3,900	5,900
	Total	17,700	21,700
Cost of fuel burned due to	Heathrow	1,792,000	2,391,000
Carrying extra fuel (£)	Gatwick	503,600	922,000
	Total	2,295,600	3,313,000
Total additional fuel burned due	Heathrow	22,700	24,600
to arrival congestion (tonnes)	Garwick	2,800	3,400
	Total	25,500	28,000
Total cost of fuel burned	Heathrow	2,951,000	3,721,700
due to arrival congestion (£)	Garwick	366,300	530,900
	Total	3,317,300	4,252,600

Note: Heathrow fuel cost £151 per tonne and Gatwick £155 per tonne for the year 1996/97; for 1995/96 a figure of £130 per tonne was used for both airports. For 1995/96, fuel burned due to carrying extra fuel; figures are estimated based on the last six months.

Congestion

Congestion is viewed by BA as 'the most immediate problem facing the aviation industry in Europe. It is estimated that delays in the air and on the ground cost the industry some $5 billion per year...and could rise to $10 billion per year by 2000' (BA 1992 : 22) and in 1996/97 BA spent £4,252,600 on fuel due to congestion at Heathrow and Gatwick (BA 1997 : 38). Congestion increases fuel consumption, resulting in additional emissions, particularly where a lack of airspace, air traffic control problems and inadequate runway capacity delay flights. BA has estimated that in 1996/97 aircraft burnt an extra 28,000 tonnes of fuel due to holding (stacking) in the air at Heathrow and Gatwick (Table 5.7). An additional 15,800 tonnes of fuel were also burnt due to carrying excess fuel in case delays occurred at Heathrow, while a further 5,900 tonnes were burnt for the same reason on flights to Gatwick. This is accentuated by taxiing delays prior to takeoff and after landing. Measures to improve airport capacity at Heathrow are currently being evaluated in terms of the proposed Terminal 5. The public inquiry for Terminal 5 entered its third year in 1997 and is expected to conclude in 1998. This is expected to delay the governments response until the year 2000, with the new terminal opening no earlier than the year 2004 if permission is granted. The brief discussion of the Terminal 5 public inquiry outlined by BA (1997) is interesting in the light. It highlights the lobbying by the British Airports Authority (BAA) and BA, given BAA's announcement in May 1997 that BA would be the main occupant of Terminal 5. BA has intimated that if approval for Terminal 5 is granted, it would work with BAA to reduce vehicle pollution and congestion on the ramp by using automated baggage and cargo handling systems and other stand services. In BA's view, the consolidation of all its services in one terminal would also reduce congestion by alleviating inter-terminal transfers of passengers and baggage, though congestion would not be entirely elimi-nated as BA passengers also travel on non-BA/BA-alliance airlines. BA also summarises the infrastructure implication of providing new transport links to Terminal 5 to reduce potential congestion. For example, this includes extending the Heathrow Express rail service from Paddington and involves various feasibility studies associated with the London Airports Surface Access Study, published in 1996. But it is inevitable that Terminal 5 and an additional runway may lead to increased environmental impacts in terms of the landtake and effect on the local community.

Tourism

BA (1992) acknowledges that the environmental impact created by tourists travelling to destinations by air is an issue which falls under the remit of its environmental management programme. BA (1992 : 25) perceives its role as one of environmental eduction by :

Table 5.8 : Tourism and conservation objective 1996/97 in British Airways environmental report.

Last year's objectives/targets	Status
To assess the British Airways Assisting Conservation programme in terms of benefits to conservation and the costs and benefits to British Airways.	Review carried out by an external consultant, programme largely endorsed. (Met)
To develop the contribution of British Airways Tourism for Tomorrow Awards to responsible tourism.	An additional away was given in 1996 to the British Airways Holidays Hotel displaying the best environmental performance. (Ongoing)
To work within British Airway and the industry to improve understanding and awareness of the interaction of tourism with the environment.	Seminar held at the Royal Geographical Society to discuss the relationship between tourism and conservation. Some 150 individuals from industry, academia, and other parties attended (Restated).
To undertake an additional destination audit of St Lucia with Britich Airway Holidays in 1996-97 and communicate recommendations for improvement.	Audit commenced in March, 1997. Results will be published later in the year. (Ongoing)

Newo or restated objective/targets
To lead improvement in the environmental performance of the tourism industry.
To improve communication on the airline's assistance given to conservation efforts worldwide.

- Raising awareness of the [environmental] issues within the industry and with customers.
- Persuading governments and tourist authorities to impose discipline and appropriate planning regulations and management procedures to ensure future tourist development is managed in an environmentally responsible way.

Table 5.8 outlines BA's objectives and achievements in relation to tourism and conservation. Its aim to lead in the environmental performance of tourism is evidence of Forsyth's (1997) argument on the benefits of self-regulation. Figure 5.1 illustrates the scope and geographical distribution of the Tourism for Tomorrow awards which have been in operation for seven years. In 1996/97 there were 100 entries

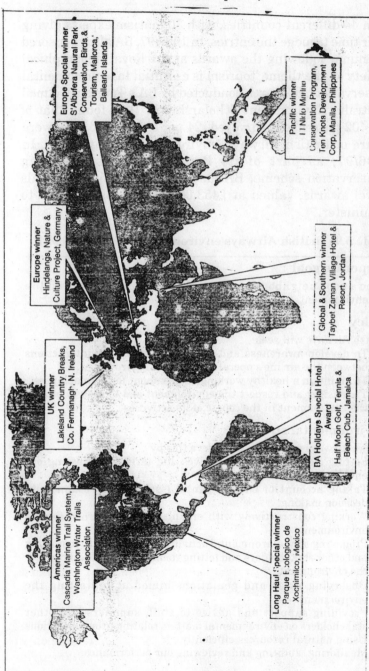

Fig. 5.1 : Distribution of British Airways Tourism for Tommorrow Awards in 1996/97.

from 44 different countries, with 30 tourism experts giving their time to judge the entries. In 1997/97, BA also sponsored a seminar following the awards at the Royal Geographical Society on the theme 'tourism is essential to environmental conservation'. Research conducted by BA's Tourism Council Australia Environment Scholarship in 1996 found that of the 402 passengers surveyed, 24 per cent stated they were aware of British Airways' environmental programme. In 1996/97, as part of its British Airways Assisting Conservation scheme, BA also offered, 3,055 individuals travel awards, valued at £453,000, which cost £22,000 to administer.

Table 5.9 : British Airways environmental policy 1996/97.

Corporate goal

To be a good neighbour, concerned for the community and the environment.

Policy

British Airways will seek:
* To develop awareness and understanding of the interactions between the airline's operations and the environment.
* To maintain a healthy working environment for all employees.
* To consider and respect the environment and to seek to protect the environment in the course of its activities.

Environmental strategy

British Airways will strive to achieve this by :
* Setting clearly defined objectives and targets addressing out environmental issues.
* Taking account of environmental issues in our commercial decision making.
* Working constructively with organisations concerned for the environment.
* Promoting our environmental activities with our staff, customers and other stakeholders and letting them know of our concern for the environment.
* Observing rules and geulations aimed at protecting the environment.
* Providing support and advice to staff, suppliers and other stakeholders on environmental matters relating to our operations
* Using natural resources efficiently.
* Monitoring, auditing and reviewing our performance.

Responsibilities : Staff

All staff are responsible for safeguarding, as far as they are able, both their working environment and the greater environment surrounding our operations. This includes:

- complying with environmental standards and procedures
- notifying management and supervisors of potential hazards
- avoiding needless wastage of energy and materials.

Responsibilities : line management

All line managers, in relation to activities under their individual control, are responsible for identifying and ensuring compliance with environmental regulations affecting our environment. Each director shall address environmental matters regularly, identify items requiring action and make sure they are followed up. Line managers must.

- Establish individual responsibilities, objectives and accountabilities for subordinate staff in environmental matters.
- Develop and maintain procdures to protect the working and external environment.
- Develop and maintain procedures to protect the working and cerernal environment.
- Monitor implementation of procedures and working practices and take swift and appropriate steps to put deficiencies right.
- Ensure that a statement of environmental impact, tailored to specific requirements, is prepared as part of the planning of facilities and operations, and for modifying or abandoning them.
- Provide channels for employees and contractors to be consulted on environmental matters.
- Investigate and report all environmental incidents and near misses and take necessary follow up action.
- Set quality standards covering relevant discharges and disposals including any that are not covered by statutory requirements.
- Review regularly the use of materials and energy in order to reduce waste, optimise recycling and select materials compatible with environmental objectives.
- Maintain accurate and comprehensive records of discharges and other waste disposals to the environment, including breaches of compliance limits.
- Report any breaches to the relevant regulatory bodies or internally as appropriate and take action to bring operations with compliance.

So how can one evaluate BA's performance in the environmental management of tourist transport? One initial issue to consider is BA's stated environmental policy, which is reproduced in Table 5.9. This illustrates an integrated approach to environmental management so that the company complies with all existing environmental regulations. It also highlights the corporate ethos-to ensure 'all staff are responsible for safeguarding, as far as they are able, both their working environment and the greater environment surrounding our operations' (BA 1997 : 51). Table 5.10 also provides a useful summary of BA's overall environmental costs. Investments and savings in 1996/97.

Figure 5.2 outlines the way in which BA manages its environmental performance, with the Environment Branch playing the lead role to 'advise, support, stimulate and monitor environmental performance' (BA 1997 : 10). To assist with communications between each department in the organisation and the Environment Branch, there are 'environmental focal points' in each department. Within BA, the network of 'environmental champions' within the organisation enables staff to take part in environmental initiatives. In 1996/97, there were 305 such champions within BA. The champions and the Environment Branch communicate by means of an 'environment letter' which is produced three to four times a year.

In evaluating the scope of BA's environmental measures, it is evident that the organisation is establishing a benchmark by 'taking the lead [but] it is up to other sectors of the industry to extend the initiative' (Sommerville 1992 : 1773), Environmental researchers have also developed a greater interest in the future impact of tourist transport systems in terms of the requirement for additional infrastructure and its impact on the environment, which is now considered in relation to Environmental Assessment.

Table 5.10 : A selection of environmental costs, investments and saving made by British Airways 1996/97.

Project / Initiative	£000s
Environment Branch including consultancy work, sponsorship and publications	587
Acquisition of aircraft over next four years (Boeing 747-400, 777, 757-200 and 737-300.	2,800,000
A significant part of the expenditure will relate to noise, emission and fuel efficiency performance	

Extra fuel burned as a result of congestion delays at Heathrow and Gatwick	4,250
Replacement of chillers utilising CFCs at Technical Block A, Heathrow with non-ozone-depleting alternative	1,000
Investment during the next two years on sub-metering (should be almost 1,000 meters).	200
Halon replacement progamme	250
Recycling of halons from ground systems for essential use in aircraft fire protection systems	50
Noise infringements at Heathrow and Gatwick, (1995/96)	75
Charges for the three months January to Match 1997 for operating GPUs on stands at Heathrow with serviceable fixed electrical ground power	5
Specific noise charges at airports from operating Chapter 2 aircraft (1995/96)	7,230
With HAL, British Airways is sharing support of £30,000 for research on active noise of Cranfield University	15
Investment over the next two years on sub-metering	200
Heathrow maintenance base gas heating project-conversion of oil-based district heating system to a more efficient local gas system (investment over next two years)	7,700
Roof replacement and wall cladding project to New Services Hangar, Heather, to improve building efficiency and insulation	2,800
New high efficiency lighting system for New Service Hangar, Heathrow	270
Support for improvements to the 105 bus route (frequency doubled and rerouted past Compass Centre)	83
Support for improvements to bus services serving the Cargo Centre and southside Heathrow (H26, 140, 555, 556, 557)	300
Support (with HAL) for free travel zone for everyone between Heathrow Central Terminal Area and northside	25
Contribution to the costs of two feasibility studies into western rail links from Terminal 5, Heathrow	20
Soil and ground water investigation at Heathrow maintenance base as part of the British Airways Maintenance Base Initiative (BAMBI) to return leased areas back to HAL	107
Waste disposal costs at Heathrow and Gatwick	1,775
Improvements to drainage system at Heathrow maintenance base	158
Money generated by recycling programme	98
Value of travel assistance to individuals through British Airways Assisting Conservation	450
Administration charge for British Airways Assisting Conservation	20
Donations to environmental organisations	50
Contribution to UNEP publication on children's conference	5
Recycling revenues donated to staff charities	25
8 additional GPUs have been replaced in 1996-97 at Heathrow and Gatwick to meet the higher noise performance standard. All new models meet Stage 1 of the European Directive for Engine Emissions. Purchases for other locations will also meet these standards	200

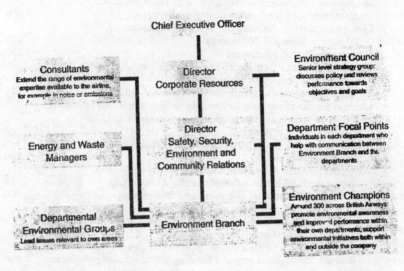

Fig. 5.2 : The structure of environmental management at British Airways

Environmental Assessment and Tourist Transport

An understanding of the past and present effect of tourist transport systems on the environment is critical to the long-term management of environmental resources, but there is also a need to consider the likely effect of future transport development projects. It is within this context that the significance of research methodologies such as Environmental Assessment (EA) can be examined to show how future tourist transport infrastructure projects may be evaluated. Within the existing literature on the environmental impact of tourism and transport (see Farrington and Ord 1988)), a number of research methodologies exist, which are documented by Williams (1987) in terms of their analytical function and the techniques they employ.

There are three levels at which EA of tourism and transport projects can be undertaken; 'identification', 'prediction' and 'evaluation'. Williams (1987) summarises five main methodologies used to assess the impact of tourism on the environment, in which transport is a significant component. These range from 'ad hoc' teams of specialists describing impacts within their professional field of study, through the 'map overlay approach frequently employed in land use planning, to 'check-lists' of different impacts associated with physical development related to tourism, 'networks' to assess the secondary and tertiary effects associated with action relating to tourism projects and lastly, more sophisticated matrices of impact with the confines of EA (see Wathern 1990 for a more detailed discussion). Although EA was not specifically designed with tourist transport projects in mind, it is a useful methodological tool to examine the direct and indirect effects of a project on the existing and future tourism environment within an integrated research framework. (See Department of the Environment 1989 for a guide to the scope and complex range of issues which EA in the UK must address as a legal requirement.)

A recent study by Perl et. al., (1997) moves the EA research frontier forward in the methodology it devised for pricing aircraft emissions at Lyon-Satolas airport. Without reiterating the technical aspects of the study, Perl (1997) highlights the three principal environmental impacts associated with airport operation: air, noise and water pollution. As Perl et al rightly argues :

One important variation concerns the degree to which these impacts mobilise public participation in, or demands for influence over, airport planning and development....an impact like aircraft noise, which is spatially concentrated in certain areas, has motivated much greater public protest than the air or water pollution impacts from airports, which diffuse more broadly and mix with pollutants from other sources.

By linking EA techniques with economic cost evaluations, Perl et. al., (1997) estimated the cost of air pollution for 1987, 1990, 1994 and 2015. The methodology involved pricing the pollution cost from the landing-takeoff cycle, which includes taxiing, idling, queuing, takeoff and climbout. For 1994, Perl et. al., (1997) estimated the cost of air pollution at

US\$3.6–6.6 million. This was projected to rise to US\$9.5–17.4 million in 2015 (assuming the aircraft engineering technology did not improve). Such reach can be extended to other airpots and can certainly assist in scenario planning for possible environmental costs of pollution. It certainly has the potential to make EA a more systematic rather than descriptive method in dealing with tourist transport impacts. To illustrate how an EA has considered a tourist transport impacts. To illustrate how an EA has considered a tourist transport system and some of its potential shotcoming, the case of the Channel Tunnel is now examined.

Case Study The Environmental impact of a new tourist transport infrastructure project-the Channel Tunnel

The Channel Tunnel is currently the largest tourist transport infrastructure project in Europe, which cost in excess of £8 billion at 1990 prices. According to SERPLAN (1989), the Channel Tunnel has the potential to generate an additional 450,000 tourists for the South East of England, using various modes of transport to travel through the tunnel to mainland Europe. It is evident that the tunnel project has created a new tourist gateway between the United Kingdom and mainland Europe, thereby facilitating more choice in the available modes of Cross-Channel travel for tourists. The extent to which the opening of the Channel Tunnel has directly and indirectly affected physical and man-made tourism environments in the 1990s is largely overlooked in recent research on Channel Tunnel.

The environmental dimension of the project has not received a great deal of attention, with the exception of the controversy surrounding the routing of the Channel Tunnel high-speed rail link through Kent (Goodenough and Page 1994 for more detail). In the UK, the environmental lobby is particularly concerned with the physical impact, although the majority of such studies have focused on a specific impact rather than the tunnels effect of different tourism environments in the 1990s.

Environmental Assessment and the Channel Tunnel

In the UK the EC Directive (85/337/EEC) on EA coincided with the government's 'Invitation to Promoters for the Development, Financing, Construction and Operation of a Channel Fixed Link between France and the United Kingdom'. Wathern (1990) examines the recalcitrance of certain member states, particularly the UK, towards adopting the directive since the government's commitment to puts the Channel Tunnel project to fruition as quickly as possible in 1985. By using the parliamentary device of the hybrid bill, no public planning inquiry was needed, which avoide any obligatory participation in an EA to comply with the impending EC legislation, since 'the Directive does not apply to projects... which are authorised by a private of Hyorid Bill' (Department of the Environment 1989 : 23), although 'the promoter of such a Bill should provide an environmental statement which can be considered by the select or standing committees...on the Bill' (Department of the Environment 1989 : 23). The latter situation applied to the four shortlisted promoters of the Fixed Lind project (Channel Tunnel Group, Channel Expressway, Eurobridge and Euroroute) which were required to comply with the EC Directive in 1985. This meant that a detailed EA rather than a simple environmental statement was required from each promoter, minimising the cost to the government by obliging the private sector to fund a detailed environmental analysis, As a result, the EAs of the Fixed Link project are a landmark in the UK since they were the first to comply with the EC Directive 85/337.

The four shertlisted promoters' EA reports submitted in 1985 who reviewed both the content, coverage, accuracy and presentation of the reports in relation to their ability to meet the requirements of the draft EC Directive 85/337. Evaluating EAs is a complex process in view of the problems of understanding and forecasting the secondary effects and consequential development such projects may generate. For example, the Channel Tunel Group's EA (Channel Tunnel

Group 1985) understimated the potential impact of a new mode of tourist transport on tourism, arguing that the tunnel would not in itself directly stimulate a growth in the demand for cross-Channel travel. Planners failed to recog-nise how the cross-Channel ferry industry would respond to the competition through mergers, acquisitions and the development of new routes (Figure 5.3). The promoters also overlooked the new tourism markets which will be more accessible to the UK and Europe as a result of the tunnel and improvements to the high-speed European rail network and road (Page and Sinclair 1992b; Page 1993d). Thus, while the Channel Tunnel Group's EA dealt with the physical impacts involved with construction of the tunnel, it failed to make a detailed assessment of the consequences of a growth in visitor arrivals induced by the Fixed Link. Criticisms of the Channel Tunnel Group's EA have also pointed to the voluminous and unintelligible nature of the study (Lee and wood 1988). Although the EA failed to consider the potential environmental impacts associated with a sustained growth is visitor arrivals and departures once the tunnel opened, it is possible to identify a number of ways in which tourist use of the tunnel would affect the environment.

The Environmental Impact on Existing Tourism Resources

The construction of the tunnel has aroused the concerns of amenity bodies such as the Council for the Protection of Rural England and the Nature Conservancy Council. Ardill (1987) examines the conservation lobby's concern for the impact on the landscape and the land damaged or lost in the process of constructing the tunnel, the terminals and associated infrastructure. The effects of consequential development on the South East resulting from selective land releases for tourism or motorway service area provision at interchanges are also considered, as are concerns that the visual amenity of the Kent landscape would be affected by the tunnel and that tourism resources might be affected by consequential development. The Channel Tunnel Joint Consultative Committee (1986) argues that only a limited environmental impact would result from consequential development associated with the tunnel, based on the fact that since 1970 there has been a threefold growth in the demand for cross-Channel travel but this has both generated any consequential development or led to any dramatic change in Kent's economic geography.

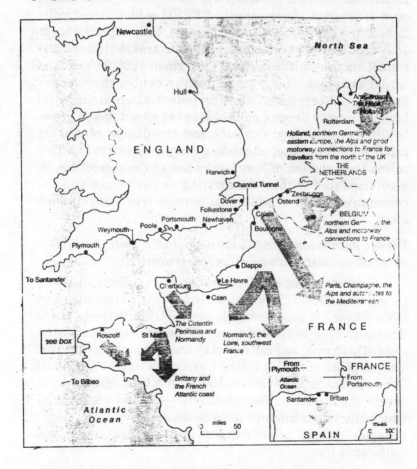

Fig. 5.3 : The pattern of channel crossing, 1998

Tourist use of the tunnel and the potential effects on the environment

According to hand Use Consultants (1986 : 49) the Tunnel could affect tourism in terms of employment and induced development, but tourism and recreation would need to be controlled and managed to reduce their impact on the environment. Their general assessment is important in terms of the scale of the potential impact of tourism in relation to how many tourists will travel through the tunnel once it is open. According to SETEC (1989), the traffic forecasting consultants to Eurotunnel, they expected up to 15.8 million road-borne passengers to travel through the tunnel via the shuttle service (Vickerman 1995 for detail on actual arrivals). This would virtually double the capacity for Channel crossings, and the potential environmental impacts largely depend on the extent to why demand grows to fill this increased capacity and the degree of market capture by Eurotunel of existing ferry and air traffic. This raises the question of how tourist use of the tunnel can be accommodated within the existing environment and the cumulative effects of additional tourists travelling through kent.

Direct environmental costs associated with tunnel-related tourist transport infrastructure

The actual impact of major road and rail infrastructure to serve tunnel traffic, was assessed within Belgium as part of its EA for the proposed high-speed TGV link from Lille to Brussels. This examines some of the real environmental costs of both road and rail travel by tourists and non-tourists. The purposes of the EA by the European Centre of Regional Development of the Walloon Region (CEDRE 1990) was to assess the 'micro-ecological effects'—the environment in which the infrastructure is to be established. The 'micro-ecological effects' are of interest in his context since they considered the :

- Aboiotic impact (i.e., the effect on geology, hydrology, noise and vibration).

- The biological impact (i.e., the effect on flora, fauna and the interactions between the two).
- The human impact (i.e., the effect on agriculture, residential areas, traffic, transport: the human elements in the landscape).

Their assessment of pollution reveals the potential impact tourist travel may have on the environment through which they travel-in this case a dedicated trasport corridor (Table 5.11). Tourist travel by rail and road produces pollutants, through on balance, rail is considered to be the most 'environmentally friendly option', as it is more energy-efficient and less intrusive, though it still generates a degree of noise pollution.

The environmental costs and benefits of tourist use of the international passenger terminals (IPTs)

Visitors using the Channel Tunnel who travel by Rail or road generate an environmental impact on their destinations. In the case of London, this impact in largely related to the international passenger terminal (IPT) at Waterloo (Page and Sinclair 1992a). In Kent, many of the direct environmental impact occur at the tunnel terminal and at the planned Ashford IPT, which is the focus for rail and car-bone travellers from the South East wishing to board the Eurostar rail services. A further environmental impact is that of increased tourist traffic in Ashford town centre. Consultants for BR identified a problem of potential congestion in and around Ashford town centre related to traffic generated by the IPT, which is likely to intensify in view of the predicted 45 per cent growth (1990-2006) in rail travel from Ashford to London and European destinations. Congestion and the provision of car parking may concentrate the environmental problems, especially pollution, in a small area of the town and forecast demand for 5,000 car parking spaces in the town illustrates the scale of the IPT development. However, since such forecasts have subsequently been found to be too optimistic, such an expansion is not as problematic as was once though.

Table 5.11 : A comparison to pollution from the TGV and car-borne traffic using the motorway in Belgium'.

Pollutant	Mass of pollutment (g) per Kilometre travelled	
	TGV	*Car*
Sulphur diodie[2]	0.124	0.090
Nirtous oxide[3]	0.071	1.460
Aerosol	0.044	0.049
Carbon monoxide[4]	0.005	1.109
Hydrocarbon[5]	0.002	0.179
Carbon dioxid[6]	228.907	135.000
Safety :		
Number of person killed per billion km travelled	0.8 (train) 0 (French TGV)	20.0 (roads 6.7 (motorway)

1. The accuracy of the pollution measurements listed in the table will depend on the meteorological conditions and prevailing winds as to whether pollutants concentrate at particular locations or disperse over a wider area.
2. Sulphour dioxide may impair health and it contributes to acid rain as sulphuric acid.
3. Nitrous oxide is a major component in photochemical smog and nitric acid contributes to acid rain. The major emission source is motor vehicles and power stations.
4. Carbon monoxide directly causes health-related problems and it can induce complications among people suffering from cardiac-related disease, Concentrations of carbon monoxide in confined areas are harmful as they can reduce the oxygen-carrying capacity of the blood.
5. Partically burnt hydrocarbons are carcinogenic (cancer-forming) agents and they also
6. Carbon dioxide contributes to the 'greenbouse effect'.

The indirect environmental impact of increased numbers of car-borne tourists on tourist destinations

An associated problem relates to additional car-borne visitors who may stop off in Ashford en route to the tunnel for leisure shopping and accommodation, adding to the potential congestion. Although Ashford is unlikely to suffer what Romeril (1989) calls 'saturation tourism' (i.e., seasonally induced peaks in flows of tourists), it is evident that planned visitor management strategies will not be able to overcome. All of the problems, particularly once the tunnel is open. The tourism carrying capacity in Kentish towns like Canterbury has reached saturation point in the peak season and key attractions like Caterbury Cathedral now employ visitor management tools, such as charging and monitoring visitos who use the cathedral. The tunnel has certainly generated the potential for more tourist visits to the country of Kent, but assessing where, when and the duration of these visits among domestic and overseas tourists using the Fixed Link remains a difficult process. Whatever locations the potential tourists visit, the existing environmental pressures posed by tourist travel to certain destinations in South East England are unlikely to be reduced without some attempts to spread the seasonal distribution of visitors.

The potential problems resulting from the development of a new tourist transport infrastructure project and the implications for destination areas highlight the significance of focusing on the necessity for tourist transport to be developed and managed in a sustainable framework.

Towards Sustainable Tourist Transport Systems

As mentioned earlier, 'sustainability' is a new-found term within tourism and transport literature: for services to be attractive to consumers they must now be 'sustainable' or 'green', though much of the rhetoric associated with sustainability has not led to radical changes in the operation and management of tourist transport system-merely some readjustment to accommodate green issues in most case. As transport is fundamental to tourist travel, some researchers argue that it is not possible to make tourism sustainable without a fundamental revision of the concept of tourism, holidaymaking and the role of travel in modern society. Therefore, without a re-evaluation of pleasure travel, measures designed to introduce sustainablility into the tourist transport environment debate are unlikely to address the root cause of the problem: the demand for tourism. However, since this is unlikely to be influenced in the short term, the immediate issue is to address the environmental impact of existing tourist travel.

The motivation to achieve sustainable tourist travel has resulted from the actions of pressure groups (e.g.,

Greenpeace, Friends of the Earth and Transport 2000 in the UK), and their views have permeated national governments as such groups have harnessed grassroots pressure from consumers to develop a greener economy and improve the quality of the environment. But it is at government level that commitment needs to be made to formulate, implement and resource policies to facilitate sustainable transport options. Little attention is given to the issue of tourist transport systems as it is often subsumed in the general theme of transport, which has a bias towards domestic concerns and the effect on economic development. The UK Tourism Society's response to the initial findings of the Government Task force (the final report is Department of Employment/English Tourist Board 1991) suggest that :

no analysis of the relationship between tourism and the environment can ignore transportation. Tourism is inconceivable without it. Throughout Europe some 40% of leisure time away from home is spent travelling, and the vast majority of this is by car...Approaching 30 per cent of the UK's energy requirements go on transportation.... [and]...the impact of traffic congestion, noise and air pollution...[will]...diminish the quality of the experience for visitors. (Tourism Society 1990).

How can the sustainability concept be incorporated into the tourist transport system? According to Barbier (1998 : 19, cited in Newson 1992), sustainability needs to be viewed as a process in terms of how different system interact as :

the wide objective of sustainable economic development is to find the optimal level of interactions among three systems—the biological and resource system, the economic system and the social system, through a dynamic and adaptive process of trade offs.

This means that economic activity, such as tourism, must try to achieve a balance with the natural environment so that the environment can support the activity without generating unacceptable impacts which affect the future resource base. The achieve this objective, the concept of susceptibility needs to be built into the operation of tourist transport systems and the following action is needed in terms of policy making and management :

- policy formulation,
- policy implementation,
- facilitating good practice in tourist transport,
- the evaluation of sustainable transport practices.

A systems approach is useful in this context as it helps one to understand how the decision-making process associated with the regulation, organisation and management of tourist transport systems affects different elements within the system. In terms of the sustainability concept, actions in one part of the system (e.g., policy formulation) will have repercussions for other parts of the system.

Policy Formulation for Sustainable Tourist Transport

Banister and Button (1992 : 2) recognise that the 'whole question of sustainable development...is–and likely to remain–a central concern of policy-makers and transport is but one element of this'. The rapid growth in long-distance passenger transport and its dominance by aviation at the international scale, together with the rapid expansion in car ownership within countries poses may problems for policy makers attempting to pursue sustainable transport options. Moreover, the underlying demand for travel seems set to continue to expand, as forecasts for the year 2000 suggest (Edwards 1992). The social and psychological demand for travel and holidays remains a potent force in developed countries. One result of the sustainability debate for policy makers is that the environmental impact of transport is not just a local issue: it is also a global problem, as the case study of BA indicated. This is confirmed by Banister and Button (1992 : 5) who argue that 'transport is an important contributor [to the sustainable development debate] at three levels (local, transboundary and global)'. Policy formulation therefore needs to be undertaken in a context where national governments develop transport policies and coordinate their response at a translational and global level through agencies such as the United Nations.

However, political commitment to formulating sustainable transport policies at national level may not be compatible with other political priorities. For example, many governments have facilitated the development of tourist transport infrastructure to foster regional tourism development and to encourage outbound travel (e.g. Japan). In fact, Wahab and Prgram (1997 : 285) argue that 'a growing trend in policy making in many countries is to leave tourism to private enterprise and current economic conventional thinking supports the role of market mechanisms'. Sustainable transport policies may require a re-evaluation of these national transport policy objectives in relation to tourism, transport and the cost the environment. In the context of the UK (see Banister 1992 for a discussion of national transport policies in the UK), D. Hall (1993) argues that sustainable transport is neglected in policy making since the Government's White Paper *This Common Importance* (Department of the Environment 1991) and accompanying policies have paid little attention to transport and the environment.

One recent development which is worthy of discussion in this context is Agenda 21. Agenda 21 'is a comprehensive programme of action adopted by 182 governments at the 1992 United Nations Conference on Environment and Development (UNCED), known as the Earth Summit. It provides a blueprint for securing the sustainable future of the planer' (Wahab and Pigram 1997). While it is the first document to gain widespread international commitment towards conserving the world's resources, it 'did not mention travel and tourism except in a few sections' (Wahab and Pigram 1997). However, the World Travel and tourism Council et al (1997) report *Agenda 21 for the Travel and Tourism Industry: towards Environmentally sustainable Development* does examine transport as one of the 10 areas of priority action for companies involved in tourism. The report identifies transport as a central feature of Agenda 21 in terms of controlling to reducing harmful emissions into the atmosphere as well as other adverse environ-mental impacts from tourism-related transport. In fact, the World Travel and Tourism Council et. al., (1997) argues that 'Transport is the lifeblood of the travel and tourism industry and failure to take action and improve performance in this area could result in harsh penalties for travel and tourism companies and increased costs for travellers.' To avoid such penalties, the report advocates that companies should:

- Use well maintained and modern transport technology, which may reduce emissions especially in the airline sector but and in other land and sea-based transport sectors.
- Assist less developed to acquire technology and skills to reduce environmental remissions from tourist transport.
- Develop and manage car-share, cycle or walk-to-work schemes for employees and provide incentive for successful implementation.
- Provide information of tourists to encourage the use of public transport, cycle ways and footpaths.
- Work with government to implement measures to reduce congestion in air transport and in urban tourism environments.
- Work with governments to achieve a greater integration in planning transport modes which not only reduce reliance on the private car, but reduce energy consumption in linking tourists to onward detonations.
- Use demand management tools to assist in reducing the need for polluting modes of transport in preference for more environmentally friendly modes of transport.

Table 5.12 : Possible components of a strategic, integrated approach to transport planning and investment at various organisational levels.

National/European

- A new integrated approach to transport planning in which the case for rail investment is evaluated on a basis comparable to that for roads, taking into account the full environmental courts and benefits.
- Within the framework of this integrated approach, the preparation of a long-term expansion plan for rail, with the aim of at least doubling passenger kilometres carried (restoring the situation to that which applied per-Beeching), increasing substantially rail's share of freight transport, but internationally

and domestically and in general exploiting fully the potential benefits of the Channel Tunnel link to Europe.

The region/county

- Through land use planning at the regional and/or county level, the maintenance of an appropriate balance of homes and employment to secure local job opportunities and reduce average commuting distance.
- The location as far as possible, of new settlements and other major developments along railway corridors to secure the best possible public transport access to other major centres.
- The development at regional level of long-term investment strategies for integrated public transport, using resources which would otherwise be spent on new roads.

New business developments

- The development of new policy guidelines for the location of businesses and public offices (together with suitable parking standards), with the aim of minimising total commuting mileages—such policies, which could perhaps be developed along the lines of the Dutch 'right business in the right place' strategy might then be set out in a future planning policy guidance note.
- The introduction of mileage reduction plans, to be developed and implemented by businesses and public organisations within government-issued guidelines and supported through financial incentives.

Shopping

- Continued strong support for city and town centre shopping (with new development permitted only where it reinforces existing provision) and for the maintenance of local shopping facilities.
- Major new retail developments to be subjected to a full shopping impact analysis, which would include an assessment of the traffic likely to be generated, both in terms of the absolute numbers of vehicles and total vehicle mileage, and an assessment of the public transport provision.

Accessibility to schools

- requirements on local planning and education authorities to place maximum emphasis on safe routes to school by foot, by bicycle and by public transport and to enure that new primary schools in urban areas are generally no more than a five-minute walk away from the children's homes.
- A requirement upon highway and education authorities, together with the schools concerned, to carry out comprehensive reviews of the adequacy of public transport and school buses servicing secondary schools, with a view, where necessary, to reorienting spending programmes to upgrade these services.

- The publication of an advice and good practice guide for local authorities on the development of safe routes to school and the allocation of some initial central funding for such schemes.

Access to local facilities

- Commitments through local planning policies to secure a full range of local facilities which are readily accessible by foot or bicycle, both is new residential areas and, when the opportunity arises, in older ones.
- The planning of future residential areas of any significant size around high-quality public transport routes, with homes generally no more than a five-minute walk away from a bus or light rail stop.

Integrated transport strategies at the urban level

- Requirement upon those responsible for land use and transport planning within out major cities to prepare integrated transport strategies, the aims of which would include the development of high-quality public transport service, significant reductions in overall vehicle emissions and, generally, a vastly improved environment for those who live and work there.

While such suggestions are helpful, in the self-regulation era companies need to be given incentives as such measures require mote commitment than conducting an Environmental Audit. It may be that individual countries need to formulate an environmentally based tourist transport strategy with which companies can comply. In fact, D. Hall (1993) suggests that a general environmental transport strategy needs to be formulated for the UK (Table 5.12). Although tourist transport is subsumed within wider category of transport systems in Table 5.12, Hall does suggest that coordinated action is needed in relation to :

- Regulatory mechanisms (e.g., by setting a ceiling for emissions).
- Financial mechanism (e.g., incentives to favour energy-efficient modes of travel).
- The introudction of hydrological advances in transport to encourage the use of more fuel-efficient engines.
- The development of an integrated and coordinated planning response to transport where land use and transport planning should minimise the distance to travel for economic and leisure activeness (e.g., work and shopping).

How does this affect international tourist travel? It would appear that the likely outcome of D. Hall's (1993) strategy would be the promotion of environmentally friendly modes of travel for tourists. Yet the real issue of existing tourists' travel habits is absent from the policy objectives as it is often perceived as an international problem rather than one nation's sole responsibility.

Implementation of Sustainable Tourist Transport Policies

A range of government transport policy responses to sustainability issues are discussed in Banister and Button (1992) and one recurrent theme in the need to adopt economic policies to price transport activities so that they reflect the environmental cost. There is growth evidence that countries such as the UK are now looking at controversial measures such as road pricing, which has been developed in Singapore. One approach widely used in developed countries is the differential pricing of pertrol through the level of taxation it attracts, to reduce the use of leaded petrol and to increase the consumption of unleaded petrol. A more radical solut;on advocated by the EU is the introduction of a carbon tax on energy production so that more environmentally sound energy sources are developed to reduce pollution. Yet this has been fiercely resisted by governments such as the UK because they feel it would add additional costs to the price of energy and thereby increase the costs of production. The basis of their argument in the area of tourist transport is it could make UK transport operators uncompetitive on a global basis. In this respect, concerted international government action is needed to reduce levels of pollution from transport, with certain countries taking a lead while others are forced to follow suit through international pressure. For example, in the UK the deregulation of bus services in metropolitan areas initially led to new operators using aged vehicles which contributed higher levels of pollution compared to the former metropolitan Passenger Transport Executives (PTEs) where grants were provided to update fleets, thereby resulting in the use of more energy-efficient vehicle (Knowles and Hall 1992). Yet as Button and Rothengatter (1992) acknowledge, the global nature of transport's impact on the environment is likely to intensify. The implementation of sustainable transport policies needs to be accompanied by changes in the lifestlyles of tourists so that they recognise the environmental degradation which their process of travel induces.

Good Practice in Sustainable Tourist Transport

The real debate over achieving sustainable tourist transport options is usually focused on the outcome: can such options really be put into practice or do they remain a stated policy objective of environmental planning which is little more than a paper exercise? There are various examples of good practice cited in the tourism literature where transport is a core component of tourism planning, so that conservation and interpretation of the environment raises tourists' awareness of natural habitats and the need for a delicate balance to be achieved between tourist use and preservation. The Tarka Project in Devon is one example where a tourism strategy has achieved these objectives (Department of the Environment/English Tourist Board 1991 and Charlton 1998 for more details). However, the reliance on public and private sector transport operators to implement sustainable tourism is questioned by Wood and House (1991, 1992). Although Wood and House (1991) acknowledge that transport operators need to pursue good environmental practices, they also advocate that the onus should be placed on the tourist. Their central argument is that tourists should 'environmentally audit themselves' before and during their holiday and this principles could also be applied to aspects of business travel. The environmental audit is based on a number of simple questions:

- Why go on holiday–consider your motivations and whether you really need to travel.
- Choose the right type of holiday to meet your needs.
- Consider travelling out of season to less well-known destinations.

- Choose the right travel method and tour operator after asking what the company is doing to minimise environmental impacts.
- Consider the form of transport you will use to get to the point of departure.
- Does the tour operator contract transport companies with new energy-efficient vehicles and aircraft or are they old, noisy and less efficient?
- Is public transport, cycling (Scottish Tourist Board 1991) or walking a feasible option when you are at the destination as opposed to hiring a car?

Wood and House's (1992) *The Good Tourist in Fance* illustrates how tourists can make their trip sensitive to the environment, especially in their use of tansport. Wood and House (1992) provide information on 'how to get there' but more importantly they undertake detailed research on each region of France so that tourist travel in the destination area can be based in sustainable options (i.e. forms of transport which do not have major environmental impacts). They outline details of operators and locations where you can hire or purchase travel services based on :

- rail travel,
- bus/coach travel,
- car travel,
- boating,
- cycling,
- walking,
- riding.

as well as contact addresses of local groups which encourage and support sustainable development.

Research on fragile tourism environments such as the Arctic has advocated the need of victor codes of practice (Mason 1994). Marsh and Staple (1995) reinforce such arguments. They argue that cruise ship passengers to such environments need to be educated about the impacts they can cause.

Probably the most sustainable form of transport which tourists can engage in is cycling. Cycling is comparatively neglected in the tourism literature, being discussed in generic transport studies research and in leisure contexts. For this reason, the following case study examines cycling as a sustainable means of tourist transport with a relatively low impact on the environmental.

Case Study—Cycling as an environmentally friendly form of tourist transport : the case of the UK

According to Lumsdon (1996a), the market for recreational and tourist cycling can range from day trips to part-time casual usage through to long-distance touring holidays. Toursist use is most likely to involve the oceasinsal cases usage by tourists visiting a destination who may hire a cycle for a day (see Page 1998 for a discussion of such usage on the Norfolk Broads in UK) or the more determined tourist which undertakes long-distance cycling holidays. Lumsdon (1996b : 5) defines cycle tourism as cycling which is 'part of or the primary activity of, a holiday trip...it falls within a categorisation of activity holidays'. Beyond the seminal study which incorporates cycling (Tolley (1990), there are only a limited number of studies on cycle tourism (Beoiley 1995; Schieven 1998; Sustrans 1997; Ritchie 1997). In a review of leisure cycling, Lumsdon (1997b) observes that the Department of Transport (1996) statistics suggest that up to 40 per cent of cycle journeys are for leisure purposes and if other personal trips are included, up to half of all trips are for leisure. Yet as Lumsdon shows, the prevailing literature of cycle transport pays little attention to the leisure dimension (in which tourist use is subsumed). Even the UK's *National Cycling Strategy* (Department of Transport 1996) highlights the significance for non-leisure use, though, as Lumsdon (1997b : 115) shown leisure is discussed :

> Leisure cycling has great potential for growth, it can be a stimulus to tourism, it is a high quality way to enjoy the countryside and a good way to introuce people to cycling for their everyday transport needs. To encourage leisure cycling there need to be small

scale improvements, especially near where people live, followed by better signposting, marketing and information. Flagship leisure routes, using quiet roads or disused railway paths, can increase the profile and boost leisure cycling in town and countryside.

But who are the typical cycle tourists and what motivates then to use this form of transport? The Scottish Tourist Board's (1991) innovative study *Tourism Potential of Cycling and Cycle Routes in Scotland* indicated that cycling had grown in popularity as a recreational activity in the 1970s and 1980s, with the membership of the Cyclists' Touring Club standing at 40,000 in the UK, having grown 10 per cent in the previous decade. The more recent study by the Countryside Commission (1995) *The Market for Recreational Cycling in the Countryside* identified some of the main motivations for cycling, including :

- keeping fit,
- fun,
- fresh air,
- access to the countryside.

Lumsdon (1996b) simplifies the market segments involved in cycle tourism to include :

- *Holiday cyclists* comprising couples families or friends who seek a holiday where they can enjoy opportunities to cycle but not necessary every day. They seek traffic-free routes and take their own bikes on holiday, a proportion will hire bikes and are likely to cycle 15-25 miles each day, a feature examined in New Zealand by Ritchie (1997).
- *Short-break cyclists,* who seek to escape and select packanes which will provide local knowledge (with of without cycle hire) and comfortable accommodation. They are likely to travel in groups and will cycle 15-25 miles a day.
- *Day excursionists* are canal cyclists who undertake leisurely circular rise of 10-15 miles and are not prepared to travel long distances to visit attractiones or facilities. They prefer to seek quiet country lanes which are signpostey. They tend to comprise 25-30 per cent of the market for cycling and are increasing using their own bikes rather than hiring them.

However, Lumsdon (1996b) also provides a more detailed analysis of the market for cycling as Table 5.13 shows. Lumsdon (1997b) cites the continued rise of adult cycle sales in Europe as evidence for the growth of interest in cycling for recreational purposes. Lumsdon (1997b) indicates that in Austria, Denmark, Germany, the Netherlands and Switzerland, tourism and recreational networks are now developing which also enhance the image of cycling. The Scottish Tourist Board (1991) outlines some of the constraints on and needs of cycling tourists in Scotland (Table 5.14). Table 5.14 highlights a range of needs and constraints, but probably the most important issue is that of approrate infrastructure and opporturnites for cycle tourism, an issue recently reviewed in New Zealand by Ritchie (1997). Although the Royal Commission on Environmental Pollution (HMSO 1994) identified the impact of other forms of tourist transport on the environment and the role of cycling as a mode of personal transport, it was recognised that it has a limited environmental impact.

The UK's National Cycle Network

The Royal commission on Environmental Pollution (HMSO 1994) recommended that cycle trips should be quadrupled to 10 per cent of all journeys in the UK by 2005. Wardman et. at., (1997) review some of the measures needed to achieve the target of 10 per cent by 2005, using behavioural model-based research. This research has important implications for infrastructure provision. One of the impor-tant findings of the royal Commission (HMSO 1994) was that local authorities in the UK should have a central role is meeting the 2005 targets are in infrastructures provision. In a planning context, this was to be achieved through the existing planning mechanism the local authority's annual Transport Policies and Programme (TPP) submission. While the purpose of this was to improve the level of cycle use, it has implications for tourism, which can utilise any infrastructure put in place for residents and leisure users in local areas. It may also assist reducing fatalities among cyclists (McClintock and Cleary 1996).

Table 5.13 Segmentation of the cycle market

Type	Profile/Nature	Use of infrastructure	Trend	Spend in local economy	Potential for growth
Day excursion					
1 Half-day day Casual home-based tourer	Occasional rider from home base. Single and couple, age 24-45. Also families. Increasingly using cars to transport bikes. Cycling approx. 10-20 miles. Socioeconomic spread.	Using back lanes or recognised cycle trails.	Sustained increase	Estimated little expenditure	High
2 Half-day and day Casual mountain biker	Occasional rider from home base. Age 24-25. Higher proportion of males and fewer families. Cycling approx. 10-20 miles. Increasingly using cars to transport bikes. Socioeconomic spread.	Seeking off-road routes of easy to moderate terrain. Potential to saturate popular routes in National Parks, etc.	Sustained increase	Estimated little expenditure	Moderate/High
3 Half-day and day Cycle hire	Infrequent-rider - more likely not to have bicycle or use when on holiday. Wider age profile of 18-55. Families strong market. Cycling 10-20 miles. Socioeconomic spread.	Seeking publicised off-road road and quiet country routes or historic town trails, (such as Oxford, York).	Strong upward trend in late 1980s. Static at present with growth of cycling Ownership	Spend in local facilities more likely	Low in most localities, high in key tourist cones, high potential in historic towns if traffic calming introduced.
Holiday market					
4 'Do it yourself' cycle tourer	Organises day rides or cycling tours from an independent base, Keener cyclists, young people, hostellers increasingly using car to transport bikes. More likely to be professional/managerial. Use of guidebooks.	Mainly country lanes	Slow growth local facilities than day market	Higher spend in	Moderate.

contd

	Description	Impact on routes	Growth	Spend	Overall impact
5 'Do it yourself' mountain biker	As in (4) but seeking more strenuous routes. Fewer families and slightly younger age profile. Use of leaflets and guidebooks. More likely to be professional and mangerial.	Heavier impact on off-road routes in sensitive areas.	Moderate and sustained growth means less time at attractions, tea rooms, etc.	Not quite so high as tourers given nature of activity	Moderate/High
6 Organised independent self-guided, cycling holidays/tourers, mountain bikes	Participants book an organised holiday, (routes, accommodation, etc.) but travel as couple or group of friends. They are more likely to be professional and managerial.	Companies offer towns, country lanes or mountain bike options. Impact minimal present.	Moderate growth	High spend in local economy	Moderate
7. Organised group cycling	As above, but participants make up a group for a guided tour.	As above	Static	High spend in local low economy	
8. Group holidays	As above but booking made for group as part of multi-activity or cycling holiday. Incorporates day hire of cycle fleets by school and youth clubs.	Usually minimal as leaders choose specific routes e.g. through YHA	Static	High spend in local economy	Low
9. Club riders	Keen riders; knowledgeable, self-arranged, long-distance day rides and holidays.	Mainly touring, minimal impact	Static	High spend on holidays	Low
10. Sports competitors	Mainstream cycling as a sporting activity.	Heavy impact, e.g. Kellogg's Tour of Britain, Milk Race.	Static	Limited potential for spend by	Spectator sport
11. Events riders	Cycling for charity mainly.	As above	Spectators, media, back-up teams Increasing	Greater potential for spend	Moderate

Note: Estimates in the table are based on evaluation of cycle hire holiday company brochures, qualitative comment by companies.
Source: Lumsdon (1996: 6-7).

A number of UK local authorities have appointed cycling officers, who have developed strategy documents for local use, but one of the principal catalysis for facilitating the development of a national cycle network in the UK is Sustrans.

Sustrans is a national sustainable transport and construction company operating as a charity 'which designs and builds routes for people'. One of this early aims was to develop a 2,000-mile national cycle network to link all the main urban centres in the UK, using a combination of traffic-calmed roads, cycle paths and disused railway lines and river/canal paths. This aim was realised in 1996 by a grant of £42.5 million from the Millenium Commission to create a 6,500-mile route on the basis of Sustrans' original vision, which would become the UK's National Cycle Network (Figure 5.4). Initial estimates seem to indicate that the network has the potential to generate 100 million trips per annum, 45 million of which will be cycle-based, of which 40 per cent will be leisure-based (18-20 million journeys a year). Sustrans (1995) argues that the network has the potential to generate £150 million in tourist receipts annually and to create 3,700 jobs. This has to be viewed within the context of cycle tourism, since Beoiley (1995) estimated that it generates £535 million a year from leisure day trips, domestic holidays and overseas trips. The C2c route illustrates the generative effect which new cycle routes can have on tourism.

It is a 170-mile coast-to-coast route in Northern England which Sustrains (1995) estimates attracted 15,000 mainly cycle tourists in an economically marginally area (West Cumbria and the North Pennines). Sustrans (1995) also has a pan-European perspective on cycle tourism, with its Europeart. Cycle Route Network (Figure 5.5). Some of the principal routes are :

- The 5,000 km Atlantis route (Isle of Skye in Scotland to Cadiz in Spain).
- The 470 km Noordzee route (Den Helder in the Netherlands to Boulogne-sur-mer in France).

Table 5.14. Characteristics and needs of different types of recreational and tourism cycling

Category of cycling activity	Characteristics of users	Nain constraints	Main needs	Growth potential
Day touring	Home (or holiday based excursions for whole or part of day. Traip of 20 miles upwards. mainly experienced users.	Few constraints although safety reaching minor sed network may be a problem. Design of roads a problem in some areas. Rail travel can be restricted.	Safe town/ country links, alternatives to busy main trunk roads. Improved access to rail network. Off-road cycleways.	Medium/High
Cycle hire	Causal cycling usually holiday-based for whole or part of day. Experienced and cyclists.	Lack of cycle hire centres in some areas. Problems of catering for diverse cycle types and sizes. Only a short season.	Off-road cycle routes in popular areas. Improved publicity and marketing. Need for information on where to cycle.	High
Cycle touring	Extended day touring requiring overnight accommodation. Mainly experienced cyclists which good knowledge.	Difficulties of transporting cycles by rail. Need for alternative routes in town centres/ on trunk roads. Accommodation sometimes a problem and conflict with cars in the summer. Cycle repair shops infrequent.	Good rual road network. Varied accommodation from campsites to hostels. Some off-road routes. Improved tourist information.	Medium/High
Organised cycle touring	Extended day touring requiring overnight accommodation. Less experienced cyclists and overseas visitors.	Difficulties of transporting cycles by rail.	Need for back up services. Quiet rural road network.	High
Mountain bikes	Major growth; car-based and hire-based activity.	Availability of off-highway facilities. Cost of bikes and hire. Lack of certainty about where cyclists can and cannot cycle. Conflict with other users.	Extensive network of off-road routes, e.g. forestry tracks. Improved information on rights of access. Signed trails. Cycle hire.	High

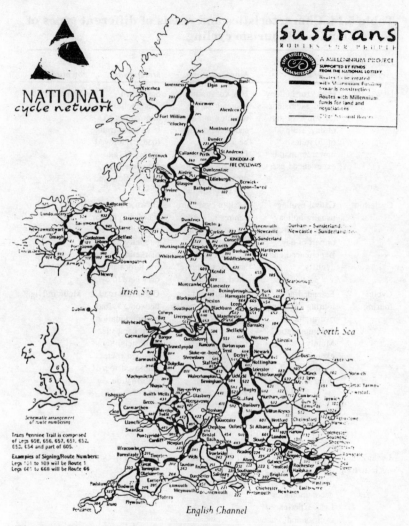

Fig. 5.4 : The national cycle network in the UK

Some commentators might view Sustran'(1996) work as making a valid contribution to local Agenda 21 initiatives, with its close working relationship with UK local authorities. It is also argued that since almost 75 per cent of leisure trips on the national Cycle Network are expected to be new or switched from other modes of transport (Susrrans 1995), it can make an important contribution to sustainable tourism

Fig. 5.5 : The national cycle network in the UK

and community-based strategies for environmental
management. In fact, the launch of the Kingfisher Trail in
Northern lowland in 1998, as part of the National Cycle
Network, is evidence of how the network can also contribute
to rural tourism initiatives. The Kingfisher Trail evolved from
a desire to harness the popularity of the Shannon-Ern
Waterway, using a network of quiet country roads. As a result

the trail is marketed as an activity-based rural tourism corridor with cycling as the vital transport link. It is similar in many ways to the widely cited Tarka Trail in Devon (Charlton 1998), which is a 180-mille walking route with a 30-mile cycling route incorporated within it. The scale of cycling on the Tarke Trail was estimated to be 75,000 cyclists in a four-month period, based on evidence from cycling businesses. Therefore, how sustainable is cycle tourism?

According to Lumsden (1996b : 10–12), there are three ways in which the National Cycle Network may contribute to sustainable tourism:

- By encouraging tourists to switch from cars to cycles at their destination, although it needs a cycle fluently culture to implement such changes in tourist attitudes. Lumsdon (1996b) argues that this could reduce recreational car journeys at the destination by 20-30 per cent.
- By reducing car-based day excursion, particularly at honeypot attractions or sites near to resorts and urban areas. Lumsdon (1996b) views the National Cycle Network as offering tourists 'escape routes' as evidence from the UK's Forest of Dean and Eye Valley implies (Lumsdon and Speakman 1995).
- A growth in cycle-based holidays in both the short break and longer duration category by UK residents are overseas visitors.

Lumsdon (1996b) also provides a detailed study of :

- The market for cycling opportunities.
- The supply of cycling opportunities.

Which is an excellent analysis of the marketing issues that need to be addressed to assist in promoting cycle tourism. However, Lumsdon (1997b : 126) views the development of a cycle culture as vital to encourage the growth of recreational and tourist cycling. Cycle tourism, as the examples of the Tarka Project and Kingfisher Project suggest, is able to make a valid contribution to sustainable tourism development, encouraging less environmentally damaging form of activity to be developed. Cycle tourism is certainly beginning to assume a much higher profile in the

UK, and if leisure use encourages people to become more avid cyclists and to reduce car usage, it will certainly make a valid contribution to Agenda 21 objectives in transport and tourism at a variety of spatial scales.

But how can one evaluate the extent of which sustainable tourism and tourist travel are realistic propositions in the next millenium?

The Evaluation of Sustainable Principles for Tourist Transport

During the 1980s the concept of mass tourism came under greater scrutiny as a range of influential books questioned whether the economic benefits of tourism were adequately compensating for the increasing environmental impact. As Wahab and Pigram argue, 'mass tourism, with the detriments it may inflict on the environment, has been severely criticised as a major environ-mental predator. It is therefore necessary that tourism adopts a different perspective that should be compatible, for all practical purposes, with the environment and the community in which it is active.' This close scrutiny of mass tourism was followed by the development of 'sustainable', 'responsible', 'green' or 'soft' tourism and a growing recognition that tourism cannot easily be managed where the carrying capacity of the environment is greatly exceeded. Marketing strategies with 'sustainable' in their title have emerged as a response to this interest in the environment, but all too often they have failed to grasp the carrying capacity and absolute numbers of tourists which different locations can support. Consequently, tourist transport has contributed to growing pressure on tourism environments by the provision of services to locations that have outgrown their carrying capacity. Therefore, it is not surprising to find criticisms of the sustainable tourism movement, which has been manipulated by certain commercial interests as a new trend they can use to sell tourism and transport services to the more discerning and environmentally aware tourists. Yet as Wahab and Pigram argue :

Tourism sustainability is a by-product of a multitrade of factors that contribute to the successful present integration and future continuity of tourism at the macro and micro level in the destination. As all socioeconomic, cultural, political and environmental factors are subject to change in time and space, sustainability is therefore a relative term and not an absolute fact.

Despite sustainablity being a relative term, there is growing evidence that tour operators and tourist transport providers have seen the positive benefits of appearing to offer sustainable products.

Wheeler (1992a) argues that it is difficult to visualise sustainable tourism as a realistic solution as the world is now experiencing 'megamass tourism', which is viewed as the next stage on from mass tourism. Although sustainable tourism (Wheeler 1992b) is emphasising small-scale individual tourist activities at specific locations and the substitution of the term 'traveller' for 'tourist', a rather elitist movement has developed, supported by a small number of more 'progressive tourists'. Herein lies a major contradiction is the sustainable debate: the insatiable demand for tourist travel is incompetible with the rather up-market, small-scale and expensive form of tourism which only a limited number of tourists are likely to be able to afford. As a concept, sustainability is still in its early stages of development and is unlikely to lead to major changes in the tourist transport system, being more appropriate as a marketing tool for 'new tourism' (Poon 1989). In all probability, sustainable tourist travel cannot be achieved until the concept has been researched further and the fundamental problem of megamass tourism is addressed.

Although the design of resort areas and man-made tourist attractions able to meet the demands of meagamass tourism may be able to deal with a high throughput of tourists in a restricted geographical area there will be a growing demand for tourist transport to reach these artificial and synthetic tourism environments. This may have the temporary effect of reducing pressure on other more fragile tourism environments while the needs of tourists are met by these staged tourist attractions. But the real prospect of environmental damage will emergy if mass tourism trends are based on the search for a more authentic experience (MacCannel 1976). The fundamental problem of environmental impacts is likely to remain and future technological advance may offer a lifeline for the environment if staged tourism can be developed further for the mass tourist, using new ideas such as 'virtual reality to meet the tourists' need for entertainment, excitement and pleasure.

As tourist transport operations are usually characterised by private sector ventures, voluntary agreements have typically been the basis for environmental management policies. Government organisation can assist in this process by ensuring that legislation is in place to encourage a reduction in environmental pollution from transport. Government commitment to sustainable transport policies in developed countries seems to have floundered as the decision to dergulate transport is unlikely to see such options implemented, given the reliance on profitability in tourist transport provision rather than environmental issues. Pigram (1992) argues that in the process of policy formulation and implementation of sustainable tourism options, it is important to recognise the role of major decision makers such as transport operators in influencing the long-term success of such schemes. Even so, Wahab and Pigram (1997) identify a very worrying trend which may militate against developing sustainable tourist transport system because :

> A growing trend in policy making in many countries is to leave tourism to private enterprise and current economic conventional thinking supports the role of market mechanisms, the pendulum shown signs of change in theory and in application...contries such as Canada and the United States have reduced or abolished the role of the public sector in national tourism administration in favour of private enterprise. State tourism bodies remain as promotion agencies at the macro level.

In other words, those public sector bodies able to understand and make the links between transport, tourism and sustainability at a policy-making level are no longer able to fulfil that role. This is certainly the case in New Zealand in relation to sustainable tourism.

Ultimately the tourists' desire for international and domestic travel may need to be the focus of long-term educational strategies to identify some of the problems travel, tourism and transport pose for the environment, and codes of practice may assist in that respect. One radical solution may be to increase the cost of travel and introduce government regulations to restrict the demands in order to reduce the impact on the environment. Yet there are many political and ethical objections to such an approach since it is reminiscent of the situation in some Eastern European bloc counties before the collapse of communist rule and it would be tantamount to an infringement of individual freedom in democratic societies. Increasing the cost and restricting the opportunity to travel has other social implications because it may run contrary to the objectives of social tourism which aims to make travel and holdiday accessible to all social groups. A partnership approach between responsible transport and tour operators and governments committed to making tourists more aware of their own actions may be one way forward. Instead of tourist travel being regulated, tourists should be encouraged to exercise greater restraint in their demand for travel, though it is evident that there is no short-term solution to preventing the environmental impact of tourist transport systems.

Summary

The human effects and environmental consequences of tourist transport have led to a greater awareness of how tourist transport system interact with the human and physical environment. The concept of 'sustainable tourism has burdened itself with incompatible conflicting objectives–small scale sensitivity and limited number to be achieved in tandem with economic viability and significant income and employment impacts' (Whaler 1991 : 95). In other words, sustainable tourism's implicit assumption that smaller-scale tourist activities will result from such development could pose threats to the economic threshold at which tourist travel services anr provided. It sustainable tourism were viewed as the only legitimate form of tourism, it would have unrealistic social impacts by limiting travel to a privilege minority. This a appeases the guilt of the thinking tourist while sumultaneously providing the holiday experience they or we want. The industry is happy because the more discerning (and expensive) range of market can be catered for by ligitimately opening up new areas to tourism.

This highlights the rather superficial nature of the sustainabilities concept (Wheeler 1994), which does not really offer any long-term solutions to the tourist and the transport provider because it fails to address the global impact of tourism, which is too large a problem for governments and transport operators to address in isolation. Even if tourist transport providers and tour operators withdrew from carrying tourists to sensitive environments, the competitive nature of tourist transport provision in market economies would mean the another rival operator, with less interest in environmental issues, might enter the market. Environmental Auditing and Environmental Impact Assessment are moving the transport business towards considering the consequences of transporting tourists to different environments but the reliance on private sector cooperation in minimising their impact may only result in action :

> Where the benefits [of environmental auditing] are largely enjoyed by third parties or the general public....if consumers' search for quality embraces an increasing environmental awareness, the tourism industry would face demanded pressure to adopt environment auditing more widely.

Even so, the growing interest in alternative modes of transport, such as cycling and government commitment to fund infrastructure such as the National Cycle Network, are econuraging signs for more sustainable forms of tourism transport for the next millenium. Change does not take place rapidly, as a major culture shift is needed in tourists' and transport providers' attitudes, so that more environmentally sensitive and sustainable tourist activities are promoted.

6

Prospects and Challenges for Tourist Transport

Introduction

The relationship between tourism and transport by developing the concept of a tourist transport system as a means of analysing the processes shaping the provision and consumption of transport services by tourists. Throughout the book, transport is emphasised as a dynamic and active element in the tourist's experience of travelling because it is a vital part of the process of tourism. Some of the first-generation tourism textbooks (e.g., Mathieson and Wall 1982) regarded tourist transport an essential part of tourism but not worthy of study in its own right. In fact, a number of subsequent texts (e.g., Cooper et al. 1993, 1998) continue to view transport as a passive element in the tourist experience (Ryan 1996) and it remains a descriptive feature of most texts.

In the scope of multidisciplinary research on tourism and transport is reviewed in terms of the concepts and methods of each discipline (economics, geography, marketing and management) use to analyse tourist transport. However, the different philosophical backgrounds of researchers from these disciplines mean that their approach to tourist transport is not easy to synthesise into a holistic framework. Moreover, the tendency for researchers to retain their disciplinary training–whether in economics, geography, marketing or management–has simple contributed to the growing body of knowledge on transport and tourism. For our understanding of tourist transport systems and the tourist's experience of travel to grow, a greater degree of coherence and a theoretical basis needs to be developed. This means that research will need to be interdisciplinary in nature. Interdisciplinary research requires people from different disciplines to collaborate and focus on a specific research problem, where different questions are asked about the topic without each researcher losing sight of the problem under consideration. This may help to integrate the contributions which different disciplines can make to the analysis of tourist transport systems in order to achieve a more holistic understanding of the operation, management and use of transport services by tourists.

Although there is not space within this introductory book to undertake a comprehensive review of transport and tourism, it has sought to focus on how the consumer, provider and other agencies (e.g., national governments) interact in different transport systems. The concept of a tourist transport system was developed as a framework in which to understand the interrelationships between different elements in such systems. Using a system approach to the analysis of tourist transport also highlighted the importance of *inputs* to the system (e.g., the demand and supply) as well as *controlling influences* (e.g., government policy) and *outputs* (the tourist travel experience) and the effect on the environ-ment. The book has also sought to identify a number of process which characterise the tourist transport system. For example, deregulation and privatisation is a process now affecting tourist transport systems in North America, Western Europe and Australasia (Button and Gillingwater 1991) as well as communist states such as China (Tapling 1993). Within the existing literature, the discussion of tourist transport systems has remained fragmented and dependent upon generalised and empirical studies or extremely specialised studies of both tourism and transport. The interface between tourism and transport has not been integrated into a holistic framework. Wilst tourism is now regarded as a complex phenomenon by educators and researchers, its frequent association with transport has meant that social science researchers have failed to integrate these issues in a framework where the complementarity between tourism and transport could be explored further. The tendency within tourism research to focus on typologies of tourism and tourists has led to a critical separation of the tourist from the mode of transport they use. This has the effect of contributing to the separation of tourism and transport research , with tourist motivation to travel viewed in isolation from the process of travelling. The result is that tourist travel is divided into two discrete elements (transport and the tourist) rather than being conceptualised as a continuous process using a systems approach. But what are the process shaping tourist transport in the new millennium?

Tourist Transport Provision in the late 1990s and the New Millennium

One of the overriding themes affecting the tourist transport system is globalisation especially in those sectors which deal with the management and logistics of international travel (Lovelock and Yip 1996). Globalisation inevitably produces 'winners and losers's in the pursuit of business and four distinct processes are associated with it. There are :

- *Deregulation,* where the entry barriers to many sectors of the tourist transport business have been removed and large oligophilies are challenged the new entrants (Pearce 1995b). As the example of the US domestic airline industry illustrates, in newly deregulated indicters, competition increased at a rapid pace. However, there is debate within the American domestic airline industry as to whether consumers have been the main beneficiaries, with lower prices. Goetz and Sutton (1997) explain that the benefits of deregulation have accrued to those passengers travelling on trunk routes, while business travellers and passengers travelling to/from more peripheral locations have experienced higher fares.

- *Technological change,* which has revolutionised the organisation, management and day-to-day running of tourist transport businesses with the introduction of information technology (IT). IT has also helped reduce some of the costs of business operations. The introduction of CRSs and GDSs have certainly assisted with the globalisation of the supply of tourist transport services. The introduction of the Internet has also had a major impact on the supply of transport services (Macdonald) Wallace 1997). In fact many of the world's airlines now have Internet sites and as Whitaker and Levere (1997) show, some are being used for bookings, but 'the scope and standard of airline-related material on the Internet varies drama-tically'. In fact the evolution of Internet sites and their use in marketing has now moved beyond a tool simply to advertise and sell tourist transport services. This traditional use, based on sales and marketing, is reflected in the UK express coach network site—http://www.national-express.co.uk. However, there is evidence that some companies (e.g., Red Funnel Ferries is Southampton) are developing a more holistic approach to transport and tourism and using the Internet to address the impact of competitive force such as rival carriers. The company's Internet site –http://www.redfunnel.co.uk contains the traditional sales and marketing function. But it also moves into a tactical marketing role where bookings can be auctioned and place-marketing is undertaken in relation to the main destination they serve–the Isle of White. The website provides ideas for theme itineraries and the main attractions to visit which complement the tourism marketing activities of the public sector (e.g., the Southern England Tourist Board). This is certainly leading the way in providing a seamless tourism experience facilitated by technology and the activities of the transport operator. Some airlines also often sophisticated system allowing passengers to plan book and pay for their flights other can master little more than sketchy corporate information (Whitaker and Levere 1997 : 27).

- *Regional change :* The highest costs for air travel remain in Europe and North America whereas in other trading blocs such as ASEAN, lower costs exist. For tourist transport providers in the global economy, it can mean airliners are competing on a different cost basis as Halon (1996) observes in terms of regional wage rates and remuneration of airline employees.

- *Hypercompetition:* Within the global marketplace, tourist transport provider are facing pressures continually to improve products and to remain competitive. In some case, organisation and constantly struggling to remain in business as experience in the international airline industry suggests. As the privatisation characteristic of the 1990s and deregulation (see Meersam and van de Voorde 1996) seem set to continue, established industry leaders and find their position challenged or destroyed by fierce completions. According to D'Aveni (1998), this hypercompetition is typified by :

- Rapid product innovation.
- Aggressive competition.
- Shorter product life cycles.
- Businesses experimenting with meeting customers' needs.
- The rising importance of alliance.
- The destruction of norms and rules of national oligopolies.

  D'Aveni (1998) identifies four processes which are fuelling hypercompetition :

- Customers requiring better quality at lower prices One of the innovations airlines have pursued to develop improved quality at lower prices is in-flight catering (Jones 1995)

- Rapid technological change, especially the use of IT.

- the rise of aggressive large companies willing to enter markets for a number of years with a loss-leader product in the hope of destroying the competition and capturing the market in the long term.

- Government policies towards barriers to competition are being progressively removed. This is evident in the tourist transport sector throughout the world, albeit to differing degrees depending on the political persuasion and commitment to deregulation.

At first sight, D'Aveni's (1998) processes are not particularly different from those listed under globalisation (e.g., deregulation, technological change, consumer preferences and regional change). But the fundamental different lies in the business strategy of hypercompetitors. As D'Aveni (1998) argues, hypercompetitors tend to destroy the existing competencies of businesses. Those affected by such change are often trapped by an inability to think laterally and to adopt new competencies. Even when new competencies are introduced, businesses often have difficulty in diffusing them throughout their organisation. Some belatedly look towards the concept of 'change management' but this can sometimes be too little action too late. Often firms are so severely affected by hypercompetions and their action, that their reponses are bound by age-old relactions based on previous rules of completion, However, the hypercompetitor can only remain in a competitive position while it retains the advantage.

According to D'Aveni (1998), hypercompetitors enter the market by disrupting the competition in some of the following ways :

- By redefining the product market, thereby redefining the meaning of the quality while offering it at a lower price. This is the strategy adopted by EasyJet in the UK which entered the market with low-cost air travel from Luton Airport to challenge the market leaders (e.g., BA, British Midland and KLM UK).
- By modifying the industry's purpose and focus by bundling and splitting industries. BA's response to EarJet was to reduce fares in the short term, but then it provided a splitting action by establishing a similar low-cost operation based at London Stansted, with lower landing fees. This avoid eroding profit margins and using high-cost airline capacity from Heathrow and Gatwick. In other words, BA can

operate a loss-leader small business to compete head on which FasyJet on equal terms. A similar response occurred in New Zealand in the mid-1990s when Air New Zealand established a low-cost airline (Freedom Air) to compete with the Hamilton-based airline Kiwi Air.

- By disrupting the supply chain by redefining the knowledge and know-how needed to deliver the product to the customer.
- By harnessing the global resources from alliances (see Dresner and Windle 1996) to compete with the non-aligned businesses. This in particularly acute in the airline industry although to data the term 'hypercompetitor' has not been used to describe the business strategy of key players.

The process of globalisation and hypercompetition are powerful forces affecting the tourist transport sector and a number of themes emergy which are worthy of further discussion :

- The role of the consumer.
- The growing significance of service quality.
- The introduction of Total Quality Management Systems.

The Tourist as a Consumer

Much of the rhetoric and hype associated with the rapid expansion of popular business books and the elevation of individuals to 'guru' status in the 1980s and 1990s is characterised by one consistent theme : that businesses need to understand the customer and to get near to them as 'end-users'.

Swarbrooke (1997) reiterates the importance of consumer behaviour research in tourism, since from a tourist transport perspective it allows businesses to plan infrastructure developments, identify product opportunities, set price levels for products and identify market segments and the best marketing medium to promote the product. Consumer behaviour research also allows businesses to modify their product and its delivery to align it more closely with consumer expectations. For the tourist transport business, understanding how tourists make their purchasing decisions and the factors affecting their choice of product is critical. In particular, the travellers' predisposition towards certain forms of transport will obviously affect their overall satisfaction with the product. For the tourism sector in general, Swarbrooke (1997) identifies a number of weakness in consumer behaviour research in the UK which are particularly relevant to the transport sector (although the exception may be the major airlines who commission in-house research that emains confidential and commercially sensitive). The main weaknesses are :

- An absence of reliable and up-to-data a feature emphasisted.
- A lack of longitudinal studies to trace the evolution of consumer behaviour in tourism through time.
- The methodologies and techniques used to collect data on consumer behaviour in tourism remain relatively crude and unsophisticated.
- The most robust data collated by private sector companies remains inaccessible to researchers.
- Methods of segmenting the market remain outdated due to a reliance on the lifecycle concepts and age, despite major societal and value changes which have questioned their validity in the late 1990s.
- Cross cultural differences in tourism markets and a predisposition towards using specific tourist transport mode remain poorly understood. The research identified by Lumsdon (1997), in prt, addresses some of these issues in relation to cycling.
- There are few media available to disseminate results to the practitioner audience.

As a result, consumer behaviour is one area which tourist transport operators will need to focus on if they seek to understand what motivates tourists to travel and to select specific modes of transport.

Tourist transport systems are likely to be affected by various opportunities and constraints on tourist travel in the late 1990s and beyond. For example, congestion of airspace in developed countries such as North America and Western Europe (French 1994, 1997b) will remain a persistent problem for policy makers and transport planners in late 1990s and new millennium. At the same time the demand for long-haul travel is developed for transports provides and tours operators if cohstraints cannot be covercome, Environmental issues will also feature more prominently in tourist transport systems as a new generation of travellers, having become familiar with green issues in the 1980s, emerge as consumers of tourist transports services. Understanding the relative importance of these factors in shaping the tourist's desire to travel on different modes of transport will be a major challenge for service providers, as the sustainability debate (Weiler 1993) focuses on more environmentally sensitive and novel modes of transport.

Increasingly, the patronage of tourist transport service is going to depend upon the ability of providers to differentiate their services on the basis of image market positioning and reputation for service quality. The 1990s are emerging as the decade of the consumer in relation to tourist travel, the providers responding to legitimate requests for higher standards of comfort, reliability and courtesy as part of the travel experience. The new millenium is also set to see a continuity and intensity of these processes of change, while the discussion of globalisation and hypercompetion indicates the pressure on transport provides will intensify, Passengers are now recognised as customers and their rights and needs are beginning to gain a higher profile in the provision, quality and management of tourist transport services.

Service Quality Issues in Tourist Transport

The concept of service was introduced in the context of marketing. While that discussion provided a broad overview

of the importance of service issues in tourist, transport, it is
evident from the processes affecting the tourist as a
consumer, that service quality is assuming a greater role in
their purchasing decisions any travel behaviour. Irons (1994)
argues that services are relationships and that whether that
relationship is a transient one or a longerterm proposition,
it needs to be conducted in a professional and consistent
manner. As Irons (1994 : 13) shows,

> Such a relationship will be based on a series of contacts
> or interactions. It is from these interactions with the
> organisation that consumers form their perceptions...
> to assess value, decide to buy, repeat purchase or
> recommend to others.

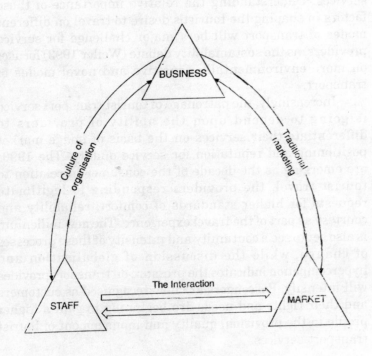

Fig. 6.1 : Iron's service quality triangle.

˙ .Such interactions are also repeated within the organisation and Irons (1994) expresses this process as a triangle (Figure 6.1) Irons explain the triangle in the following way:

- An organisation need to associate its internal culture with the one it portrays externally and this underpins the relationships evident in Figure 6.1.
- Within the organisation, power needs to be devolved so that the relationships can be developed and the appropriate skill and know-how is provided at the point where costumer satisfaction is met.
- The organisational values and culture need to be clearly understood by all employees so that they affect their actions and activities in ralation to customers.
- Managers need to lead the process, empowering people at the various levels in the organisation to achieve customer-related targets. In other words, managers need not only to exercise a degree of control in the management function, but also to lead the organisation in this era of the consumer.
- A customer focus is critical rather than a focus first on the product and then its purchasers.

To create a service culture in an organisation, Irons (1997) identified the following key points :

- Service businesses need to identify what the priorities are for the customer. Irons (1997) cites the example of Southwest Airlines in the USA which saw a set or priorities–reliability, low fates, personal treatment– and set about 'rigorously building the airline around meeting these needs and cutting out those things the customer did not want's.
- Organisations need to develop a clear vision of 'what they stand for and where they aspire to go...This vision should be for the customer, for the staff and for the owners'.
- Organisations and employees need to communicate so that they understand what is to be achieved, why, how and the role of employees in the corporate vision.
- The organisation needs to learn from its experience through problem-solving and how this can benefit its vision.

- The service culture needs to be led from the top in the organisation rather than through passive forms of managerialism.
- It is at the point of interaction between the market and the consumer that value can be created.
- Service delivery is an integral part of the process for service organisations and it should drive the business.

While the principle outlined by Irons (1994, 1997) may be useful in outlining how businesses may create a service culture, at a practical level the service requirements of the tourist transport sector need to be examined in more derail. This is because in certain sectors of the tourist transport business, service qualities offer particular challenges to operators because of the nature of the service interaction. It should also be emphasised that in some case, tourists' expectations are rising beyond the reach of mass transport providers and their ability to meet these needs.

Within the literature on tourism and transport there are comparatively few systematic reviews of service quality. While studies reviewed on rail travel highlighted the experience of InterCity prior to privatisation, few other reviews exist. Those studies which have been undertaken have largely focused on the airline sector (e.g. Ostrowski et al 1993, 1994; Van Borrendam 1989(. Probably the most influential publication to date is that by Witt and Muhlemann (1995) which not only reviews the previous research in the area, but also identifies the idiosyncrasies and conditions which influence service quality in airlines.

Service quality : Conceptual Issues

Ostrowski et al (1993) argued that service quality issues were comparatively poorly developed in the airline industry, based on a survey of 6,000 travellers using two US airlines. They concluded that there was considerable scope for improvement. Hamill (1993) places this in the context of changes in the aviation sector in the 1990s, with deregulation and privatisation forcing companies to become more customer-oriented. This process is continuing in the late

1990s in Europe with liberalisation (Graham 1998), since Lufthansa prepared itself for privatisation in 1997. By January 1998, at least four other European flag carriers had prepared for privatisation (Air France, TAP Air Portugal, Alitalia and LOT of Poland). Hamill (1993) also points to the strategies pursued by some airlines, where the use of computer reservation systems (CRSs) was seen as improving service. Yet this development has no direct impact on the actual service encounter and such a perception is futher evidence of the need for a focus on service quality issues.

Witt and Muhlemann (1995) explore the problem of establishing a working definition of service quality. Gronroos (1984) introduced the idea of a *technical quality* dimension (the customer interaction with the service organisation) and a *functional quality* dimension (the process through which the technical quality is delivered). As a result, the consumer's perception of service is a result of the service dimension combining technical and functional aspects. In contrast, Gummesson (1993) argued that four qualities affected customer perceived satisfaction. These were:

- design quality,
- delivery quality,
- relational quality,
- production quality.

A further model of quality was developed by Zeithmal et al (1990) which was based on gap analysis and focused on four dimensions :

- customers not knowing what to expect,
- inappropriate service quality standards,
- a service performance gap,
- company·promises not matched by delivery.

To evaluate quality, Zeithmal et. al., (1990) used ten dimensions which were reduced to five elements :

- tangibles,
- reliability,
- responsiveness,
- assurance,
- empathy.

which are combined in the SERQUAL model used to evaluate customers' perceptions of quality. While SERQUAL and measures of perceived quality were certainly dominant elements in the research agenda in the late 1980s and early 1990s Witt and Muhlemann (1995 : 34) argue the 'the successful organisation will be one which establishes a total quality culture' based on total quality management (TQM). But what is TQM, where does it originate from and how will it affect tourist transport providers?

Total Quality Management

It is widely acknowledge that the 1980s was many service providers and North America respond to a perceived 'quality' crisis posed by products and services offered by rivals in the Pacific Rim (Deeming (1982). Many service providers responded with corporate strategies focused on quality issues as a method of retaining market share. Yet if the late 1980s were characterised by a business environment committed to quality, the 1990s were dominated by total quality management (TQM) as a more sophisticated form of recognising customers' needs as an integral part of an organisation's goals. TQM developed as a corporate business management philosophy and it even has an academic journal—TQM—devoted to research in this area. Why should this be of interest to the tourist transport system in the 1990s? The growing concern for consumers, quality and total supply management in the tourist transport system is part of the move towards TQM among service providers. Furthermore, TQM is likely to assume a greater role in academic and commercial research on tourist transport in the 1990s.

TQM is an all-embracing approach which enables an organisation to develop a more holistic view of consumers, quality issues and service provision as an ongoing process. Yet one of the principles of TQM—the concern for quality—is explicitly dealt with in detail in this book. One difficulty is in establishing a universal definition of quality which could be applied to tourist transport system. Dotchin and Oakland (1992) provide an excellent review of this issue, citing the work by Townsend and Gebhart (1986) which distinguishes between the subjective evaluation of quality be the customer (quality of perception) and the provider's more objective assessment (quality of fact). Chearly the meaning of quality will very according to the context and the perception of who is establishing what can be deemed as quality, as the discussion of conceptual issues of quality showed. While the journal TQM contains many interesting discussions of this issue, opeationalisings TQM in a tourist transport context requires organisation to work towards specific goals forcused on an agreed concept of quality. Corporate commitment is required so that TQM permeates all areas of the company's business. TQM also provides an organisation with the opportunity to monitor and implement internal procedures and to control supplies using established quality standards such as BS 5750.

One of the real challenges for TQM in tourist transport systems is to establish what the customer considers as excellece in service provision and the design of service delivery systems to deal with individual tourists' requests requirements and needs. Many corporation involved in tourist transport provision are trying to make individual tourists feel more valued as customers but, until delivery systems are able to deal fully with this issue, operatcrs will be unable to claim success in TQM. It is at the strategic policy and planning stage that organisa-tions may need to agree on how to improve continuously and strive for quality in service provision so that the tourist's travel experience is enhanced. One challenge is to ensure that the process of travel is not perceived as such a mundane and stressful experience for some tourists.

Implementing a TQM strategy is no easy task for organisations where it may involve a change in corporate culture. Nevertheless, a number of critical factors charac-terise success in TQM in service provisions. As Table 6.1 shows, senior management set on developing a policy for TQM will need to follow certain principles and management strategies. Many of the principles discussed in Table 6.1

expand the ideas developed by Irons (1994, 1997) on
developing a service culture, while TQM is a more systematic
attempt to ensure quality is dealt with in a consistent
manner. Witt (1995) cites Oakland's (1989) route to
implementation as a series of steps which are outlined in
Figure 6.2. Oakland (1989) explains that the CEO of any
organisation must begin by *understanding* the concepts of
TQM and the route to implementation. This then needs to
be followed by *commitment and policy* to set out what the
organisation hopes to achieve from its quality strategy.
Following this, it may be necessary to alter the
organisational structure to fit which the new ethos. In terms
of *measurement,* the inputs (raw materials), output
(product), performance of employees and any costs of failure
need to be quantified. Even though it is often hard to
measure intangible elements in a service, the SERVQUAL
survey tool might be used. The process of *planning* is the
next step, to assess the nature of the service process, who it
serves, when and where. This is a good point to use the
results of the SERVQUAL survey to plan changes to the
delivery of the service. The next stage is called *system,* where
a quality manual is produced to explain how the company
undertakes its quality policies, with the manage-ment
system in place. This is also an opportunity to specify the
nature of the product being delivered and how it is produced.
The term *capability* refers to be next stage where the
organisation can assess whether it has the ability to meet
each customer's set of requirements or if modifications are
needed. This is followed by a *control* function to ensure the
service is delivered in a consistent manner within acceptable
tolerance levels, on each occasion. Since service delivery
often involves more than one person, the role of *teamwork*
needs to be considered. This may also involve the use of
quality circles in the organisation, where employees work
in teams to solve problems and promote a commitment to
quality. To ensure a continuous improvement in quality,
training is essential. At the top of the steps is TQM
implementation. Porter and Parker (1992) notes that

management behaviour and their willingers to carry through such programmes is often the key to the successful implementation of TQM.

Table 6.1 : Implementing a Total Quality Management programme.

Senior management in an organisation seeking to implement a TQM programme should consider :

- An organisation needs long-term commitment to constant improvement.
- Culture of 'right first time' is required.
- Employees need to consider more than just the price–they must also consider to total cost.
- Improvements in delivery systems need to be managed.
- The introduction of methods of supervision and trading needs to the explained to avoid fear and inteansigence.
- Breaking down interdepartmental barriers by managing the service process to improve communications and teamwork.
- Eliminating.
  – goals without methods
- – standards based only on numbers.
  – fiction, get facts by using the correct tools (e.g. by using appropriate research techniques)
- Developing an ongoing human resource management strategy to develop experts and 'gurus'.
- Developing a systematic approach to managing the implementation of TQM.

The implementation of a TQM programme can be shaped using these principles to achieve: *outcomes* which involve:

- The identification of customer-supplier relationships.
- Managing processes.
- Cultural change.
- Commitment.

which may needs to be accompanied by management necessities including :

– systems based on international standards.

– teams to monitor and improve quality throughout the systems,

– tools to analyse and predict what type of corrective action is needed to improve quality.

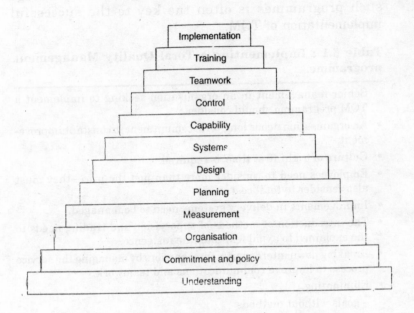

Fig. 6.2 : Implementation of a TQM programme for a tourist transport operator.

However, interest in TQM is not substitute for the organisation and logistical skills involved in coordinating and managing rourist transport systems. Conveying large numbers of people over short and long distances for pleasure and business is a complex process requiring a great deal of planning and organisation on a day-to-day basis as well as in the longer term. Adding a concern for quality provision in this process makes the delivery of service a more complex undertaking and it is not surprising that service interruptions occur due to the sheet volume and scale of people handled in tourist transport systems. But when things do go wrong, companies and their front-line staff must be empowered to deal with incidents, or systems must be in place to deal with crises when they occur. Whether a tourist transport provider prefers a gradual improvement approach to quality or a TQM approach, it is worth considering some of the impediments to quality improvements in relation to the airline sector.

Quality Issues in the Airline Industry

Witt and Muhlemann (1995) identify two persistent problems to meeting travellers' requirements :

- How may a quality service be defined, what factors influence the customer's experience and how may these factors be identified?
- How may performance or delivery of the product be measured or contoured, given the intangible nature of services? (Witt and Muhlemann 1995 : 35)

Witt and Muhlemann (1995 : 35) identify the following five factors which may pose particular problems

- The mixed nature of airline markets where leisure and business travellers may be mixed on any flight, each with different requirements
- Lack of direct control over factors contributing to the traveller's experience, including:
  - ticket purchases from travel agents, which can involve mistakes in ticketing.
  - experiences at the airport (e.g. air traffic control problems and weather conditions)
  - the impact of airline alliances, where partner airlines may not have harmonised standards of service to ensure a consistent quality throughout the journey regardless of the carrier.
- Congestion and slot availability, where large carriers dominate the main slots at a time when air travel in Europe and North America is becoming more congested
- Restrictions versus deregulation, where spatial inequalities occur in service provision depending upon the traveller's location in the system and choice of route, as Goetz and Sutton (1997) observe in the USA

- Differentiation in the product, where the airlines seek to segment the market and attract more travellers through the use of marketing tools such as frequent flyer programmes (Mason and Barker (1996 ; Beaver 1996).

Some airlines, such as SAS, have implemented quality management systems moving hear to TQM and BA is a further example of an airline which has attracted a great deal of attention in the research literature for its focus on quality (see Hamill 1993 for example). KLM is also implementing a full TQM scheme (Van Borrendam 1989). However, as Witt and Muhlemann (1995: 39) suggest, 'Singapore Airlines is probably the best known for customer focus'. Aside from quality issues, there are a range of other themes likely to affect tourist transport in the next millennium.

Government policy, planning and investment in infrastructure assume a significant role in facilitating the efficient movement of people for the purpose of tourism. In this context, the London Tourist Board's (1990) *At the Crossroads: The Future of London's Transport* reaffirms the essential relationship between transport and tourism dealt. The London Tourist Board study is unique in this respect since it recognised that :

- An efficient transport network is necessary for tourists to gain access to a destination such as London; tourism would not exist without a transport network as it is part of the tourism infrastructure.
- An integrated transport network with convenient transfers between different modes of transport is essential, with reasonably priced travel options.
- Within the destination, tourists need a choice of transport to transfer between the port of arrival and their final destination.
- Investment in public transport provides social, economic and environmental benefits for both residents and tourists alike. Investment in transport infrastructure is a long term proposition and is unlikely to

yield tangible benefits in market economies in relation to tourism. Yet without it, tourism would not be able to develop.

As the London Tourist Board Study notes, the development and long-terms prosperity of tourism depends on transport both to make destinations accessible and to facilitate tourist travel within the destination area. Efficiency, safety and ease of travel and convenient inter-changes are likely to be viewed as important performance indicators by users of tourist transport systems. These principles apply to the wider context of tourist travel and making the travel experience more rewarding is one major challenge for all parties involved in providing tourist transport systems.

Withing the airline sector, concerns with dropping yields and moves to secure, the loyalty of economy travellers contune to face many companies. In terms of consumer behaviour, economy class travellers tend to seek the cheapest fare, which means a great emphasis on securing the loyalty of commercial passengers, regardless of whether they travel economy or business class. Even some of the British railway companies, such as Midland Mainline, which operates London to the East Midlands/ South Yorkshire services, have recongnised this. Their introduction of a premium business service follows the same principle for securing the commercial traveller. Many of the world's airlines have turned to the creative flair of advertising agencies to appeal to their prestige markets such as the business traveller. For example, in August 1997 Air New Zealand launched a new advertising compaign designed by Saatchi and Saatchi. At the same time, a database marketing company worked with Air New Zealand to identify its Koru Club and Air Points members. A 'teaser' was then set to select a few members and encourage them to watch the advertisement when it was first screened, motivated by a prize opportunity. The chosen few then received a follow-up mailing some weeks after the advertisement extrolling the virtues of flying Air New

Zealand. At the same time Air New Zealand customer support staff also received a newsletter to explain the focus of the campaign on business travellers, highlighting what they needed to do to show that Air New Zealand is unique.

What such campaigns show is that the marketing activities are selective and based on the concept of hand-picking. While the airline continued to use powerful national icons, such as the Koru image which is displayed on the tail of every aircraft, it is apparent that the targeting of high-yield travellers is now becoming the key focus for airlines. Such activities are likely to continue in the transport sector, as businesses seek to improve yields.

In a similar vein, airlines are also securing software which will improve yields. For example, Air New Zealand already uses Sabre Technology solutions in yield management and flight planning systems. In December 1997, Air New Zealand was in the process of signing a contract with Sabre to build a new Internet site and to introduce new software to replace its flight operation and crew management system. This illustrates that IT is enabling tourist transport operators to remain competitive and hopefully to reduce operational costs.

Transport operators are also turning to new solutions to reduce other components of their operational costs. For example, in May 1997 Cathay Pacific launched new Airbus A340 services on its Auckland–Hong Kong route–Airbus Industries claims that the fuel cost per seat of the A340 is 40 per cent of that for a Boeing 747. This was part of a US9 billion fleet replacement programme for Cathay Pacific. Fleet replacement costs represent a perennial problem for many airlines. The capital cost of fleet replacement means more innovative solutions need to be sought such as lease-buy schemes, manufacturer funding and straight lease schemes. This frees airlines from major sunk capital counts over and above those needed to service debt repayment on leases. Even so, cash -rich airlines such as Singapore Airlines continue to purchase aircraft and options on future aircraft rather than seeking leasing options.

Table 6.2 : The potential for cost reductions among airlines.

| | Cost drivers | | |
Cost items	Route network	Fleet composition	Company policies
Aircraft crew costs	XXX	XXX	XXX
Engineering overheads	X	XXX	
Direct engineering costs	X	XXX	X
Marketing	XXX		X
Aircraft standing	XXX	X	
Stations and ground services	X		X
Passenger services	X		X
General and administrative costs	X		X
Fuel		X	
Airport and en route costs	X		
Direct passenger service			X

Notes

XXX Significant cost reduction potential

X Some cost implications

A recent study by Seristo and Vesalainen (1997) offers a number of insights into the actual cost and revenue factors associated with airline operations. This is important in an age of cost-competitiveness, especially when airlines have been trimming staffing levels (Alamdari and Morrell 1997) and salaries in the 1990s to remain afloat. Yet as Sersto and Vepsalainen (1997 : 11) argue, 'for many a carrier even more critical measures will be needed to achieve sustainable profitability', which is also relevant to the wider tourist transport sector. In the analysis of cost derivers in 42 of the world's airlines, a number of variables were examined :

- The fleet composition of airlines.
- The flying personnel used, particularly the number of flight crew per aircraft.
- The route network.

- Cost drivers, operating expenses and profitability in terms of :
    - the composition of traffic,
    - route structure,
    - salaries/remunerating levels.

Using quantitative research methods (e.g., factor analysis), the variable were analysed and a model was built (Figure 6.3). This model highlights how various factors and variables were interrelated and as a result, it identifies the cost items and the factors where cost reductions were possible. Such analyses highlight that transport operators will need to focus on systematic appraisals of costs in a climate of increasing customer expectations, competitiveness amongst providers and declining yield per passenger through time. One strategy which airlines have followed is the pursuit of cost savings by divesting themselves of non-core activities such as in-flight catering operations. In June 1997, for example, Air New Zealand sold its catering business and planned to involve IBM in running its computer centre in a contracting-out of specialist non-core activities. These changes were identified in the company's 'Project Save' in the 1997/98 financial year, which is expected to save up to NZ$100 million in operating costs. Such savings are also expected to liberate capital to be reinvested in core business activities (Hanning (1997).

Interest in environmental factors such as sustainability in tourist transport seems set to continue as a powerful theme embracing tourism well into the next millennium. A growing interest is the use of public transport inrastructure to support tourist travel (Charlton 1998) is evident, with initiatives such as the Devon and Cornwall Rail Partnership, which has attracted leisure travel to offset losses in the non-leisure local rail market. Such rail tourism projects certainly have the potential to offer an alternative to the ingrained role of the car in recreational and tourist travel (Page 1998). Public transport certainly has a valid role to play in achieving sustainable tourism objectives in local areas. Such initiates not only make a contribution to the reduction of congestion and environmental pollution in areas of natural beauty, but also offer access opportunities for but disabled, cyclists and casual travellers in place of the car. Even in urban areas, the development of public transport system may offer the tourist more opportunities to enjoy the urban evvironment without the stress of parking and driving a car is congested cities. Brooks (1995) documented the reintro-duction of historic Victorian trams in Chrstchurch, New Zealand, where the five vintage trams cover a 2.5 km inner city track. By 1997 it was obvious that they were not profitable. While the trams undoubtedly offer an attraction for the tourist, like those used in Blackpool and Fylde in Lancashire, UK, it is evident that transport systems may sometimes need to be subsidised to generate tourist business for other sectors of the urban economy (as is the case with the tourist tram service in Melbourne) (Page 1993a, 1995b). Yet this seems to run somewhat contrary to the political policy-making environment of the late 1990s where transport users, particularly tourists, need to pay the economic cost of transport.

Within an international context, there is also evidence to suggest that with the globalisation of the airline industry and other transport sectors there is a growing need for an agency to ensure fair competition. According to downs and Tunney (1997), European completion law for the air transport industry may 'become the foundation stone for global competition rules for aviation' (Downes and Tunney 1997 : 76) The World Trade Organisation is seen as the most likely body to ensure competion rules are upheld. At the same time tourist transport providers are facing an operating environment where increased health and safety regulations (Caves 1996) and airport risk controls as well as measures such as the EU's (1995) *Protection of Tourists* (European Parliament 1995) place a greater onus on the operator and package to provide accurate information to travellers. These types of measure are likely to encourage transport operators to consider the tourist experience within the context of ever-increasing demands for quality improvements.

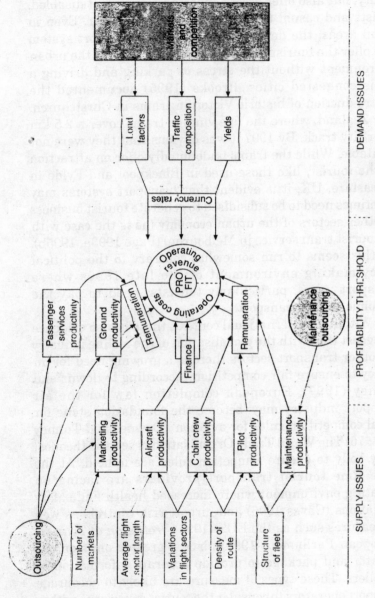

Fig. 6.3 : Interdependencies in the factors and variables affecting airline costs.

One worrying trend in the airline sector is the rise in 'on-board incidents' where violent passengers disrupt the flight. Skapinker (1998b) reports that while BA only encounters 10 to 15 such incidents a year, they can endanger the lives of hundreds of people. It is likely that their is only the tip of the iceberg and it is certainly a concern for both airline employees and passengers alike, as the authors found when observing such an incident. One of the contributory factors is alcohole consumption and BA now empower the staff to prevent drunk passengers from boarding and to stop serving passengers who appear drunk on board. Airport delays and inadequate information may lead to increased alcohol consumption and at least one Asian airline has even issued cabin staff with restraints to prevent disorderly conduct. Although such events usually occur on long-haul flights, airlines are imposing heavy fines on passengers, especially where pilots divert to eject passengers. It is just one additional issue with which airlines now have to deal. Managing such situations in an appropriate manner can also result in commitment and customer loyalty if the emphasis is on the enhancement of a quality experience for all passengers.

7

Marketing for Tourism

Introduction to Marketing

The complexity of the many different organisations and industries which provide services and products for visitors or travellers of all types. This mixed bag of service providers is often termed 'the travel and tourism industry' or 'the tourism industry', despite the fact that it encompasses many different classifications of industry and organisation, and serves many different consumer groups. This chapter will, therefore, refer to other industries, such as accommodation and tour operations, as 'sectors' within the more global definition 'tourism industry'.

Hotels, restaurants, tour guides, tour operators, tourist boards and other businesses or organisations involved in tourism often act cohesively in order to market their products and services more effectively. Indeed, many of the major tourism marketing events, as well as more general promotional activity, are undertaken jointly by tourism organisations, such events or activities including tourist board promotions; overseas trade missions (for example, those undertaken by the British Tourist Authority); trade shows, such as the The World Travel Market, and joint advertising. As Seaton (1996) observes, those business defined under the 'tourism industry' banner are able to achieve greater visibility by acting cohesively together, although in subsuming them under one label, we ignore the fact that there are few common denominators aside from their provision of services for tourists or local visitors.

From the outset, therefore, it should be recognised that each industry involved in the activity of promoting tourism has slightly differing characteristics and approaches to marketing. Assistance in understanding these differences can be found in texts which examine the subject of marketing in more detail. However, it is beyond the scope of this chapter to exa-mine these differences in depth and, therefore, further reading on distinct areas are suggested at the end of this chapter.

Definitions of Marketing

Firstly, it is important to define what is meant by the term marketing, for to do so helps to clarify its overal purpose as well as presenting a more holistic picture of the marketing process. The Chartered Institute of Marketing, a professional and awarding body for practioners in marketing, defines it as follows:

> *Marketing is the management process responsible for identifying, anticipating and satisfying customer requirements profitably.*

This statement has a number of important indicators as to the scope, purpose and process of marketing. Firstly, a business must identify for whom it is designing products and services, and it must anticipate the needs and wants of both existing and potential and consumers. Assuming that these needs and wants of consumers have been forecast correctly and that a product has been designed to suit them, the business should then focus on satisfying their needs successfully satisfy so that they will want to return and give the company more business. More simplistically, therefore, marketing can also be described as providing the right product, at the right place and the right time.

The central focus of marketing, then, is the consumer. In other words, the popular notion that marketing is to do with advertising and promotion, or that it is really selling in disguise, oversimplifies the total process. In reality, marketing is a broader, logical process consisting of many activities which are central to satisfying the consumer and ensuring the future prosperity of the organisation.

Marketing Activities

Marketing involves not just the deparment or function responsible for marketing activity but whole organisation, and marketing planning takes the form of both strategic and operational (or tactical) planning. Whilst the operational plan for any business or organisation usually covers a period of approximately one year, the strategic plan covers a longer time scale, generally three to five years. However, a particular feature of some sectors of the tourism industry where competition is most intense, for instance tour operating, is the emphasis on tactical planning - it could be argued that the dynamic nature of the business renders longer-term strategic planning an almost impossible task. Therefore, this chapter will concentrate on the marketing activities which are considered to be primarily operational or tactical. Nevertheless, this specific focus helps to highlight and explain the preliminary and formalised planning processes that most market oriented companies undertake. McDonald explains the relationship between the two planning (operational and strategic) stages as follows:

> *A written strategic marketing plan is the backcloth against which operational decisions are taken on an ongoing basis (McDonald 1995).*

The former part of the planning process, therefore, involves preparing for strategic planning - a simple explanation of this process is that it explains 'where we are now' as an organisation and 'where we want to be' at a point in the future. This chapter is more concerned with the processes which follow strategic planning and the techniques which marketing can employ to determine 'how' the organisation's objectives can be achieved, or how it can get to where it wants to be.

The activities associated with longer-term strategic planning and operational planning are fully outlined in McDonald (1995). However, the key activities in marketing are summarised in the following sections.

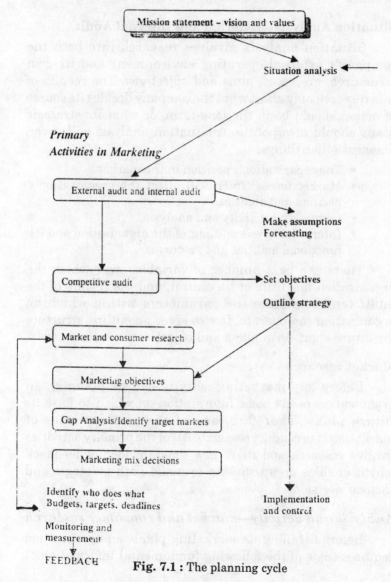

Mission statement – vision and values

Situation analysis

Primary Activities in Marketing

External audit and internal audit

Make assumptions
Forecasting

Competitive audit

Set objectives
Outline strategy

Market and consumer research

Marketing objectives

Gap Analysis/Identify target markets

Marketing mix decisions

Identify who does what
Budgets, targets, deadlines

Implementation and control

Monitoring and measurement

FEEDBACH

Fig. 7.1 : The planning cycle

The Planning Cycle

Figure 7.1 presents a simplified adaptation of the planning cycle, describing the primary planning phases and the important activities undertaken within the marketing process.

Situation Analysis—External and Internal Audit

Situation analysis involves research into both the company's external operating environment and its own structures, processes, aims and objectives. The results of this research may affect what the company decides its course of action should be in the long-term, or what its strategic plans should incorporate. A situation analysis will cover, amongst other things:

- The organisation's position in the market.
- Market forces which will affect the organisation's position and abilities.
- Competitive activity and analysis.
- Internal analysis or audit of the organisation and its functional abilities and resources.

There can be a number of variables over which the organisation has little or no control, and the results of the audit tend to dictate the parameters within which an organisation can operate. It also gives an outline structure for future short-term plans and objectives.

Market research

Before any marketing activity can be planned, an organisation needs basic information on which to base its future plans. Therefore, one of the primary roles of marketing is to conduct research. All of the primary activities involve research and there is a constant loop or feedback which enables organisations to make both strategic and tactical decisions.

Analysis and activity—market and consumer research

Before detailing its marketing plans, an organisation requires some of the following fundamental information.

(i) **Market research**

- The size and nature of the market.
- The nature of products and services on offer.
- The nature of competing products and services.

(ii) **Consumer research**

- Identifying consumer groups to whom the product will appeal.
- Identifying the validity (size, reachability, etc.) of target consumer groups.
- Identifying consumer tastes and preferences.
- Identifying consumer behaviour and changes—i.e. forecasting.

The results of this research will largely determine what the organisation produces, for whom, when and in what quantities. In other words, it principally determines how and on what the activities of the organisation will be focused.

The Marketing Plan

Based upon the market and consumer information derived from the research and the subsequent strategic plan, the organisation must now decide on a more immediate course of action. These actions should enable it to achieve it to achieve its more long-term objectives. This operational marketing plan tends to cover a shorter period (usually one year), and its purpose is to determine in more detail how the company will achieve its objectives.

The marketing plan incorporates activities generally referred to as :

The Marketing Mix

Marketing mix is the term normally used to refer to the combination of tools and methods adopted by an organisation to achieve the desired outcomes of the marketing plan. These tools, often referred to as the four 'Ps', are summarised as:

- *product*—the type of product the organisation produces, its characteristics, brand identity/image, and so on;

- *price*—the anticipated costs of production and distribution and the return that will achieve at the price
  which the market finds acceptable and which achieves
  the corporate objectives;
- *promotion*—the way in which the product is marketed
  the product to the consumer, deciding the nature of
  its appeal;
- *place*—the way in which the product is distributed to
  the consumer and its general accessibility.

In addition, there are other variables which organisations, particularly those in a service related industry such
as tourism, can manipulate in order to change the nature of
the offering and stimulate demand. These include areas
such as people and processes, and are discussed later in the
chapter in the context of the marketing mix and the extended
marketing mix.

The nature of marketing planning is cyclical and
should easily respond change. In other words, constant
change in the external environment or in consumer
preferences means that marketing must be a flexible
process which incorporates ongoing feedback and research.
Owning to the dynamic nature of tourism, it is particularly
essential that organi-sations are able to be proactive and
flexible.

Segmenting, Targeting, Positioning

A primary purpose of marketing is to identify those
groups of people for whom the organisation will produce
products or services. An important element of this proces is
to corectly identify those groups to be specifically targeted,
knowing that they bring a greater chance of the product or
service being successful (where the product is designed
specifically to their requirements). Correct targeting of
priority groups will also result in the organisation itself being
more successful, as the purpose is to target those groups
which will enable the organisation to meet its objectives.
These priority or target groups may have more individual
characteristics which help to define what the specific appeal

of the product or the organisation might be. This, in turn, helps the organisation to:

- Position the product in the consumers mind.
- Position the product against competing products or services (product or competitive positioning).
- Design campaigns which highlights the benefits to the consumer.
- Re-position the product (for example, to a new segment of consumers).

Segmentation

If the organisation is to utilise its marketing resources correctly or efficiently, it must have a clear picture of the groups of individuals who will use its product or services. The process of identifying and describing these groups of individual consumers is called segmentation. A segment is a group of people who have similar characteristics.

The marketing effort must be sufficiently different and appealing to these groups of consumers or segments so as to stimulate a recognition of a need or desire for the product or service. Thus, those organisations which do not correctly identify their market segments are likely to waste money by producing what has been termed 'a blanket approach' - that is, by treating everyone the same. The majority of organisations find that they need to adopt a differentiated approach to individual consumer groups or segments and to design products for their specific needs and, of course, to tailor their marketing campaigns to them.

What is a market segment?—criteria for identification

According to Engel *et. al.,* (1993), the objective of segmentation is to identify groups within the broader market that are sufficiently similar in characteristics and responses to warrant separate treatment. They suggest that there are four basic criteria which can be employed to identify a segment (Engel *et. al.,* 1993. 693-6):

- *Reachability:* can the group be identified and can it be isolated into a distinct group?

- *Identification of causal differences:* is it possible to identify the motivations and influences which define the group?
- *Economic potential:* is the segment large enough or valuable enough to warrant individual attention?
- . *Possession of required marketing resources:* will the resources or effort required match the return?

Segmenting the market—methods and practices

There are many methods used by marketers to segments the market, some of which are more recognised or widely used than others. Government data collected through census or by similarly rigorous methods are often used as an initial basis for identifying groups by, for instance, age, socio-economic group, size of group of percentage of the population. These methods are not, however, sufficient on their own to describe the many different characteristics of consumer segments. Therefore, most organisations seek to use a number of methods to build up a clearer picture of their target audience. This is generally termed multivariate analysis ; that is, the use of more than one method. Marketing text books refer to and describe many different forms of segmentation, some of which are designed and researched by advertising agencies, which are useful for particular consumer or product markets. Some indication of size of segments is necessary and advertising agencies or professional research companies are sometimes in a better position to research and identify the size of specific product or consumer markets and the characteristics of groups contained within them.

Since there are many different types of organisation which make up the tourism industry, many different methods of segmenting consumer markets are used. However, only some of the more common methods are reviewed here (for more detail, see Engel *et al.* 1993).

(i) Demographic segmentation

Demographic segmentation allows marketers to divide the market by known factors about the population, such as age, gender, occupation, education, nationality, family size, family life cycle or life-stage. These tend to be reliable and measurable factors as they are primarily contained in regular government data or census details.

(ii) Socio-economic Groups

Socio-economic groupings are often referred to in marketing text books as the familiar categories of A, B, C1, C2, D and E. This classification has, however, become outdated, primarily because this segmentation method was used to link a household with an individual's (the head of the household) occupation and, therefore, income level. The household's socio-economic category was linked to class structures and, for marketers, was useful in identifying their likely purchasing habits or needs, level of education and so on.

However, a vareity of social transformations, such as changes in types of occupation, the level of education required and relative salary levels, have changed household characteristics, with the result that these traditional segmentation methods are no longer applicable. Therefore, the government has revised the old classification system into the current National Statistics. Socio-Economic Categories or Classifications (NS-SEC) system. Details of the methods and reasoning behind this can be found on the government website (ONS—Office for National Statistics) and on the website for the Institute for Social and Economic Research at the University of Essex (see www.open.gov.uk; and www.iser.essex.ac.uk).

From 2001, the reference for the household is now the person with the highest income, whether male or female. The new national statistics for socio-economic classifications contains 17 categories in eight sub-groups these can be aggregated to produce approximated socio-economic groupings. It is still essentially, an occupational-based classification but it has been adapted to cover other groups in the adult population who cannot be classified by occupation, such as full-time students and the unemployed. This method of classification provides a useful method of segmenting the market, but would generally be used in conjunction with other methods.

Socio-economic group: old classifications	Socio-economic groups: new classifications
A: Professional classes	1: Higher Managerial and professional occupations
B: Managerial/technical	1.1: Large employers and higher managerial occupations
C1: Skilled blue-collar	1.2: Higher professional occupations
C2: Skilled and manual	2: Lower managerial and professional occupations
D: Semi-skilled	3: Intermediate occupations
E: Unskilled	4: Smaller employers and own account workers
Other	5: Lower supervisory and technical occupations
	6: Semi-routine occupations
	7: Routine occupations
	8: Never worked and long-term unemployed or sick

Note: Full details of the 17 sub-groups (fourteen functional and three residual operational categories) representing the variety of labour market positions and employment statuses can be obtained from the web site www. Statistics. gov. uk.

Source: Office for National Statistics

Fig. 7.2 : The national statistics socio-economic categories.

Age

Sometimes, large portions of a consumer market can be identified by age grouping. According to Yale (1998), tour operators providing for the holiday market in the UK can be seen to provide for three distinct groups identified by age and life-stage, or early middle and late adulthood. These are:

- The Youth Market (18-30 years old).
- the Family Market (25-50 years old).
- The Third Age Market (50+ years old).

Within each of these broad notional age boundaries, there exists of course a myriad of similarities and differences which tour operators must provide for. Sub-groups may include, for example, the more active, the wealthy early retired, older parents, fixed-income singles, single parent families, and so on.

A gland at a range of tour operator brochures provides some clues as to what additional methods are used to further segment each age group. Take, for instance, a range of brochures catering for the 'third age' or over 50s group. This group could potentially cover an age range of 40 years and, not surprisingly perhaps, different brochures tend to illustrate the other variables which describe the target segments. At the same time, the actual names of the tour operators' programmes, such as 'Golden Years', 'Young-at-Heart' and Thomsons 'A la Carte' also give an indication of what these variables are (see also the Saga Holidays case study below). Nevertheless, segmenting according to one variable, such as age, remains an over-simplistic approach which may result in, for example, the provision of holidays which do not take into account the varying needs of consumers within particular age groups—it is feasible, for example, for a 50 year old to enjoy the same leisure lifestyle as a 30 year old.

Family life cycle

A method which overcomes some of the pitfalls of segmenting by age along is the family life cycle or life stages. This method recognises that some people may be in the same life stage but at different ages. For example, many people are choosing to have children later in life and have more in common wiith other people in the same life stage (i.e., younger married couples with dependent children). It is also recognised that a high incidence of divorce has created a new category of the bachelor stage, namely, the 'second-time-around single'. However, these singles may not be in early adulthood. Many marketers in the holiday industry are, therefore, interested in identifying the life-stage rather than age of consumers. Many of their brochures reflect this by

Bachelor stage:	Young and single
Newly married:	Married couples, no children
Full Nest 1:	Married couples with dependent children (sub categories toddlers and children over 6)
Full Nest 2:	Older married couples with dependent children
Empty Nest:	Older married couples with no children at home (sub categories of working and retired)
Solitary Survivors:	Older single people (sub categories working or retired)

Fig.7.3 : The Family Life Cycle

using older models with young families, or by portraying images of youthful and wealthy older age groups (Figure 7.3 for the Family Life Cycle).

Case study: Saga Holidays

Saga have been in the holiday business for more than 40 years and specialise in holidays for the 50+ market. Despite a stereotypical image of catering for the older market, the type of product that they produce is varied and geared to a very wide age range of people. They claim a customer base whose ages range from 50-90, and provide holidays from coach tours using student accommodation, to luxury cruises. (They do believe, however, that the majority of their client base consists of the more economically well off).

Saga identify target groups via a number of methods, including those which give an indication of their socio-economic status and lifestyle. Some of this information is available to Saga from other sections of their company which deal with products designed for retired people, such as investments and insurance. They also use geodemographic indicators, such as Acorn and Mosaic, to pinpoint households. They also identify some of their most important target consumer groups by regular or occasional usage, whilst lifestyle descriptors, such as 'independent elders' and 'better off retireds', are also used to segment their market. The changes in life expectation and the general health and wealth of the 50+ market have meant that Saga's product and marketing policies have had to keep pace with this changing group of people, which no longer consists of one segment but many differing segments, all of which require different approaches.

Segmentation by geodemographics

Groups of consumers living in similar housing may well have similar incomes, similar lifestyles and similar wants and needs, as they often share common demographic characteristics. Geodemographic segmentation, which combines a number of geographical and demographic details, is a commonly used method of pin-pointing specific geographical locations or types of housing which contain potential groups of consumers with similar characteristics. ACORN and MOSAIC are two commonly known systems

ACORN

A	Agricultural areas
B	Modern family housing, higher incomes
C	Older housing of intermediate status
D	Poor quality older terraced housing
E	Better off council estates
F	Less well off council estates
G	Poorest Council estates
H	Mixed inner metropolitan areas
I	High status non-family areas
J	Affluent suburban housing
K	Better-off retirement areas

Fig. 7.4 : Geodemographic segmentation methods.

Categories and Components:

ACORN Category	ACORN Group		% of Population
A: Thriving	1:	Wealthy Achievers, Suburban Areas	15.1
	2:	Affluent Greys, Rural Communities	2.1
	3:	Prosperous Pensioners, Retirement Areas	2.6
B: Expanding	4:	Affluent Executive, Family Areas	4.0
	5:	Well off Workers, Family Areas	7.8
C: Rising	6:	Affluent Urbanites, Town and City Areas	2.5
	7:	Prosperous Professionals, Metropolitan Areas	2.2
	8:	Better off Executives, Inner City Areas	3.7
D: Settling	9:	Comfortable Middle Agers, Mature Home Owning Areas	13.5
	10:	Skilled Workers, Home Owning Areas	10.7
E: Aspiring	11:	New Homeowners, Mature Communities	9.5
	12:	White Collar Workers, Better Off Multi-ethnic areas	4.1
F: Striving	13:	Older People, Less Prosperous Areas	3.7
	14:	Council Estate Residents, Better Off Homes	10.9
	15:	Council Estate Residents, High Unemployment	2.8
	16:	Council estate Residents, Greatest Hardship	2.4
	17:	People in Multi-ethnic, Low-Income Areas	2.0

(Figure 7.4). Companies which specialise in collating this data offer a method of identifying the characteristics of households, consumer behaviour, and lifestyle types. Many tourism companies find it useful to identifying postal areas where potential client types may exist, as this assists them in planning promotional activities such as advertising and direct mailing.

Specialist tour companies, such as Cox and Kings may, for instance, wish to identify the 'high status non-family areas', and Saga the 'better off retirement areas' profiled by Acorn. Geo-demographics can also be useful for organisations in identifying where shops or services should be located.

Lifestyle and psychographic segmentation

These methods of segmentation aim to probe deeper into the characteristics of the consumer by identifying such things as their interest in life, their attitudes, values and aspirations. They attempt to identifying the type behaviour consumers may demonstrate and to predict behaviour based on a knowledge of similarity of lifestyles, attitudes and motivations. Lifestyle segmentation assumes that we can relate certain products or services to certain types of lifestyle and consumer. Sometimes, these reflect aspirations or the type of 'lifestyle' some groups or individuals would like to lead, and many tourism organisations, such as hotels, can use this knowledge to target consumers.

Benefits and behavioural segmentation

These methods attempt to describe groups of consumers by the way in which they use products and the benefits they seek from them. Many organisations identify regular and occasional users, both of whom may require differing product characteristics. For example, regular users of an airline may be prepared to pay extra for a product, or anticipate added value, in the form of additional services such as a special business lounge.

Knowledge about the usage habits of consumers can assist with loyalty schemes or pricing structures. They are also useful for highlighting the way in which tourists use and choose products or services. For example, special occasions are often a time to dispense with usual buying routines, hence consumers may be more likely to use a different type of hotel for a honeymoon, or take additional treats such as champagne and flowers in the room on anniversaries. The benefits that groups of people seek from the product may also change the way in which products are designed - for example, all-inclusive holidays offer the benefits of a carefree holiday with little budgetary planning.

Analysis of Market Segments and Selection of Target Markets

The detail of some market segementation methods could lead marketers to over-rate the value of some of the more descriptive lifestyle classifications, or to believe that all information on the consumer is relevant. Engel *et. al.,* (1993) offer some advice regarding the trend towards greater multi-variate and descriptive analysis of market segments: 'Ask yourself of what practical value are the descriptors? Is the information interesting but irrelevant? And what will I do differently now that I have this information?.

Conversely, however, a business which choose to describe its market segments in overly simplistic, out-of-date terms, or by product alone, may find itself 'out of step' with its customers and, hence, it may fail to communicate with them effectively.

The selection of the most appropriate target segments for some travel and tourism organisations can be a difficult process. For example, in the case of tour operators the majority of large companies will produce packages for a wide variety of differing segments and generally try to identify those which assist in profit objectives. That is, they seek the most lucrative segments or those which assist in the achievement of startegic advantages, such as market share.

For tourist destinations, the choice of target segments may be limited to those which the tourism development strategy has identified as being the most beneficial guests (although not all destinations, off course, enjoy the luxury of being able to 'choose' their customers. Frequently, it is the tour operator that determines the characteristics of tourist flows to a destination). Their choices may focus on aspects other than finance, such as socio-cultural benefits, and may require some of the more immediately financially lucrative target markets to be ignored. Generally, however, watever the options, the organisation must decide which segments have the greater priority, as the development of the marketing mix and complementary budgets will be tied to those priority groups.

Characteristics of the Tourism Industry and Positioning Strategies

The tourism industry, like many others, reacts to the particular nature of the environment and the structure of the market in which it operates. This brings about differing approaches to segmenting the market, and differing strategies for segments and product groups. Companies sometimes work on determining 'competitive market structures'—that is, grouping products or brands on the basis of competition boundaries. It can be recognised that, in the tourism market, there are specific areas where brands compete more strongly with one another than with other similar products.

For example, stronger brands and vertically integrated organisations, such as JMC or First Choice, may concentrate their marketing effort on dealing with the competition offered by others operating on a multi-market, multi-product basis (such as Thomsons or Airtours), rather than on smaller operators using the same destinations and offering similar packages. Similarly, major tourist destinations in the world, such as Greece and Spain, may compete more directly with one another for various tourist segments from the UK than do France and Spain as two of the largest destinations for UK tourists.

Differing Market Strategies and Mixes in a Fragmented Market

A recent feature of the market for tourism is that many tour operators and destinations which catered for what was termed the 'mass market' are now attempted to respond to the growing trend towards a more fragmented market and tourists who require more individually tailored holidays (niche markets). This they have done by bringing out a wider variety of products to suit individual market segments and, as a result, in some product areas the larger operators might see their more direct competition to be a specialist or smaller operator. This highlights the need for distinctly different marketing strategies for particular market segments and products, with a different marketing mix.

As an example, the competition between JMC and Thomsons for their main multi-product summar programme might be such that they are forced to manipulate price rather more than other elements of the marketing mix. They might also have to concentrate a higher degree of their marketing budget on advertising and promotion. On the other hand, a smaller specialist operator, such as Abercrombie and Kent, competing with Thomsons in a tourist location may offer added value and expertise and a greater personal service element to the product. Thomsons may, in turn, may have to manipulate its product mix or perceived value in order to compete with the smaller operator. In this case, either operator may invoke the extended marketing mix (see below) and the emphasis may be on elements other than price, such as people and the service they give. Similarly, destinations such as Spain have the challenge of remaining appealing to the established market segments of the 'Costas' whilst promoting to smaller, and potentially more lucrative, segments who require differing product benefits. The marketing mix they invoke for these segments may therefore have to be very different.

The Control of Variables—The Nature and Characteristics of Services and Tourism Marketing

In the marketing of tourism products, it is acknowledged that there are a number of variables over which the industry has little control and which characterise the tourism product. These variables tend to focus on economic and political influences over which organisations in the tourism field have either little or no control. These variables, such as PDI (personal disposable income), are used by market intelligence agencies, such as Mintel, to forecast the nature of the market. Mintel maintain, for instance, that pdi has a direct correlational effect on the number of holidays the consumer is able to take in the year, and anticipated growth or decline in PDI will, therefore, have a direct influence on trends in holiday taking (Mintel 2001).

The level of activity and spend in the tourism market are also affected by potential changes in the economic and political environment, including inflation, levels, mortgage rates, interest rates and exchange rates, all of which may have a greater or lesser effect on consumer confidence and spending. Other variables of particular concern to those involved in tourism are wars and political instability. All organisations, therefore, seek to reduce risk by research; that is, they undertake economic forecasting and acquire other market intelligence which enables them to make realistic strategic and tactical plans.

Once organisations have defined those variables which will have most influence over the ability of the consumer to purchase, they must decide upon ways of overcoming some of the difficulties and then decide upon more direct activities. These direct activities focus on those variables which marketers are more able to control and are more widely known as the marketing mix, the extended marketing mix or services marketing mix. Marketers must seek to find the correct 'mix' which will achieve success for the organisation and satisfy consumers.

The marketing mix and extended marketing mix

As discussed above, the most widely accepted and used definition of the marketing mix is the four 'Ps', which incorporates product, price, place (distribution) and promotion. In service industries and in tourism in particular, it is considered that this mix can be extended to include other activities and that these can assume just as much importance. Indeed, the four 'Ps' approach has been widely criticised for its limitations and many commentators have offered advice on the application of an extended mix and the nature of services.

Cowell emphasises that the marketing mix is a guide and a framework for action, not simply a theoretical idea. Marketers should, therefore, be prepared to adapt and adopt the correct mix according to their particular industry and organisational conditions and, most particularly, according to the needs of the target market segments they have decided to cater for. One of the principal reasons for adopting an extended mix is the nature of the delivery of services, such as tourism, where in order to differentiate one product from another, factors such as the management of service quality through *people, processes and physical evidence* are important. These additional variables in the production process can affect the response of the consumer more readily. As far as possible, marketing must influence performance and delivery of the product.

The role of customer service and the control of quality are, therefore, heavily emphasised in tourism organisations. Companies such as British Airways spend sizeable portions of their marketing budget ensuring that the product is made more tangible and that customer experiences and percep-tions are more consistent. The extended marketing mix of people, processes and physical evidence provide more ways in which marketers can control the delivery (see Zeithaml and Bitner (2000) for further reading).

Product

The nature and characteristics of the tourism product

(i) **Inseparability and heterogeneity :** As has already been observed in the discussion of marketing mix, one of the features of tourism products is that production and consumption are not entirely exclusive. This inseparability is created because services which are part of the production process are only 'produced' at the time of consumption. For example, a night in an hotel or a flight on an aeroplane only occurs the service is 'consumed'. Because people are so much a part of this production process, another feature of tourism products is their lack of standardisation or 'heterogeneity'. As previously stated, marketers must try to make the product conform to the same standard so that it perceived the same by all users.

(ii) **Intangibility :** Tourism products incorporate many elements, but a particular feature of tourism is that many of these elements are intangible - they are not physical goods, but experiences and feelings. In short, the nature of many holiday products is such that consumers could be said to buy on trust. As demonstrated in the above section, the producer seeks to control as many of these intangible variables as possible in order to make the product more tangible for the consumer.

(iii) **Perishability and seasonality :** Tourism products are highly perishable; unlike manufactured goods, they cannot be stored and sold at a later date. Therefore, the costs involved in their production can increase if, for example, tours are not filled to capacity, some departure dates remain unsold, or aircraft seats remain unsold. These are some of the factors which affect the pricing of tourism products, since producers must sometimes allow for a level of unsold capacity which can increase the individual costs of a holiday.

It is sometimes the seasonal nature of the tourism product which increases the risk and, therefore, tourist attractions and tour operators must ensure that they are able to make the most of peak seasons. Cash flow tends to be poor and sometimes non-existent in shoulder and off-peak seasons, whilst for those with high fixed costs or assets which remain dormant (aircraft, ships, coaches, hotels), the problem of seasonality is greater. Marketing efforts must, therefore, be focused on achieving prices which achieve the highest rate of return in peak season, and prices which stimulate demand in low seasons, thus increasing the likelihood of full use of assets.

Product analysis

Product analysis is an element of the marketing process that helps an organisation to identify the ways in which it can adpt and improve products in relation to customer needs and competitor products. It also assists the organisation in identifying features and benefits which can be highlighted in promotional campaigns.

Shoashtack (1977) has attempted to analyse products by identifying their relative importance to the core service, demonstrating how important some of the more peripheral services are in making the product more tangible for some consumers. The importance of components within the structure may change for different consumers—with airlines, for example, business class travellers may value reclining seats and more leg room, whilst a leisure passenger may value speed of service and ancillary services, such as duty free shopping. Both, however, experience the same core service—the flight.

The concept of a core which satisfies the most fundamental or basic needs arises from Kotler's (1994) Five Product Levels model, in which he suggests that marketers should attempt to enhance the set of attributes and conditions that customers normally expect with and augmented level, one which distinguishes their product from others. By augmenting the product, marketers will be satisfying more than the basic needs of customers and be supplying additional benefits which also differentiate the product from its competitors.

There are many other useful models which assist organisations in comparing and improving upon products. A SWOT analysis (strengths, weaknesses, opportunities and threats), for instance, may prove useful in comparing competing products. Alternatively, an analysis of the benefits which consumers derive from products helps the organisations to distinguish them from the integral features, thus providing marketers with material for promotional campaigns.

It is harder is to develop new products for the tourism market, as opposed to other markets, since it is generally much more difficult to pre-test service related products. Some tour operators will pre-test new products by pilot launches to specific geographical regions or release programmes with limited departure dates. Hotels and purpose built attractions may test concepts and reactions to interior decor. The retail trade and tourist boards can attempt to simulate the holiday experience through videos and computer generated graphics. In general, however, much of the industry relies on experience and the post-purchase evaluations of consumer satisfaction. When compared to some industries in manufacturing, the costs of the research, introduction and testing of new products for tourism are relatively low.

Product life-cycle

Since manipulating the features and design of the product is one of the primary ways in which marketers can ensure success, it is inevitable that they will also be interested in how much adaptation of the product can take place before consumers tire of the product and it becomes obsolete. The product life-cycle concept proposes that every product has four basic stages, namely, *introduction, growth, maturity and decline.* It is the job of marketing to assess the life of individual products in order to:

- Assess and predict the length of the adoption stage of a new product.
- Determine at what stage in the process each product in the organisation's portfolio is.

- Adapt products to stem the decline or renew interest (extending the lifecycle).
- Assess when products need to be deleted.
- Assess when new products need to be introduced.

There are a number of pitfalls in predicting the life-stages of products, and the intense competition in the tourism industry with its characteristic price wars could lead to a misinterpretation of the pattern of growth and decline. The popularity of products is clearly not just influenced by their path to obsolescence and caution is needed in interpreting the pattern of sales.

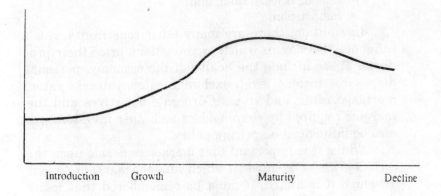

Introduction   Growth   Maturity   Decline

Fig. 7.5 : The Product Life-cycle.

At the introduction stage, cost is the primary factor and it is not until the growth stage, when sales begin to rise, that marketing can be sure of some return on their investment. A mistake that some companies make is to underestimate the length of the adoption process and pull to the plug on new products too early. Equally, overestimation will increase costs with no return. Growth may also be affected by a number of other factors, such as the introduction of competitive products. At the maturity stage, it may be that a smaller number of producers battle it out for market share, during this stage it may be difficult to tell whether sales have reached saturation and a decline is likely.

Price

Influences on pricing

There are many influences on pricing, including:
- demand;
- supply (availability);
- costs;
- competition;
- government policies on pricing;
- consumer legislation; and
- competition.

In addition, there are many other constraints which influence the way in which organisations price their products. These include the health of the economy, personal disposable income level, exchange rates, interest rates, mortgage rates, and so on. Corporate objectives and the margins required by shareholders and other investors will also be influential on pricing policy.

Whilst it is important that marketers decide upon the correct price for the product which suits the market segment at which it is aimed, it must be remembered that many constraints influence their ability to use price as a tool to manipulate consumer response.

Supply and demand pricing policy

Some sectors of the tourism industry are said to be characterised by price was. These are, sometimes, the inevitable result of over-capacity in airlines, shipping, and to a lesser extent, hotels, and reflect the extent to which supply or demand influences pricing. Principles or producers with spare capacity resulting from lower demand or increased supply will sell at cheaper rates in order to cover existing or high fixed costs, or cut prices in the belief that a reduction in price will lead to a subsequent increase in sales.

Market share and pricing policy

In recent years, price wars and discounting have been the major characteristic of the larger, vertically integrated companies who combine the functions of tour operator, travel agent and charter airline. These reflect the extent to which both perishability and the fight for market share influences pricing.

These larger companies have produced larger tour operating programmes, sometimes flooding the market with products, in order to preserve or win market share. When these efforts fail, products often have to be put back on the market in different forms or through different distribution channels and, generally, at lower or discounted rates.

Those companies without adequate resources cannot generally price products for market share. Nor should companies with either substantial borrowings and poor performance pursue pricing for market share, as banks may 'pull the plug' at the wrong time whilst shareholders may object to policies which reduce margins. Thus, market share is not a realistic option for many companies; indeed, some markets may remain stagnant with little growth in volume. Nevertheless, growth can be achieved not only by selling more of product but also by selling the same volume, but at higher prices. For some, but relatively few, organisations in the tourism industry, this is the only option.

Pricing methods

(i) **Target rate of return :** Prices are decided on the basis of achieving a particular return on the assets employed in an organisation. Investors in a business may simply set a target with which they will be happy.

(ii) **Cost based methods :** Based on accounting disciplines of costing, this method is easy for many organisations to understand and use. Costs can be split into two types, fixed and variable. Fixed costs are those which do not vary with 'output', or the amount of the service provided. Variable costs, conversely, are those which do increase as more of a service is provided.

These two cost elements can be combined with revenue - which should increase as the service is sold - to give a picture of when an operation becomes profitable. Known as Break Even Analysis or Cost/Profit/Volume (CPV) Analysis, the interaction of these elements can be shown graphically.

In reality, in some businesses it may be difficult to allocate overheads or fixed costs to some products. Some businesses may want to be flexible and operate differing prices and pricing methods to achieve different objectives which stimulate demand. Therefore, contirbutions to cost (marginal cost pricing) is a more realistic proposition for some companies, as the range offered may support the sale of other products, or utilise spare capacity (e.g., transportation).

(iii) **Promotional and psychological pricing** : Promotional pricing may be employed to destroy rival products or pricing policies. It may also be used as the lead-in price for a brochure where, for example, £399 is perceived as removing a barrier price of £400 or over. However, it would normally be viewed as a short term strategy as its objectives are achieved at the cost of profit.

(iv) **Competitive based pricing** : Some industries are constrained in the way they price products and can only sell at what is termed the going rate, that is, the rate which the competition is charging. However, this method should be used with caution as it also means that costs should be relatively the same for both parties. Many organisations are forced into this situation when competition is intense and the public have got used to what they consider to be the 'going rate' for a product—as is very much the case with the mass, package holiday market.

(v) **Premium and destroyer pricing** : These methods represent the opposite ends of a scale. More successful companies with well-known brands and highly regarded products are in a position to be price leaders in a market and achieve a premium price over others. Generally, there are good reasons for being able to achieve this, such as providing a higher quality service or providing a specialist or unique service.

At the opposite end of the scale, destroyer aims to undercut competitors in order to remove them from the market. This type of pricing can result in negative implications for the consumer as, once competition is removed, so too are the barriers for increasing prices and, therefore, such actions may be swiftly followed by price rises.

Place

Distribution and promotion often play inter-related roles in the marketing of travel and tourism products. The decisions facing most organisations are either to market direct to the consumer or to market their products via an intermediary, such as a travel agent. This still leaves the problem of how to distribute information and inventory (available capacity) to the travel agent. The nature of distribution services has changed considerably in the past twenty years as more and more ways of delivering the product direct to the consumer or more speedily business to business have been developed. For example, on a business to business basis CRS's—global reservations networks—allowed travel agents and producers to access inter-related products, such as airlines, hotels and other services and for organisations to communicate. These systems are now becoming redundant as agents are able to access inventory and information on the Internet via separately controlled networks (which the public are not allowed access to).

Importantly, time is often saved and fewer bruchures are needed if the public is able to access information direct from producers' web-sites and make some decisions before contacting travel agents. In these instances, the consumer is going direct to the producer for information but is still using the agent for booking purposes. Many organisations have developed call centres for the same purpose.

There has been much discussion on the value of the Internet tool. Before making any decisions on more direct methods of distribution and promotion, it is necessary for marketers to decide what use the majority of people will make of the these services. For example, it must be ascertained whether consumers will use services, such as the Internet, as a tool for collating information (accepting promotional material) or whether they would with to undertaken transactions using the Internet (a distribution tool).

Air travel is one product which has been successfully distributed on the Internet. Ryanair, for example, have achieved 70 percent of their bookings through their web site another 23 percent are made by phone and only 7 per cent through agents (Mintel 2001b: 11).

One of the major advantages of the Internet is that it may lower the cost of distribution for many organisations. For products such as ferry crossings, it offers another method of distributing information on fares and sailing times which are quicker than brochure distribution and more flexible. The Internet has also provided an opportunity for new types of distribution service which differ from retail agents. These distribution services may concentrate on one type of service or one consumer segment. They aggregate services to capture whole product or consumer markets, whilst providing an opportunity for a more efficient service for consumers wanting to compare services, prices and times (Barrass 1998). Thus, sites such as Ferrybooker.com are able to offer information on all ferry services on one site (Mintel 2001: 23).

Keynote maintain that four times as many tourists considered the Internet and travel books a better source of information than travel agents and tour operators (Keynote 2001: 51). Nevertheless, many organisations still believe that there are limitations to distributing products through the Internet. These limitations are: a reluntance to use technology; security concerns (with credit card transactions, bank details); ease of access to inventory; ease of access to correct information; and the lack security associated with dealing face-to-face or verbal communication.

Travel agents are still the primary method by which people in the UK access information on holiday products and make reservations. Agents can provide a professional service with additional information and advice, which should be impartial. There has been much discussion as to how impartial this advice can be when many agents are part of vertically integrated companies who have an interest in promoting their own products. Therefore, the European Competition, Commission have taken an active interest in the growing integration of the European travel industry and have issued guidelines for agents which enable the public to identify where an agents is offering products which are owned by the group. The nature of travel agents is changing and many companies are developing new types of agency which no longer perform traditional roles but, which offer the benefits of new technology, such as the Internet alongside personal contact.

Whilst it is the marketer of tourism products who must decide on the best method of distribution for their product, it is still the consumer who makes the decision which method they prefer to use. Most organisations now seek to determine how particular market segments will react to and use different distribution systems and the preferences of important target market segments are taken into account. The type of holiday product and the typical consumer give some indication—for example, the Internet is apparently the ideal method for adventure travel operators as the profile of their consumers closely matches that of consumers likely to participate in adventure travel. It also suits the many small companies involved in this area, as distribution through agents would be difficult if not impossible. Indeed, approximately 85 per cent of sales for adventure travel companies is by direct booking (Millington 2001). Specialist tour operators in general are hoping to develop their brands via the Internet, whilst the Association of Independent Tour Operators (AITO) has used it to raise the profile of its members and their products and as a communications tool (Mintel 2001).

In addition to consumer preference, tour operators and others must consider the cost of distributing products. If distributing through travel agents, they must decide whether they will distribute on a blanket approach to each agent or whether they will selectively distribute to a small number of agents or selected chains. Many organisations do not have the choice as, with such a wide variety of products on offer, travel agents must be selective about how many they stock and some producers may have no option but to sell direct.

Promotion

It is the responsibility of marketing to communicate factors about an organisation and its products. The purpose of communications can vary; for instance, it may be used for establishing an identify for a product, creating a corporate image for an organisation or creating awareness of a destination. The promotional efforts of organisations should generally be focused on their selected target market segments. It is one of the responsibilites of marketing not only to identify the various audiences but their characteristics. They also need to analyse the characteristics of their products and the appeal they have for their audience. This knowledge will enable clear directions to be given to those preparing the promotional plan as to the purpose of the campaign.

The purposes of campaigns are very varied. Tour operators or destinations, for example, may find it necessary to place advertising which raises awareness of a destination whereas established consumer segments, who are already knowledgeable on products and destinations, may need more persuasion to choose the product in preference to others. The purpose of the campaign, therefore, may be to create more favourable attitudes or to stimulate consumers to purchase.

As discussed shortly, there are a number of ways in which we can communicate with chosen audiences. However, the choice of the promotional effort or mix of the commu-nications package will depend upon many factors, including:

- the size of budge;
- the objectives of the promotional campaign;
- the size and nature of the target audience; and
- the geographical spread of the target audience.

The primary concern is to establish clear objectives or goals for the campaign and then to monitor and measure the responses to it. Without monitoring and measurement, no organisation can clearly determine whether its success is due to marketing effort and the cost effectiveness of that effort.

Elements of the promotional mix

(i) **Advertising** : Marketing must carefully select media by identifying the typical readership, viewers or listeners and matching the medium to their target audience. There are many considerations which affect choice and it is suggested that marketing must look not only at the absolute cost of adver-tising (time or space purchased) but also at the relative costs of advertising, 'that is, the cost of contacting each remember of the target audience' (Fill 1995: 310). A wide range of media may be used for advertising, including:

- TV
- Radio
- National and local press
- Trade and professional journals
- magazines
- Posters/bill boards
- Direct mailing

For each method, details of advertising rates, readership and each are published and part of the research and planning process is also to determine the medium most likely to be cost effective and which the audience is most likely to identify.

(ii) **Public and press relations** : Press and public relations campaigns form a major part of the additional

activities which can enhance communications strategies. The influence of media coverage, in particular on the holiday product, has proven to be enormous. It is not just consumer programmes which review holiday products that are influential - the image of destina-tions created by TV programmes have also been instrumental in developing tourism and have been shown to have a far more powerful effect than traditional advertising (for example, 'Heartbeat' on Goathland and 'Peak Practice' on Crich/Amber Valley area of Derbyshire). Marketers know that filming in a location is likely to enhance or build an image for a destination and arouse awareness and curiosity.

(iii) **Direct marketing** : Direct mail, telemarketing and the Internet are all forms of communication which are increasingly used in the travel and tourism industry. Direct mail and telemarketing have the advantage of being more easily monitored and, therefore, the response more directly measurable. Direct response methods, such as promotional coupons, are also used successfully to promote holiday products. Unlike the Internet, the cost of these is more directly measurable.

(iv) **Brochures and printed materials** : The brochure is still the primary selling tool for the majority of the travel and tourism industry, including destinations, although the Internet is bringing about change on this front. The nature of the holiday product means that it is information intensive and the brochure has been the primary tool through which all information is distributed. It is, however, a costly business and marketers must consider how many brochures they need to distribute. The real cost of brochure production and distribution can be measured by assessing the number of bookings received to the number of brochures distributed. The conversion rate for most orgnisation is, in fact, staggeringly low and the real costs of 'wastage' (brochures taken but not used as a booking medium) are high.

(v) **Direct selling** : A large proportion of business to business activity is undertaken by direct sales. However,

the role of selling in the travel industry is often a controversial one, especially when considering the role of the travel agent. Face-to-face selling, therefore, has less of a role than, say, telesales throughout most of the industry. In reality, the purchases of holiday products involves complex decision-making, often by groups of people, some of whom take differing roles (for example, buyers or influencers). The direct selling role can therefore be controversial. However, some organisations have attempted to use direct selling when people's responses are known to be less guarded, such as in the selling of time-share in holiday resorts.

8

The Accommodation Sector

Introduction

Accommodation is a fundamental part of the domestic and international tourism product. Moreover, the selection of accommodation and associated product expenditure is a major part of the tourist decision process. Medlik and Ingram (2000:4) state that 'the primary function of an hotel is to accommodate those away from home and to supply them with their basic needs'. Recent years have witnessed increasing diversity in the provision of accommodation for the tourism industry which, in terms of scope, certainly makes this an interesting sector to study. At the same time, however, it is also challenging to keep pace with developments within the sector as the industry structure is in a constant state of flux.

The study of accommodation is inextricably linked to the concept of hospitality. Jones (1996:1) states that 'hospitality is made up of two distinct services - the provision of overnight accommodation for people staying away from home, and the provision of sustenance for people eating away from home'. Here, we are concerned only with the former service, the latter being well beyond the purpose of this chapter. The importance of the accommodation sector to the tourism industry in terms of share of total expenditure in shown in Table 8.1.

Table 8.1 : Tourism expenditure as a percentage of the total, 1999.

	Overseas Visitors in UK	Domestic visitors	All visitors
Accommodation	33.3	34.0	34.0
Eating Out	20.6	26.0	23.5
Shopping	26.0	13.0	18.9
Travel in UK	9.2	19.0	14.7
Services	7.1	1.0	3.4
Entertainment	2.9	6.0	4.4
Other	0.9	1.0	1.0

History of the Accommodation Industry

Overnight stays and the provision of accommodation are, of course nothing new. Not only can we look back as far as Roman times and even further to the renowned. 'Inn' in the Bible for evidence of the provision of accommodation for travellers, but also the development accommodation has long been linked with the growth in travel. Journeys in the very early centuries were made on foot or horseback and often took many months to complete, necessitating overnight stays to rest. Many accommodation outlets at that time also supplied alcohol and were associated with unruly behaviour (threats to public order and temptations to indulge in adultery-perhaps not so different to today:). It was this that gave rise to the first regulation of the trade in the twelfth century, even prior to the introduction of taxation and licensing.

Throughout the Middle Ages, the first inns and guesthouses were developed primarily for travelling merchants and pilgrims. These would usually be established alongside the primitive road system and in private residences, offering hospitality for a small charge. However, as time progressed, the provision of accommodation developed in accordance with its markets as comparatively well off merchants began to seek more comfortable accommodation. Thus, the seventeenth and eighteenth centuries

witnessed the emergence of the coaching inn and the spread
of these throughout Europe. Travellers motives varied, of
course. Merchants travelling for trade and business purposes
obviously needed accommodation Leisure travel and the
European Grand Tour were increasingly popular at this
time. Travellers were also undertaking religious pilgrimages
or, for health reasons, visiting spas and resorts in Europe
and so accommodation facilities were developed to meet the
needs of all these different groups.

The development of the railways in the nineteenth
century impacted hugely on the provision of accommodation.
From the 1860s onwards, railway companies and related
steamship companies began to build hotels at terminal
stations in order to capitalise upon the regularity of rail
services and the public's increasing desire and ability to
travel for pleasure—indeed, reminders of this era remain
evident today in some of the fabulous hotel buildings in cities
throughout the world. Interestingly, international airlines
were to have a similar influence on hotel development over
a century later. The Le Meridien chain, for example, was
originally established by Air France.

Following the patterns of innovation in transport, the
structure and distribution of accommodation provision has
been heavily influenced by the massive growth in the use of
the private motor car. Roadside accommodation is, of course,
very much in evidence today,but ever-increasing car
ownership has meant that tourists can go wherever they
want, thus spreading the demand for accommodation to some
very out-of-the-way places. Where no accommodation is
available, tourists often take their own, in the form of
caravans, tents or boats.

As society has become more affluent and more leisure
time has become available over the last century, the
accommodation industry has developed to meet changing
needs. In the UK, for example, the Holidays with pay Act of
1938 stimulated the demand for 'mass tourism'and meant
that, from the late 1940s, holidays could become a reality
for many. As a result, holiday camps such as Butlins

flourished and, indeed, many ideas from this period form the basis of holiday provision today. Sharpley (1999 : 55) states that Butlain's first holiday camp, which opened in Skegness in 1936, was relatively luxurious. 'It comprised 600 chalets, dining and recreation facilities, a swimming pool, a theatre, tennis court, services such as child-minding and organised entertainment and, perhaps most important of all modern sanitary arrangements'. In short, then, the accommodation sector has developed and diversified to meet the evolving and changing needs of tourists and it is now a vast and complex industry which lies at the very heart of travel and tourism.

Categorisation of Accommodation Demand

The accommodation sector meets the needs of a number of different markets:

Business or leisure market

When examining the motives behind the selection of accommodation, a simplistic division can be made between accommodation for business or for recreation and tourism purposes. In reality, of course, such a clear cut division does not exist and many people travelling for the purpose of business or attending conferences will add on leisure time and become 'a tourist'.

Domestic or international market

Visitors from both markets are clearly important to the accommodation sector. Visitors from overseas, however, generate crucial foreign exchange earnings. Britain receives approximately 25 million overseas visitors each year, who spend nearly £13 billion (British Hospitality Association Election Manifesto 2001). The British Tourist Authority (BTA) has predicted that international tourists to the UK will spend in excess of £18bn a year by 2003, although there is concern that, in recent years, the number of incoming visitors has remained broadly static. Moreover, given the developments in the early half of 2001 related to the outbreak of foot and mouth disease, as well as the events of September 11th in the USA, the BTA's fore cast would seem to be optimistic.

Commercial and non-commercial accommodation

Non-commercial accommodation can be defined as accommodation that is only concerned with the recovery of costs as opposed to making a commercial profit, such as privately owned holiday homes and yachts, tents, caravans and motor homes. Youth hostels and centres for young people's activity holidays can also be included in this category. Conversely, the commercial sector covers all forms of accommodation run as a business.

Serviced and non-serviced accommodation

A further distinction must be made between serviced and non-serviced (i.e. self-catering) accommodation. This is fairly obvious in the case of a four star hotel which relies heavily on its provision of service in attracting customers, whilst a rural bed and breakfast would also fit into this category. However, the distinction is less clear in the case

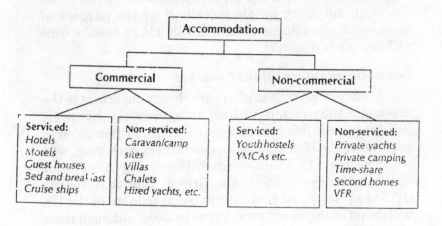

Fig. 8.1 : Categorisations of accommodation

of, for example, a French self-catering farmhouse holiday where the owner offers the provision of an evening meal and, more generally, there has recently been an increase in the demand for what is essentially non-serviced accommodation but with the option and flexibility of service provision if required. 'Apart-Hotels' fall into this category - the accommodation component is basically of a self catering nature, but the location of the apartment within an hotel means that the occupants may use hotel leisure facilities, restaurants and bars if they wish. Figure 8.1 summarises this categorisation of accommodation.

The Variety and Diversity of the Accommodation Sector

Accommodation has developed enormously since the first roadside inn and the present-day heterogeneity of the sector makes it difficult to produce managers with the relevant skills to run it. For example, the operation of managing and cooking for a chalet in a ski resort based on personal service for eight guests requires very different skills from that of the General Manager of a large multi-national hotel chain (although the underlying principals will essentially be the same). Similarly, the physical nature of one of the properties owned and let by the Landmark Trust (Figure 8.3) is very different from a city centre Marriott Hotel. It is, therefore, difficult to categorise such a range of accommodation types, examples of which are given below :

• Hotel - budget, mid-market, luxury	• Home Exchanges
• Club Hotels	• Second Homes
• Bed and Breakfast/Guest house	• Timeshare Homes and Apartments
• Pubs	• Cruise Liners
• Holidays Houses, Cottages and Apartments	• Yachts/Boats
• Camping and Caravan	• Train Accommodation

Within these accommodation types there are naturally a huge number of variables, such as location, markets, ownership (small family run business to multi-national

chain), and levels of service provision. Table 8.2 compares
the different types of accommodation used for domestic
holidays in the U.K.

Table 8.2 : Accommodation used for domestic holidays.

	Trips		Nights		Expenditure	
	m	%	m	%	£m	%
Home of friend or relative	22.0	33	85	29	1,650	15
Hotel, motel, guest house	15.5	24	55	19	3,750	34
Own/timeshare property/static caravan	6.5	10	25	9	450	4
Camping/touring caravan	6.5	10	35	12	900	8
B&B, farm, hostel, university	3.5	5	10	4	550	5
Holiday centre (serviced or s/c)	3.5	5	12	4	650	6
Boat	0.5	1	3	1	200	2
Other self catering*	8.0	12	65	22	2,850	26
Total	66.0	100	290	100	11,000	100

*Flats, houses, cottages, chalets; rented static caravans/mobile homes.

The Economics of Accommodation

The profitability of commercial accommodation is
greatly influenced by occupancy rates. These represent
the level of usage of hotel rooms or bed spaces and are
usually expressed as a percentage figure. Care must be
taken to differentiate between the four main types of
occupancy rate, all of which will produce very different
figures.

- The basic occupancy rate measures the percentage of
  rooms used by guests on a given night.
- The average occupancy rate measures the percentage
  of rooms used over a period (i.e., over a month or a
  year).
- The bed occupancy rate establishes how many guests
  are physically accommodated as a percentage of the
  maximum capacity; that is, is there one person or two
  in a double/twin room?

- The revenue occupancy rate, which compares the room revenue on one night with the theoretical maximum that could be charged. Therefore, it takes into account any discounted prices that may be offered.

Hotels generally have a variety of different charges for any one room. The published tariff of the hotel is known as the 'rack rate' which represents the price the hotel would ideally like to charge. In practice, however, the rack rate is often not used and prices vary according to whether they are for a tour operator, who often reserve rooms on 'allocation' for their guests, a corporate client for a conference or incentive stay, a large group booking, cr simply because the demand for the hotel beds on that night is low and the market dictates a discounted price. Thus, the two key components of rooms revenue are the level of occupancy and the average achieved room rate. The latter only represents the price achieved on rooms sold, however, and bears little resemblance to the full or rack rate' (Knowles 1994 : 86).

In addition to rooms revenue, hotels also earn income from direct and ancillary services, such as food and beverages, telephones, dry cleaning, currency exchange and in-house retailing. Frequently, such services are more profitable than the basic business of selling rooms.

Factors Affecting Profitability and Pricing in the accommodation Sector

Perishability

The accommodation product is highly perishable—if a room is not sold on a particular day, the opportunity to generate any avenue from that room will be lost for ever. Therefore, it is important for managers to be able to forecast demand as accurately as possible, to be aware of the external environment and to adjust prices accordingly. One common 'solution' is overbooking in the expectation that cancellations, for one reason or another, will offset this although yield management systems, which will be looked at later in this chapter, are increasingly being used to address the problem of perishability.

Seasonality

Tourist accommodation is subject to seasonality, which must be taken into account when pricing. For example, business and conference clients can often be an important source of business during the low season in resort hotels whilst, in city centre hotels which depend upon the business sector during the week, prices may be adjusted to attract short-break leisure customers over weekends and holiday periods. The importance of target marketing and tactical pricing is, therefore, crucial ensure a balanced flow of customers throughout the year. In fact, this is one of the most challenging areas for those involved in the management of tourism accommodation.

High fixed costs

The accommodation sector has very high fixed costs and these are proportionally far greater than the variable costs. Fixed costs are costs that are fixed irrespective of levels of occupancy achieved, such as capital costs for bank loans, finance arrangements, building maintenance and equipment. Variable costs, on the other hand, increase as occupancy levels increase, and include items such as food, drink and the cost of additional staff. The high level of fixed costs means that the break-even point is also relatively high, whilst revenue from sales will, in the longer term, need to be sufficient to cover both fixed and variable costs.

It is only once the accommodation unit has reached this break-even point (Fig. 8.2) that it can begin to make a profit. The break-even point represents the point at which total revenue is equal to both fixed and variable costs. A hotel will have a certain level of occupancy (calculated from revenue generated, not necessarily physical occupancy) that represents its break-even point. As the occupancy level is increased beyond the break-even level, profits accumulate as revenues exceed costs.

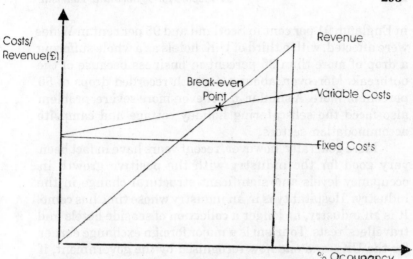

Fig. 8.2 : The economics of accomodation: the break-even point

The external environment

One of the major problems facing the accommodation sector is the uncertainty and unpredictability of the external environment. This includes not only the business environment with its fluctuations in the economic cycle, where both leisure and business demand will drop sharply during periods of economic down-turn, but also events and factors which may dictate market circumstances. For example, a study of 193 UK hotels by consultants Pannel Kerr Forster Associates found that, during a recessionary year in the early 1990s, profits fell by almost a quarter, occupancies fell by an average 8 per cent nationally, whilst average achieved room rates fell by an average 2.5 per cent. This situation was reflected in the European hotel market generally. The Gulf War, also at that time, exacerbated the problem and many accommodation businesses suffered as a result of cancellations, in particular within the American market. More recently in the U.K., the strong pound and a global economic slowdown has not helped in attracting tourists to the U.K. whilst, in early 2001, the foot and mouth outbreak had a disastrous impact on accommodation bookings. According to one survey in Aprit 2001, 78 per cent of hotels in England, 91 per cent in Scotland and 95 per cent in Wales were affected, with a third of U.K. hotels as a whole suffering a drop of more than 25 percent in business because of the outbreak. Moreover, about a seventh recorded drops of 50 percent or more. A similar, if not even more severe, problem also faced the self-catering holiday cottage and campsite accommodation sectors.

More generally, however, recent years have in fact been very good for the industry with the positive growth in occupancy levels and significant structural change in the industry. 'Hospitality is in an industry whose time has come. It is an industry, no longer a collection of seaside hotels and travellers' rests. Tourism is a major foreign exchange earner for the UK—and one now recognised by the government, if its reaction to the present foot and mouth outbreak is anything to go by' (BHA 2001).

Taxation

British accommodation providers face one of the highest rates of VAT on accommodation and restaurant meals in Europe and this is affecting the industry's ability to compete internationally. Issues such as this, coupled with the impact of substantial increases in property taxes in recent years and the introduction of the minimum wage, have compounded to make the accommodation sector a challenging area in which to achieve consistent profitability.

The Importance of the Hotel Sector

As already noted, the accommodation sector is diverse but hotels, in particular, comprise the largest and most important category of accommodation providers. Through the provision of facilities for businesses, conferences, leisure and entertainment, hotels play an important role in society and the economy in most countries. 'In many areas, hotels are important attractions for visitors who bring to them spending power and who tend to spend at a higher rate than they do when they are at home. Through visitor spending, hotels thus often contribute significantly to local economies both directly, and indirectly through the subsequent diffusion of the visitor expenditure to other recipients in the community' (Medlik and Ingram 2000 : 4). The definition of a hotel varies according to which source used, yet it is estimated that there are approximately 60,000 hotels and guest houses in the UK alone (BHA 2001.)

The pattern and structure of hotel ownership has been changing in many countries in recent years and to an extent, now more closely mirrors other industries. Strategies have been imported from the United States and we have witnessed several companies enlarging their market share on a sizeable scale. Thus, although independently owned hotels may still be dominant in terms of number in the UK, with corporately owned hotels representing a small percentage of the total number of hotels, growth is, however, generally associated with the large hotel chains (listed on the stock exchange and with access to financial resources) utilising strategies such as mergers, acquisitions and alliances. Indeed, 'the hotel industry in the UK has changed beyond all recognition. Companies which were household names 25 years ago no longer feature in the list of top hotel groups' (Parker 1996: 39).

One of the current 'buzz words' in the hotel industry (as in many others) is globalisation; 'globalisation is popularly understood as a process which establishes a hotel company's presence on a worldwide basis. Globalisation is commonly perceived to have a standardising impact, as products and institutions originally offered only in the domestic market appear worldwide (Pine and Go 1996:96). This is manifested in American incursions into the UK hotel industry-Blackstone/Colony has taken over the Savoy group, Starwood has acquired Sheraton, and Marriot expanded its base with acquiring Renaissance. However, the British hotel industry has been similarly active. For example, Bass bought Inter-Continental to enhance its Holiday Inn holding and thus became the second largest hotel group in the world, whilst Whitbread has acquired the master franchise for Marriott and also founded Travel Inn. At the same time, the recent merger of Granada with Compass has led to the sale of all the Forte Hotels except Travelodge and has opened up new opportunities for other companies (BHA 2001). In short, what we are seeing is transnational hotel corporations based in Europe, Asia and North America investing abroad, thereby creating a global market place (Table 8.3).

Table 8.3 : Top 10 hotel groups worldwide.

Hotel Group	Rooms	Hotels
1. Cendant Corp. (USA)	542,630	6,315
2. Bass Hotels & Resorts (UK)	471,680	2,886
3. Marriott International (USA)	355,900	1,880
4. Accor (France)	354,652	3,234
5. Choice Hotels International (USA)	338,254	4,248
6. Best Western International (USA)	313,247	4,037
7. Hilton Hotels Corp. (USA)	290.000	1,700
8. Starwood Hotels & Resorts Worldwide (USA)	217,651	716
9. Carlson Hospitality Worldwide (USA)	114,161	616
10. Hyatt Hotels/Hyatt International (USA)	85,734	195

The UK Hotel Industry

As already noted, a lack of consensus exists with respect to the definition of an hotel. Additionally, hotels in the UK are not currently required to be centrally registered whereas, in many other countries, hotels can only be termed an 'hotel' after a compulsory inspection. Industry pressure now exists to introduce legislation making it compulsory for all hotels to be registered. This would, of course, be of considerable advantage to the Tourist Boards whose responsibility it is, by a process of independent inspection, to provide a classification and grading system. Thus, in the UK, hotels are generally defined as accommodation establishments which also have a licence to sell alcoholic drinks. This definition would also include pubs and inns with accommodation but excludes bed and breakfasts and guesthouses as they are normally unlicensed. A number of issues with respect to the UK accommodation sector deserve consideration:

Classification and Grading

A distinction needs to be drawn between registration, categorisation, classification and grading. These terms are often confused but can be explained as follows:

- **Registration**—relates to the basic listing of accommodation establishments and is not presently compulsory in the UK, with fewer than 23,000 of the estimated 60,000 'hotels' in the UK registered with a tourist board (Travel and Tourism Analyst 2000).
- **Categorisation**—refers to different accommodation types: hotels, bed and breakfast, self-catering cottages, etc.
- **Classification**—is concerned with the range of facilities and services provided by the accommodation unit.
- **Grading**—assesses the quality standards of the facilities and services provided.

In 1999, the English Tourism Council in conjunction with the AA and RAC launched new quality standards for serviced accommodation. The new harmonised scheme replaced the three separate schemes previously in existence, which were subject to much criticism on account of being complicated and confusing for consumers to understand. Thus, the new scheme is based on a scale of 1-5 and features the symbols 'Stars for Hotels,' (replacing 'Crowns') and 'Diamonds' for Guest Accommodation (replacing 'Highly Commended/Commended').

Beioley (1999) states that 'accommodation rating schemes are seen by the tourist boards as a key tool for improving the experience of visiting Britain'. The main purposes are two fold:

- To aid consumer selection of accommodation by providing meaningful criteria which will assist judgement and comparison and provide assurances concerning the quality of facilities; and
- To encourage accommodation providers to upgrade their facilities, thus improving the stock of accommodation throughout the UK. Used appropriately, the scheme can be an excellent marketing tool for service providers.

The scheme, however, remains voluntary and although open to accommodation throughout the UK, Scotland and Wales have opted for their own rating systems. This, coupled with the lack of compulsory registration, has meant that despite the launch of the new scheme, this country still does not have a universally accepted system for grading hotels throughout the UK. Critics of the existing system argue that there are a growing number of complaints from domestic and overseas visitors concerning the quality of some hotels and that compulsory hotel registration would help counteract this. Furthermore, it would enable consumers to make more effective comparisons with hotels overseas. There is also a move for a common grading scheme to be introduced for all EU member countries. However, given the problems in implementing a grading and classification schemes in the UK alone, the successful introduction of a European Scheme would seem to be unlikely in the near future.

Independent schemes

Independent grading and classification schemes, such as those of Relais and Chateau, Wolsey Lodges and Michelin, continue to proliferate, often accompanied by their own guide books. Other independent guide books, such as the 'Which? Good Hotel Guide' and 'Good Pub Guide', Alistair Sawday's 'Special Places and 'The Great British Bed and Breakfast', are also extremely popular, reflecting the growing niche of discerning consumers wishing to make their own arrangements. These guides provide all sorts of idiosyncratic information, including the owners peculiarities, pet facilities, decor schemes and local knowledge, and are often to be found in the 'Best Sellers' book listings.

Awards

Competition for special awards can help enhance accommodation quality and are popular with providers as a marketing tool. Awards have huge diversity, varying from 'Hotel (or Pub) of the year' and 'Caravan Park of the year' to 'Loo of the Year'!

Location

The hotel sector is highly fragmented; the 60,000 UK properties termed as hotels range from the small family owned and run hotel through to the large multi-national chain hotel. Location is one of the most important factors dictating an hotel's markets and, it could also be argued, success in terms of profitability. London hotels can almost be regarded collectively as a separate category, being the main destination for over 80 percent of overseas visitors (Mintel 2000) and the major centre for business meetings and conferences. London hotels have occupancy rates of over 80 percent for the last seven years, a figure unparalleled in any other European city (BHA 2001). At least 10,000 new hotel rooms were built in the capital between 1995 and 2000 and a target exists for a further 10,000 rooms before 2006 (BHA 2001.) The capital is not, therefore, as affected by the factors affecting price and profitability discussed earlier. Nevertheless, even London hotel bookings were affected by the foot and mouth outbreak in 2001, mainly as a result of negative press reporting overseas.

A large proportion of British hotels are located beside the sea, and many of these are still family owned and have been hard hit in recent times with the trend for overseas holidays. Therefore, they have attempted, where possible, to diversify their markets, in particular offering short breaks or selling themselves as conference hotels during low season.

Budget hotels

Budget hotels have boomed in the last decade in the UK, reflecting the demand for cheap, basic accommodation that has been a particular feature of accommodation provision for many years in both the USA and France. Forte were the first to capitalise on the demand in the budget sector with Travelodge chain. This brand went on to be developed by its subsequent owners the Granada Group, and is the only chain currently not being sold off by the newly formed Granada Compass group.

Table 8.4 : Ten largest UK hotel groups, 2000 (by total number of bedrooms).

Group Name	Hotels	Rooms
Forte Hotel Division (Granada Compass)	337	30,754
Whitebread Hotel Group	323	24,022
Hilton Group	81	15,869
Bass Hotels & Resorts	97	14,074
Thistle Hotels	56	10,718
Choice Hotels Europe (Friendly)	91	7,428
Corus (Regal Hotels)	97	6,764
Jarvis Hotels	65	6,635
Scottish & Newcastle	123	6,427
Queens Moat Houses UK	43	6,208

Note: At the time of writing (2001) the Granada Compass group currently consists of 47 Heritage Hotel, 7 Le Meridien, 4 London Signature Hotels and 200 Travelodge. The Compass group is however disposing of all its Forte hotel brands, with the exception of Travelodge.

Hotel branding

Market segmentation is a marketing strategy increasingly used in the accommodation sector. In particular, larger hotel chains have adopted this strategy, finding that the various segments require different product offerings that incorporate a tailored 'marketing mix'. They have, therefore, designed clearly identifiable branded products. 'Branding or, more specifically, a company's success or failure at building a brand, is perhaps one of the hottest topics for the industry at present. Operators are increasingly accepting the value of brands in delivering profits. The brand is becoming the key element of defining the market. Rather than who owns or who operates a hotel, it is the name of the brand under which it trades that is the key' (Travel and Tourism Analyst 2000: 66).

In terms of traditional consumer segmentation based on, for instance, socio demographic information, such as age or occupation, we can relate some of the brands above to the market segments to which they most appeal. For example, the budget hotel brands Travel Inn, Express by Holiday Inn and Travelodge will appeal to families on the move, or those travelling on business on a limited budget. Heritage Hotels, conversely, may appeal to 'Empty Nesters' with more disposable income as their children have left home or 'Dinkies' (dual income no kids) who want an active leisure break, for which Heritage have become well known.

Table 8.5 : Leading hotel brands in the UK, January 2000

Brandname	Owner	No. of hotels	No. of rooms
Best Western	Best Western	368	17,037
Hilton	Hilton Group	82	16,194
Posthouse	Granada	84	13,244
Travel Inn	Whitebread	230	12,461
Thistle	Thistle Hotels	51	9,789
Travelodge	Granada	178	9,350
Marriott	Marriott International	50	9,073
Jarvis	Jarvis Hotels	71	6,846
Moat House	Queens Moat Houses	40	5,779
Premier Lodge	Scottish & Newcastle	116	5,738

Similar applications of branding as a method of market segmentation occur throughout Europe and the evidence suggests that the brand grows up first with the domestic market, as in the case of the French owned Accor group, and then spreads overseas in accordance with the globalisation trend discussed earlier. Accor brands, such as Ibis, Hotel Mercure, Formule 1, Novotel and Sofitel, are to be found worldwide in the same way as British brands; research has shown that over 60 percent of adults recognise the top five brand names (Hilton, Holiday Inn, Forte Posthouse and Travelodge) Mintel (2000).

Hotel Ownership and Growth Strategies

It will by now be apparent that hotel ownership and is becoming increasingly complex, particularly with the current emphasis on globalisation strategies. Indeed, it is almost impossible to keep abreast of this very dynamic and fast moving industry, with changes in structure and ownership occurring on a seemingly daily basis. The methods and principles of expansion and diversification remain, however, the same and it is these upon which we shall now focus.

Ownership and management contracts

It is important to point out here that there is a clear distinction between the 'ownership' of hotel properties and their 'management.' An hotel may be owned by a company with no operational involvement with the hotel industry; various organisations, such as insurance companies, investment trusts and banks, are often owners of hotels, essentially viewing the financing of an hotel as a safe investment with a good return. Real estate investment trusts also often have ownership of hotels, whilst property developers, construction companies and landowners also have a logical interest in hotel ownership. However, travel and tourism organisations, including travel agencies, tour operators, airlines and theme park owners are increasingly turning to hotel ownership as vertical integration strategies within organisations are becoming more and more prevalent. For example, Airtours plc's acquisition of various hotels in recent years reflects this trend. In some developing countries, the government may invest in the purchase of a hotel and then try and engage a well known international hotel organisation to run it. The recognised brand will immediately give it a head start in terms of quality and reputation and experienced management means that it will have a greater chance of success.

Ownership is therefore both complex and various. In comparison, management contracts are, essentially, a straightforward means of running a hotel in which a hotel owner employs an agent to manage the hotel. In other words the agent—sometimes an internationally recognised hotel chain, sometimes an independent management company— operates the hotel on behalf of the owners in returns for a management fee. There are, naturally, advantages and disadvantages to both parties. However, it is an increasingly used strategy as it assists hotel chains to expand globally and rapidly whilst utilising capital provided by external investors, thereby avoiding the risks associated with ownership. Having said that, it is not unusual to find that the hotel may be partly owned by a management contract company who manages that contract, yet is also a franchisee of the hotel brand! This will be explained more fully in a moment.

Strategic alliances

Strategic alliances have become increasingly common in recent years, not only in the hotel industry but also in the airline sector. By linking up with another hotel chain, expansion can more easily and readily be achieved—very often in desired overseas markets. This strategy may take many forms, from joint marketing to a common reservation system but, generally, 'by using a common name, or one of the partners' existing names, it is possible to double a hospitality firm's portfolio overnight' (Knowles 1996: 249). Not surprisingly, partners are carefully selected, often with fairly similar properties and service standards, in order to fit in with existing or determined future markets.

Case Study

Extract from the TravelMole Insider Electronic newswire www.travelmole.com 21 May 2001

Millennium and Maritim Hotels strike global alliance

Millennium and Copthrone Hotels PLC (M&C) and Maritim Hotels have announced a combined global marketing alliance to tap into each other's main geographical markets, in other to accelerate their worldwide expansion strategies.

The move grants each chain immediate penetration into those regions where its partner is particularly strong, and at relatively little expense. M&C has a strong presence in Europe, the USA and Asia, whilst Maritim's main hold is over Germany—one of the world's largest hotel markets. M&C last year bolstered its presence in Europe with the appointment of a Germany-based Sales Director for Central Europe.

Together, the two chains have a portfolio of 128 hotels with almost 35,000 rooms in Europe, the USA and Asia. The plan is for these hotels to be cross-sold by staff at both Maritim and M&C, enabling the two chains to help maximise incremental revenues in the medium to long term.

Kwek Leng Beng, Chairman of M&C, commented: "This is a 'win-win situation for Maritim and M&C, as well as for our respective customers... Instead of buying hotel chains, this alliance allows us to compete and grow quickly. Germans are avid leisure and business travellers, and the country is ranked the top outbound country in the world. Now they will have an opportunity to stay at our hotels in Singapore and elsewhere."

The main advantage of strategic alliances is a sharing between alliance partners of their market, in particular the subs-tantial sector of the frequent business traveller who wil be able to utilise the increased number of hotels within the chain in a larger diversity of locations. Marketing advantages and economies of scale also occur and one of the major benefits is that the ownership of the property will not alter and the chain can still retain its independence. Strategic alliances are, therefore, a key route to achieve global expansion.

Joint ventures

A joint venture is an agreement between the hotel operating company (often in international hospitality organisation) and another (non-hotel) organisation. Generally, the hotel operator is in full partnership by means of joint ownership of the hotel with another company and there will therefore be joint participation in any financial result. Real estate developers are often involved in such arrangements and joint ventures have been popular methods of expansion in areas where there is a compara-tively low volume of modern hotel stock, such as in eastern Germany post-unification and in Eastern Europe more generally. The advantages are similar to those discussed under management contracts and, in this instance, the investors would be looking towards a longer-term capital appreciation.

Acquisition

Acquisition continues to remain a popular route to expansion, with the splitting up of the Granada Compass portfolio in 2001 (formerly Forte) being a good example of recent major acquisitions. Macdonald Hotels have purchased the Heritage Brand, Bass the Posthouse brand and the Japanese Bank Nomuera, the Meridien Brand. How these companies integrate their new acquisitions into their existing portfolios remains to be seen.

Franchising

Franchising is becoming almost a household word. MacDonalds, Burger King and Pizza Hut have been operated successfully for many years using this format, whilst many other internationally organisations operate on a franchise basis. In the context of accommodation in particular, the growing pressures of globalisation and greater emphasis on hotel brand awareness by customers has resulted in franchising becoming enormously popular as a method of spreading the market. It is, however, a frequently misunderstood concept and there are many definitions of it.

The relationship between the two parties, franchisor and franchisee, may be summarised as follows. 'Franchising can best be described as a system of distribution whereby one party (the franchisor) grants to a second party (the franchisee) the right to distribute products, or perform services, and to operate a business in accordance with an established marketing system.' For this there is a fee, the arrangement of which varies considerably. The franchisee can then utilise the company's brand, logo, identity and operational systems including marketing and distribution practices. There are many advantages and disadvantages on both sides:

For the franchisor

- Income from fees.
- International growth and recognition of the brand product - without the huge financial outlay involved with acquisition.
- An opportunity to sell and market their product both nationally and internationally without prohibitive expense.
- The opportunity to maximise the usage and spread the costs of an international computerised reservation system.
- A lack of quality control over franchisees and the danger that standards may fall therefore endangering the reputation of the chain.
- The costs of setting up will have to be met by the franchisor.

For the franchisee

- The opportunity to operate under the umbrella of a successful and well known brand which already has an international identity and fully functional operating systems.
- To be able to utilise a national or international organisation's computer reservation system (CRS) or Global Distribution System (GDS) thereby maximising market opportunities.
- To be able to participate in all marketing functions provided by the organisation.
- To benefit from the provision of management experience in all operational areas.
- To gain from economies of scale, guest loyalty schemes and referrals from other members of the chain.

but also

- The financial costs are considerable, not only fees, but also initial investment in ensuring that the property is converted to the franchisor's standards and staff trained accordingly.

- There is a loss of identity, sense of ownership and uniqueness in conforming to the new brand.

Critics of globalisation trends argue that hotel brands are making Europe's hotels bland. For example, an article in the Wall Street Journal (e-tid 20.04.01) entitled 'Endangered Species: Hotels with Character' suggests that, through franchising,' anonymous chains are gobbling up Europe's quaint inns'. However, there is no doubt that, as a method of expansion, franchising is a very successful format and one which will continue to grow in popularity.

Case Study

Extract from Electronic Travel Industry Digest (June 2001) www.e-tid.com

Ramada returns to UK with Jarvis franchise deal 13/06/ 01. Jarvis Hotels has signed a 20 year franchise agreement with Marriott International. 55 properties will be rebranded as Ramada Plaza, Ramada-Jarvis or Ramada Resorts. John Jarvis, chairman and founder, said that the deal gives Jarvis access to Marriott's global reservation systems and Ramada's sales network. Marriott's mid-market Ramada brand has been absent from the UK for two years since four hotels were rebranded as Renaissance.

Consortia

Although the large international hotel chains may dominate the accommodation industry, the independently owned hotel sector, in terms of numbers, is still greater. In an attempt to compete in a global market place dictated by large organisations, these independently owned hotels frequently band together and consolidate their strength in the market place by forming consortia.

The key advantages of being a member of a consortium lie in the access to central marketing and distribution systems which will introduce the possibility of new domestic or overseas markets. They are, therefore, often termed 'Marketing Consortia'.

Main Advantages of Consortium Membership

- Access to a CRS or GDS.
- Featuring in the consortium's guidebook (nationally or internationally distributed).
- Press exposure as a result of public relations activities featuring the consortium's brand name.
- Economies of scale in terms of purchasing power for hotel equipment, food, wine, etc..
- Referrals from other consortium members.
- Access to professional advice on all operational issues.
- The hotel still retains its independence, not only in name, but also in operational character.

The main disadvantage is the cost of membership, which is generally high in order to ensure that the provision of quality in terms of service and standards remains high throughout the chain and the brand name. In order for consortia membership to be effective, members seek like-minded hoteliers featuring similar products and levels of service. One of the most well known consortia is Best Western, often referred to as 'the world's largest hotel chain.' It is a membership association of independently owned and operated hotels and provides marketing, reservations and operational support to 4000 members in 80 countries. A recent advertising campaign features international landmarks, such as the Eiffel Tower and the Grand Canyon, thus demonstrating the idea that no matter where travellers go, they won't be far from a Best Western. Other well-known consortia include Les Routiers, Monotel, The Leading Hotels of the World, Small Luxury Hotels of the World and Relais & Chateaux.

Other Accommodation Types

Despite the evident importance of hotels in terms of visitor numbers and expenditure on accommodation, many of the trends experienced by the hotel industry, such as branding, franchising and consortia membership, are replicated in other accommodation sectors.

Bed and Breakfast

Often referred to as 'the great British phenomenon', the bed and breakfast (B&B) concept has been copied all over the world and is now found in such far flung places as New York City. Generally, B&Bs are family owned and run, and popular on account of their value for money, hetero-geneity (each different B&B provides a unique experience) and distribution—certainly, there are few places in the UK where some form of B&B cannot be found. This appeals to the increasing number of independent travellers packaging up their own holidays and staying somewhere economical for a short break or one or two nights before moving onto the next location. In 1998, the British spent nearly 11 million nights in B&Bs in the UK and overseas visitors over 9 million nights, together amounts to about 1 in 6 of all tourist nights. Total spend of visitors using B&B accommodation was £1 billion (Beioley 2000).

The classification and grading scheme administered by the tourist boards incorporates B&Bs and, of those registered with the ETC, 37 per cent are diamond rated and about half of these have en-suite facilities (Beioley 2000). Again, defining a B&B, as opposed to a hotel or guesthouse, is problematic and so statistics need to be treated with some caution, B&Bs generally consist of only a handful of rooms, so the distinction is made in terms of size and, often, cost as they tend to offer excellent value for money. B&Bs can, however, have a licence and many of them will now provide an evening meal.

The initial capital required to establish a B&B is often small and they are an important extra source of income to communities, particularly those in rural areas and farms in particular. The plight of many B&B accommodation providers was highlighted during the foot and mouth crisis in 2001, which seriously adversely affected many in the business.

B&B providers are becoming more knowledgeable and experienced and are increasingly segmenting and targeting their markets in order to overcome problems of seasonality. Marketing consortia also exist for B&B providers, such as Distinctly Different who offer B&B accommodation in buildings which have been converted from their original use, such as water and windmills, barns and even brothels! There is no doubt that the B&B is here to stay and that quality, specialisation and uniqueness will be the order of the day.

Camping and caravaning

This sector incorporates a wide variety of holiday types and has grown increasingly in terms of demand in recent years, both in the UK and abroad. The chief attractions are the freedom and flexibility it offers and the cost effectivenss of owning your own accommodation, although many tourists now opt for the expanding range of static mobile homes and tents provided by tour operators. General holiday trends with an emphasis on activity holidays, health and fitness have also provided a boost to this sector. Once again, membership organisations, such as the Camping and Caravan Club, and branding are becoming all-important distribution and marketing strategies. Classification and grading quality schemes also exist, accompanied by inclusion in guidebooks, and endorsed either by the tourist offices or independently run schemes, such as Alan Rogers' Cood Camps Guide.

Timeshare

The timeshare industry in the UK is growing rapidly. There was a 13.6 per cent increase in timeshare ownership between 1998 and 1999 and 1.5 per cent of all UK households are involved in timeshare ownership (Mintel 2000). Timeshare appeals to a particular type of holidaymaker who likes to return to the same place each year and prefers self-catering. The emergence of club resorts in holiday complexes means, however, that many facilities are now on hand.

The ownership of a second home has different motivations attached to it compared with purchasing holiday accommodation and a full analysis is beyond the scope of this chapter. Nevertheless, despite the continuing negative publicity associated with time share ownership, the industry has become much more sophisticated and the emphasis has switched from hard sell approaches to marketing and meeting consumer needs. The industry is also a significant source of employment and income for local communities and, it is claimed, generates a higher level of tourist spending than hotel-based tourism.

Holiday cottages

The self-catering market has developed considerably over recent years and holiday cottages represent only a part of the provision of this diverse sector. Cottages and houses are available for rental throughout most parts of the UK, (the French equivalent is the very popular *gite*), from either a tour operator, membership consortia, or directly with the owners themselves by way of an advertisement or web site. Like the bed and breakfast, they are generally privately owned and many are second homes and let out when the owners are not using them. They can provide a valuable contribution to the local economy as long as holidaymakers utilise local facilities and shops.

Case Study

The Landmark Trust

The Landmark Trust provides holiday accommodation with a difference. They are an independent UK building preservation charity who rescue worthwhile historic buildings from neglect and let them for holidays. The income from letting contributes to their upkeep.

Holidaymakers can stay in accommodation ranging from manor houses to mills and follies to forts, thus having a unique and independent holiday experience. Demand for this type of accommodation is growing in accordance with increasingly discerning customer choice and also the knowledge that visitors are participating in a sustainable and worthwhile tourism venture.

Cruise

The cruise market in the UK has more than doubled in the last 5 years, making it one of the fastest growing sectors of the outbound travel market (Mintel 2000). Cruises were previously associated with the elderly or wealthy but the traditional image is now disappearing and consumers are aware of the very broad range of holiday types which incoporate cruising. Short cruise breaks on the Mediterranean are now extremely popular and several large tour operators, such as Airtours and Thomson Holidays, have invested in cruise liners. A wide variety of other water based holidays providing accommodation is also available, such as genting holidays (either participating in a flotilla holiday or chartering a 'bare' boat and making up your own independent itinerary) and canal boat holidays.

Technology

As in all sectors of the travel and tourism industry, technological developments have had a huge impact on the accommodation sector and there are almost daily developments. The most important areas are briefly examined here.

- Yield Management Systems are becoming increasingly utilised within the accommodation sector, especially as their performance continues to improve with technological developments. They are essentially computer software systems which aim to maximise profit and revenue by interpreting demand in accordance with room types available. There is no doubt that they are becoming a key tool for accommodation providers in order to overcome the problems of perishability and seasonability, but in order for them to be effective they have to be provided with essential and accurate historical booking patterns and information.

- Computer reservation systems (CRS) and global distribution systems (GDS) continue to play an important role, particularly for hotels which are members or a consortium or an international chain. The Hotel Electronic Distribution Network Association has reported that hotel bookings made through Amadeus, Galilieo, Sabre, Sahara and Worldspan grew 11.4 percent in 2000, with 48,787,000 bookings (Travelmole, 23/03/2001).

- Utell (a subsidiary of Pegasus) is the hotel industry's largest third party marketing and reservations provider. It manages and produces very large hotel databases which provide a wealth of information on hotels around the world, as well as providing yield and other management systems for member hoteliers. The organisation has no affiliations with the hotels on their systems and acts effectively as a 'one stop shop' for travel agents. It is also linked to GDSs.

- On-line hotel reservations are expected to grow from the current rate of 4.9 per cent to 15.4 per cent within the next three years (TravelMole, 06/06/01). Hospita-lity companies are keen to reduce the currently very high costs of distribution, such as travel agency commi-ssion fees, GDS fees and the costs of multi-faceted distribution and the Internet is seen as providing limit-less opportunities for implementing successful on-line marketing and distribution strategies. However, simply having a web site will not be sufficient and the development of a formal e-strategy may be necessary to take full advantage of this new distribution channel. At the same time, evidence suggests an unwillingness on the part of consumers to book over the Internet, although consortia members have significantly benefited from

Internet business through a central web site and reservations system.

- Recent research by Hilton has shown that WAP users are not so much using their appliances to make reservations with hoteliers but rather to cancel them, or to check in. This can have a beneficial impact on re-sale of rooms and therefore perishability and it is suggested that this trend may also benefit airlines who suffer from similar problems from 'no shows'.

The Accommodation Sector and Sustainability

Accommodation providers play a very important role in providing a sustainable tourism product, not only in terms of the quality of the provision of the built environment (physical appearance and degree of harmony with surroundings) but also with respect to the volume and type of market segment that they attract and in their operational procedures. It is imperative that accommodation construction and the provision of leisure facilities, such as swimming pools and gardens, now take into account environmental factors, such as energy and water consumption, pollution, global warming and degradation of the natural environment. Accommodation providers can make significant cost savings through the adoption of environmentally friendly practices, such as a reduction in energy costs by utilising solar power where possible. Re-cycling and changes in operational practices, such as using real as opposed to paper napkins, can also lead to an improvement in quality standards. It is also becoming evident that accommodation providers are being progressively more consumer led in the demand for environmentally friendly tourism accommodation, although the success of environmental policies in the accommodation sector, as in all areas of tourism, is dependent upon the acceptance and positive support of tourists.

Case Study

Extract from the TravelMole Insider.

Sydney's Green Games inspire hotel clean up

Sydney Olympic Park's Novotel and Hotel Ibis Homebush Bay have recently completed a comprehensive survey in order to the ascertain the impact of environmental initiatives on hotel guests and how, if at all, they affect the guest experience.

The survey, which was conducted in August, of 105 guests and 345 rooms highlights the public's increasing preference for 'environmentally friendly' business.

90 percent of guests polled said they preferred to stay in a hotel that cared for the environment (compared to 8 per cent who were indifferent).

At home or at work, 91 per cent of respondents indicated that they recycle, 82 percent said they reuse plastic bags, 50 percent said they opt for less packaging and 46 per cent make compost.

Whilst 57 per cent of guests opted to reuse their towels more than once to save water and washing detergents, a growing 35 percent of guests opted to reuse their sheets more than once for the same reasons—a new trend in hotels.

During their stay, 78 percent of guests used the recycling bins in the hotel rooms correctly (as compared with 95 per cent of respondents who said they used the facility), 83 per cent chose to use the soap dispensers rather than ask for individual soap cakes and whilst 58 percent used their operable windows rather than air conditioning, a staggering 98 percent identified the windows as one of the top three environmental initiatives.

Conclusion

The accommodation sector is a vitality important part of the travel industry. On account of its heterogeneity and diversity, however, it is impossible to analyse the industry as one body. In general terms, we are seeing a move from an hotel industry that was basically a collection of family owned and run accommodation providers to one where international chains are increasingly dominating the industry. Growth strategies, such as acquisitions, alliances and joint ventures, are proliferating as the demand for a global presence becomes ever necessary and the brand is becoming all-important in terms of standardisation and quality. New products, such as designer, boutique and townhouse hotels are emerging, as are new locations such as hotels next to sports stadia.

Independent hoteliers are, however, fighting back by joining marketing consortia, segmenting and targeting their market more effectively and providing products, which meet new consumers' needs in terms of taste and current trends. Holidaymakers, seeking more independent and specialised travel, can take advantage of new technology, such as the Internet, and are able to find a large array of segmented accommodation suitable to their particular needs. Providers of accommodation as an alternative to hotels continue to grow in popularity and the line between serviced and non-serviced is becoming more indistinct. Thus, there is, no doubt that the accommodation sector will continue to diversify and, despite periodic setbacks in the external environment, it will continue to expand in accordance with the general trend in demand for travel and tourism products.

Bibliography

Abeyratne, R. (1998) 'The regulatory management in air transport', *Journal of Air Transport Management*, 4 (1): 25-37.

BA (1997) *Annual Environmental Report*, Harmonds worth : British Airways.

There is an enormours business literature on quality issues, quality management and the challenges facing service organisations involved in service delivery. However, the following offer a good starting point for a literature which is laden with acronyms, hype, jargon and repetitive massages focused on a simple set of principles.

Braithwaite, G., Caves, R. and Faulkner, J. (1998) 'Australian aviation safety - observations from the lucky country', *Journal of Air Transport Management*, 4(1): 55-62.

Bywater, M. (1998) 'Who owns whom in the European travel industry', *Travel and Tourism Analyst*, 3 : 41-60.

Berry, L.L and Parasuraman, A. (1991) *Marketing services: Competing through Quality*, New York: Free Press.

Barrass, C.(1998), *An Exploratory Study on Internet Marketing Strategy and its Impact on Passenger Shipping*, Unpublished MA thesis. University of Northmumbria.

British Hospitality Association (2001), British Hospitality: Trends and Statistics.

Beioley. S. (1999), Accommodation standards - what the customer wants, *Insights, Volume 10,* B47-B51, London: English Tourist Board.

Beioley, S. (2000), Diamonds are trumps - the bed and breakfast sector, *Insights, Volume 11* - B65-B80, London: English Tourist Board.

British Hospitality Association (2001), *British Hospitality: Trend and Statistics,* London: British Hospitality Association.

Bull, A. (1995), *The Economics of Travel and Tourism, 2nd Edition,* Harlow: Longman.

Cowell, D. (1994). *The Marketing of Services, 2nd Edition,* Oxford: Butterworth Heinemann.

Cowell, D. (1997), in Marketing, Michael J. Baker, Butterworth Heinemann 3rd ed: pg. 671

Electronic Travel Industry Digest. URL:http://www.e-tid.com [11th, 18th & 20th April, 11th May, 14th & 21st June.

Engel. J.F., Blackwell, R.D., Miniard, P.W., (1993), *Consumer Behaviour, 7th Edition,* Fort Worth: The Drydeen Press.

Fill. C. (1995), *Marketing Communications,* Trowbridge: Prentice Hall.

Fitzsimmons, J.A. and Sullivan, R.S. (1992) *Service Operations Management,* New York : McGraw–Hill.

French, T. (1998) 'The future of global distribution systems', *Travel and Tourism Analyst,* 3: 1-18.

Gronroos, C. (1990), *Service Marketing and Management,* Lexington, MA: Lexington Books.

Gnoth, J. (1995) 'Quality of service and tourist satisfaction', in S. Witt and L Moutinho (eds), *Tourism Marketing and Management Harwook: Student Edition,* Hemel Hempstead; Prentice Hall, 243-54.

Goetz, A. and Sutton, C. (1997) 'The geography of deregulation in the US airline industry', *Annuals of the Association of American Geographers*, 87 (2): 238-63.

Hall, C.M. and Lew, A. (eds) (1998) *The Geography of Sustainable Tourism*, London: Addison Wesley Longman.

Hilling, D. (1996) *Transport and Developing Countries*, London: Routledge.

Horner. S. and Swarbrooke, J. (1996), *Marketing Tourism Hospitality and Leisure in Europe*, London: Thomson International Business Press.

Ilinitch, A., Lewin, A., and D'Aveni, R. (eds) (1998) *Managing in Times of Disorder: Hypercompetition Organisational Responses*, London : Sage.

Jones, P. (1996) *Introduction to Hospitality Operations*, London: Cassell - Part A.

Jones, P. (1996), *Introduction to Hospitality Operations*, London: Cassell.

Knowles, P. (1998), *Hospitality Management An Introduction, 2nd Edition*, Harlow: Longman.

Knowles, P.(1996), *Corporate Strategy for Hospitality*, Harlow: Longman

Knowles, P. (1998), *Hospitality Management An Introduction, 2nd Edition*, Harlow; Longman

Knowles, P. (1996), *Corporate Strategy for Hospitality*, Harlow: Longman.

Keynote (2001) *Current Issues - Travel Agents and Overseas Tour Operators*.

Kotler, P. (1994). *Marketing Management: Analysis, Planning Implementation and Control, 8th Edition*, London: Prentice Hall International.

Landmark Trust, (2001), *Landmark Trust Handbook*.

Leisure Intelligence (2000), *Hotel Report,* London: Mintel International Group.

Leisure Intelligence (2000), *Holiday Property Abroad Report,* London: Mintel International Group.

Leisure Intelligence (2000), *Camping and Caravaning Report,* London: Mintel International Group.

Medlik, S. and Ingram, H. (2000). *The Business of Hotels, 4th Edition,* Oxford: Butterworth-Heinemann.

Medlik, S. and Ingram. H. (2000). *The Business of Hotels, 4th Edition,* Oxford: Butterworth-Heinemann.

McDonald, M. (1995), *Marketing Plans,* Oxford: Butterworth Heinemann.

McDonald, M. and Payne, A. (1996), *Marketing Planning for Services.* Oxford: Butterworth Heinemann.

Middleton, V. (1998) *Sustainable Tourism : A Marketing Perspective,* Oxford : Butterworth-Heinemann.

Milman, A. and Pope, D. (1997) 'The US airline industry', *Travel and Tourism Analyst* 3: 4-21.

Millington, K. (2001), Adventure Travel, *Travel and Tourism Analyst,* No. 4: 65-97

Mintel (2001), *Crossing the Channel,* Leisure Intelligence UK Report, London : Mintel International Group Limited.

Mintel (2001b), *Directly booked holidays,* Leisure Intelligence UK Report, London: Mintel International Group Limited.

Parker, A. (1996), The changing face of the hotel industry, in R. Kotas, R. Teare, J. Logie, C. Jayawardena and J.Bowen. (eds.) *The International Hospitality Business,* London: Cassell: 39-41.

Pine, R. and Go, F. (1996), Globalisation in the hotel industry, in R. Kotas, R. Teare, J. Logie, C. Jayawardena and J.Bowen. (eds.) *The International Hospitality Business,* London: Cassell 96-103.

Pender, L. (1999), *Marketing Management for Travel and Tourism,* Cheltenham: Stanley Thornes.

Seaton, A. and Bennett. M. (1996), *Marketing Tourism Products, Concepts, Issues, Cases,* London: Thomson International Business Press.

Shostack G. (1977), Breaking free from product marketing, *Journal of Marketing* 41(2) : 76

Sinclair, M.T. and Stabler, M. (1997) *The Economies of Tourism,* London: Routledge. Although this is a difficult text for the uninitiated economist, it is well worth reading for detail on supply issues.

Sheldon, P. (1997) *Tourism Information Technology,* Oxford: CAB International.

Sangster, A. (2000), The impact of branding on the UK hotel industry, *Travel & Tourism Analyst,* (2) 65-82.

Sharpley, R. (1999), *Tourism, Tourists and Society, 2nd Edition,* Huntingdon: ELM Publications,

Townsend, P.L. and Gebhart, J.E. (1986) *Commit to Quality,* New York: John Wiley.

TravelMole Insider. URL:http://www.travelmole.com[19th October 2000, 19th June 2001].

Ward, C. and Hardy, D. (1986), *Goodnight Campers! The History of the British Holiday Camp,* London: Mansell Publishing.

Walton, J. (2001), The hospitality trades: a social history, in C. Lashley and A. Morrison (eds.) *In Search of Hospitality,* Oxford: Butterworth-Heinemann:

Witt, S., Buckley, P. and Brooke, M. (1991). *The Management of International Tourism,* London: Routeledge.

WTO (1996), *Timeshare: a new force in tourism,* Madrid; World Tourism Organisation.

Yale, P. (1988), *The Business of Tour Operations,* Harlow: Longman.

Zeithmal, A. and Berry, LL. (1985) 'A conceptual model of service quality and its implications for future research', *Journal of Marketing,* Fall : 41-50.

Zeithaml, V. and Bitner, M. (2001), *Services Marketing: Integrating Customer Focus Across The Firm,* McGraw-Hill Higher Education.

Zeithaml, V., Parasuraman, A. and Berry, L. (1985), Problems and strategies in services marketing, *Journal of Marketing* 49(1): 33-46.